Theosis and Forgiveness in the Gospel of Matthew

Theosis and Forgiveness in the Gospel of Matthew

Kangil Kim

LEXINGTON BOOKS/FORTRESS ACADEMIC
Lanham • Boulder • New York • London

Published by Lexington Books/Fortress Academic
Lexington Books is an imprint of The Rowman & Littlefield Publishing Group, Inc.
4501 Forbes Boulevard, Suite 200, Lanham, Maryland 20706
www.rowman.com

86-90 Paul Street, London EC2A 4NE, United Kingdom

Portions of "A Theology of Forgiveness: Theosis in Matthew 18:15–35" in *Journal of Theological Interpretation* 16.1 (2022): 40–56 (doi: https://doi.org/10.5325/jtheointe.16.1.0040) used with permission from Penn State University Press.

British Library Cataloguing in Publication Information Available

Library of Congress Cataloging-in-Publication Data

Names: Kim, Kangil, 1987– author.
Title: Theosis and forgiveness in the Gospel of Matthew / Kangil Kim.
Description: Lanham : Lexington Books/Fortress Academic, [2024] | Includes bibliographical references and index. | Summary: "In this book, Kangil Kim reads the Matthean teaching of forgiveness through the framework of theosis. Kim argues that theosis provides a theological lens that brings into sharper focus the meaning of forgiveness, especially with respect to the dynamics of heaven and earth and of God and the human in Matthew's Gospel"—Provided by publisher.
Identifiers: LCCN 2023030183 (print) | LCCN 2023030184 (ebook) | ISBN 9781978716322 (cloth) | ISBN 9781978716339 (epub)
Subjects: LCSH: Bible. Matthew—Criticism, interpretation, etc. | Deification (Christianity) | Forgiveness—Religious aspects—Christianity.
Classification: LCC BS2575.52 .K555 2024 (print) | LCC BS2575.52 (ebook) | DDC 226.2/06—dc23/eng/20230810
LC record available at https://lccn.loc.gov/2023030183
LC ebook record available at https://lccn.loc.gov/2023030184

Contents

Acknowledgments

This book is a revision of my doctoral dissertation, completed at Fuller Theological Seminary in 2023. I want to thank God my Father for empowering me to write this book. As envisioned in the title of my book ("theosis"), this academic journey was indeed a time to walk with God and to share in his revelation (1 Chr 28:19).

I am deeply grateful to my mentor, Dr. Tommy Givens, for his helpful guidance, including the many hours he spent reading and commenting on my work from start to finish. His keen insight has enriched this project in many ways, especially with respect to the nature of forgiveness and the God-human relationship in the Gospel of Matthew. My sincere appreciation extends to my second mentor, Dr. Joel B. Green, who read my chapter drafts with great care and gave me constructive feedback. His valuable comments and suggestions have improved the overall quality of this work. I would also like to express my gratitude to Dr. Michael J. Gorman, who reviewed my work thoroughly and suggested ways in which this work can be improved.

My thanks also go to Gayla Freeman, the editorial board of Lexington Books/Fortress Academic, and the anonymous reviewer, who read and accepted the manuscript for publication. I also wish to thank Julie Lambert, the journals manager of Penn State University Press, and Dr. Tim Meadowcroft, the editor of the *Journal of Theological Interpretation*, for their permission to use portions of my previously published article ("A Theology of Forgiveness: Theosis in Matthew 18:15–35," *JTI* 16, no. 1 [2022]: 40–56) in the present book.

As always, I am thankful for the loving prayers and support of my parents, Dae Hee Kim and Joo Hee Hong, and my parents-in-law, Ho Young Kwon and Sook Young Kim. Thanks, most of all, to my wife, Jinyoung Kwon, whose love, prayers, and unflagging support have sustained me throughout this journey. She is my favorite friend and companion to heaven. It is to her I dedicate this work.

Abbreviations

BIBLE TEXTS AND VERSIONS

CEB Common English Bible
LXX Septuagint
MT Masoretic Text
NA^{28} *Novum Testamentum Graece*, Nestle-Aland, 28th ed.
NLT New Living Translation
NRSV New Revised Standard Version
NT New Testament
OT Old Testament

PRIMARY SOURCES

Deuterocanonical Works and Septuagint

Sir Sirach
Wis Wisdom of Solomon
1–2 Macc 1–2 Maccabees
3 Macc 3 Maccabees

Old Testament Pseudepigrapha

1 En. 1 Enoch
Jub. Jubilees

Dead Sea Scrolls

Q Qumran
4Q372 apocrJoseph^{b}

4Q460 Narr. Work and Prayer

Rabbinic Works

ʾAbot Avot
B. Qam. Bava Qamma
Ned. Nedarim
Taʿan. Ta'anit
Ṭehar. Teharot

Apostolic Fathers

Did. Didache

Greek and Latin Works

Irenaeus

Haer. *Adversus haereses* (*Against Heresies*)

Josephus

Ant. *Jewish Antiquities*
J.W. *Jewish War*

Justin

Dial. *Dialogus cum Tryphone* (*Dialogue with Trypho*)

Maximus

CCSG Corpus Christianorum, Series Graeca
Qu.D. *Quaestiones et dubia* (*Questions and doubts*)

Tertullian

Or. *De oratione* (*Prayer*)

SECONDARY SOURCES

ABRL Anchor Bible Reference Library
AnBib Analecta Biblica
BBR *Bulletin for Biblical Research*

BDAG Danker, Frederick W., Walter Bauer, William F. Arndt, and F. Wilbur Gingrich. *Greek-English Lexicon of the New Testament and Other Early Christian Literature*. 3rd ed. Chicago: University of Chicago Press, 2000
BETL Bibliotheca Ephemeridum Theologicarum Lovaniensium
BibInt Biblical Interpretation Series
BTS Biblical Tools and Studies
CBQ *Catholic Biblical Quarterly*
ConBNT Coniectanea Biblica: New Testament Series
CurTM *Currents in Theology and Mission*
Di *Dialog*
DJG *Dictionary of Jesus and the Gospels*. Edited by Joel B. Green, Jeannine K. Brown, and Nicholas Perrin. 2nd ed. Downers Grove, IL: InterVarsity Press, 2013
HTR *Harvard Theological Review*
HTS *Harvard Theological Studies*
HUCA *Hebrew Union College Annual*
IBC Interpretation: A Bible Commentary for Teaching and Preaching
ICC International Critical Commentary
Int *Interpretation*
JBL *Journal of Biblical Literature*
JETS *Journal of the Evangelical Theological Society*
JSNT *Journal for the Study of the New Testament*
JSNTSup Journal for the Study of the New Testament Supplement Series
JTI *Journal of Theological Interpretation*
LCL Loeb Classical Library
LD Lectio Divina
LNTS Library of New Testament Studies
NAC New American Commentary
NICNT New International Commentary on the New Testament
NIGTC New International Greek Testament Commentary
NovTSup Supplements to Novum Testamentum
NRTh *La nouvelle revue théologique*
NTOA Novum Testamentum et Orbis Antiquus
NTS *New Testament Studies*
OTL Old Testament Library
OTS Old Testament Studies
PRSt *Perspectives in Religious Studies*
SBLDS Society of Biblical Literature Dissertation Series
SNTSMS Society for New Testament Studies Monograph Series
STI Studies in Theological Interpretation

StPatr	*Studia Patristica*
SubBi	Subsidia Biblica
THNTC	Two Horizons New Testament Commentary
WBC	Word Biblical Commentary
WUNT	Wissenschaftliche Untersuchungen zum Neuen Testament

Chapter 1

Framing the Research

THE QUESTION

While various NT writings have been considered with a theosis framework, little to nothing has been written on the contribution of such a framework to the interpretation of Matthew.[1] Some scholars, like Stephen Finlan and Vladimir Kharlamov, recognize Matt 5:48 as a text that expresses the idea of theosis, but they do not examine the particular expression of theosis in this Gospel.[2] Matthew's Gospel has been known for its emphasis on forgiveness (e.g., 1:21; 4:17; 9:2; 18:21; 20:28; 26:28). In his work, *The Significance of Interpersonal Forgiveness in the Gospel of Matthew*, Isaac K. Mbabazi presents forgiveness as a matter of systematic concern in Matthew, summarizing it as "a lifestyle in which each member cares for the others."[3] F. S. Spencer similarly observes that from the beginning of the narrative (1:21), Matthew orients Jesus's "identity and mission around securing his people's salvation from sins," which involves the forgiveness of sins.[4] Yet, the theme of forgiveness includes a dynamic of relation between God's action and human action that remains unexplored, and theosis provides a theological lens that allows the meaning of forgiveness in Matthew's Gospel to come into sharper focus. While the thematic importance of forgiveness has been recognized, what has not been explored is the particular way the concept of theosis sheds light on the theme of forgiveness in Matthew's Gospel.

This study aims to read Matthew's teaching of forgiveness within the framework of theosis. By theosis, I mean our transformative participation in the divine life,[5] such that God himself is reflected in particular ways in the human.[6] Theosis is thus divinely empowered human life, a human manifestation of divine life itself. We participate in God's own life and action, thereby becoming God at work in *us*. My thesis is that theosis offers a hermeneutical key for understanding the embodied transformation of forgiveness in

Matthew, namely, our transformative participation in God's forgiving nature. Thus, theosis names our participation in the nature and will of the Father in heaven, specifically through embodying forgiveness. This study does not, however, envision forgiveness as the only way to think about theosis in Matthew's Gospel. Forgiveness names one form of participation in God's life. Forgiveness in Matthew can be conceived as a transformative action of God through particular human actions, and forgiveness as theosis in this sense helps us understand better what Matthew is saying about forgiveness. The goal of this study is thus to demonstrate how a focus on theosis clarifies and advances the Matthean teaching of forgiveness, with respect to the transformative dynamics between the action of God and the action of human beings. By considering the concept of theosis, we will see that forgiveness is a particular way we participate in God's own life.

THE CONCEPT OF THEOSIS AND ITS USE IN NT SCHOLARSHIP

Grant Macaskill points out that in modern Orthodox thought, "*theosis* functions as a comprehensive and integrative doctrine."[7] It is concerned with "the entire purpose of God for the glorification of creation" rather than "simply one important element of salvation."[8] According to Macaskill, the union of God and human beings is grounded in the biblical concept that humanity is created in the image and likeness of God (Gen 1:26–27). Because human beings bear the likeness of God, they can participate uniquely in God's life. Within humanity, moreover, Jesus's incarnation is the key point and culmination of theosis: the humanization of the divine in the person of Jesus and the deification of the human as the result of our living with Christ. It is thus in and through the person of Jesus who embodies full humanity and full divinity that human beings can fully realize their humanity and fully participate in the divine life. Vladimir Kharlamov observes that the process of theosis that reached its apex in the incarnation of Christ "requires active human participation."[9] Since human beings are distinguished from God in essence, theosis involves "a particular construal of the participation" in God's life and character.[10] Theosis is thus a transformative experience that enables human beings to "become not 'who' Christ is but 'what' he is."[11] In this light, this study assumes forgiveness as a particular mode of theosis in Matthew's Gospel. Through embodying forgiveness, human beings become what Christ is. To explore the concept of theosis in the Christian tradition, I build on patristic thought and the OT. I then examine the use of theosis in NT scholarship and its relevance to Matthew's Gospel to clarify the need for this study.

Theosis in Patristic Thought

Scholars like Stephen Finlan observe, "It is beyond dispute that a major theme in patristic thought was the deification of believers, their taking on of divine character."[12] The concept of theosis in the patristic Christian tradition begins with the famous dictum of Irenaeus of Lyons, later developed by Athanasius: "God became what we are to make us what he is."[13] Norman Russell identifies different senses of theosis in the patristic tradition—nominal, analogical, and metaphorical. According to Russell, the nominal sense simply refers to honorific status of human beings as gods, which possesses no theology of deification. The analogical sense makes the nominal sense an explicit analogy. What will be pertinent for this study is the metaphorical sense. For Russell, the metaphorical sense is further divided into the "realistic" (i.e., human beings are transformed by God and participate in God's life) and the "ethical" (i.e., human beings attain likeness of God by imitation).[14] Russell notes that the metaphor of theosis develops along two distinct lines in the patristic tradition: "on the one hand, the transformation of humanity in principle as a consequence of the Incarnation; on the other, the ascent of the soul through the practice of virtue."[15] But Russell points out that the realistic (transformative participation) and ethical (practice and imitation) senses go hand in hand in the patristic tradition, especially in Cyril of Alexander and Maximus the Confessor. Daniel A. Keating rightly captures the dynamics of these realistic and ethical senses: "We can make no progress in attaining likeness to God if we have not already been joined to Christ in a realistic sense through participation in his divine life."[16] Building on this observation, this study embraces the metaphorical (realistic and ethical) senses of theosis rather than the nominal (honorific) and analogical senses.

The language of "participation" is important for understanding the concept of theosis.[17] According to Andrew J. Byers, the patristic concepts of theosis can serve as "*articulations* and *clarifications* of biblical themes like union and participation."[18] Russell also observes that there is a "fundamental reliance on the theme of participation, which offers a way of understanding on the ontological level how Becoming can share in Being, or the created in the uncreated, without abandoning its contingent status."[19] J. A. McGuckin observes, accordingly, that the church fathers articulate theosis in terms of participation, as opposed to Platonic assimilation language.[20] While the church fathers employed Greek philosophical language and concepts, they appropriated them "in accordance to a vast array of convictions that were explicitly *Christian*."[21] That is, they "generally reworked Platonist values and concepts in accordance with their Christology."[22] To understand theosis, therefore, this study builds on the language of "participation" and the relational dynamics of God and the human found in patristic interpretation. The church fathers viewed participation as participation in God's character and attributes rather than sharing in God's essence.[23] For Athanasius, when God became human, God did not do so to make it possible for human beings to become God in essence but to transform what it means to be a human being.[24] This transformation can be understood as the healing or perfection of the human by participation in God's life. Justin Martyr, Athanasius's predecessor, articulates the nature of participation in God's life in terms of sonship. Justin takes up the theme of filiation in Ps 82:6 (*Dial.* 124) to depict believers as sons and daughters of God (cf. *Dial.* 123). Macaskill observes that for Justin, "Deification is subordinated to this controlling metaphor of sonship. The sonship of believers is developed with reference to" Israel's familial relation with God.[25] Thus, for Justin, our participation in God's family is understood in terms of God's relationship and communion with Israel. As with Justin, Irenaeus also writes that human beings share God's light in communion (*Haer.* 4.14). God's property is "given" to humanity in communion, "not one innate to it."[26]

This relational communion with God is later taken up by Maximus the Confessor. For Maximus, "Participation is in the attributes of God and his spiritual gifts (e.g., *Qu.D.* 180; CCSG 10.123)."[27] This participation does not imply "participation in God's essence."[28] Michael J. Christensen notes the observation of Maximus that the process of theosis is "perichoresis," that is, "interpenetration" of God and the human.[29] The idea of interpenetration implies a dynamic relation between God and the human. Regarding perichoresis, Russell points to Maximus's claim that "Human beings are able to deify themselves by the practice of the virtues because God has already presented them with an exemplary humanity—the 'image' which is Christ."[30] The important principle in the idea of perichoresis is that the essential distinction between creator and creation remains: "God and [the hu]man are *paradigms* of each other."[31] In patristic thought, "[e]ach retains his or her own nature and personal identity."[32] Thus, human beings become like God "through a participation in him, such that they reflect divine attributes."[33] In articulating theosis, Maximus uses "the imagery of a sword placed in the fire," such that "the sword remains iron" in the fire but "takes on the properties of light and heat from the fire by its participation (*Ambiguum* 7; cf. *Opuscule* 16)."[34] The relation between God and the human is thus not one of absorption. In line with this thought, Russell observes that while theosis is a "metaphor" and "a poetic figure of speech" in the sense that human beings cannot participate in God's essence, theosis is a "real and intimate relationship with God."[35] Regarding this intimate relationship with God, Macaskill observes that when the church fathers "draw upon the philosophical concept of *theosis*, they do so in relation to the controlling metaphor of filiation, or sonship, which is a relational concept. Platonic concepts are certainly encountered in the Fathers, but they are firmly subordinated to this driving theme of filiation."[36] Thus, a relational dynamic between God and the human is crucial to prevalent patristic concepts of participation.[37] Building on a relational, participatory, transformative dynamics of God and the human as found in patristic interpretation, this study presses further to articulate a relational dynamics of heaven and earth in Matthew, especially revealed in Jesus's forgiving power. Interpenetration in Matthew's Gospel follows the triadic pattern of "Father-Son-Disciples," similar to that found in John's Gospel.[38] With Jesus, the disciples exercise God's own forgiving power; Jesus does this and, by extension, other human beings do this in relation to him. Thus, Jesus as God-with-us provides a way to conceive of Jesus's action in and through us as our participation in God's own life.

Additionally, in explaining the patristic concept of theosis, Robert W. Jenson points out the nature of human participation in God in conjunction with God's plurality: "We can become God because the true God, the triune God whose unity is founded by his mutual *plurality*, has *room* in himself for others."[39] Byers similarly observes that "plurality is constitutive of divine unity. In other words, Jesus is correlated with God but not in such a way that the two dissolve into one another."[40] It is not about our becoming additional instances or an approximation of the divine nature. It is about our becoming sharers in God in that we jointly live the divine life wrought by Jesus in the power of the Spirit. Thus, we participate in the life that God is, and so we become like God. The way the human participates in the divine life is thus the way the triune God shares the divine life in the divine family. Byers rightly points out that we are "*not within the divine identity*, but within the *divine family*."[41] This affirms "a gulf between the divine identity comprising Jesus and God and the divine family into which human beings are integrated."[42]

In sum, for the church fathers like Irenaeus, Athanasius, and Maximus, theosis does *not* mean that the line between God and human beings can be erased, as human beings cannot participate in God's essence. A Greek philosophical conception of divinization is conceived "in terms of *methexis*," namely, "mixture of being," but a Christian tradition of theosis is conceived in terms of participation or "*koinōnia*."[43] The nature of divine-human relation, then, neither "presupposes identification of human beings with God nor human dissolution into the divine" in patristic thought.[44] Thus, for the church fathers, theosis is to be understood as our participation in and communion with God's own life without ceasing to be human. To have communion with God is to share in God's life. Building on the church fathers' conception, this study uses the terms "participation," "communion," or "union" to refer to theosis.[45] Moreover, in line with the patristic view, this study does not articulate theosis as an ontological fusion with the divine essence but a dynamic relation whereby the human is transformed by participating in God's forgiving power, which is an expression of God's life. Thus, the distinction between God and the human remains, even as human beings assume certain divine prerogatives and thus exercise divine action.[46] That human beings participate in God's character is clearly revealed in Matthew's Gospel, where Jesus invites his people to take on the divine character: "Be whole, as your heavenly Father is whole" (5:48).[47] Finally, as the church fathers envision, since participation in God's life is relational in nature, our participation in God's life in Matthew's Gospel happens as we enter into a relationship with Jesus (e.g., 11:25–27).

A Brief Survey of Scholarly Discussion on Theosis in the OT

Although a patristic idea of theosis will be brought to Matthew's Gospel, the conceptualization will be shaped by the particular Matthean usage evident in the text. Thus, this study does not aim to recount patristic readings of Matthew but to describe the theological vision set forth within the text of Matthew through a hermeneutical lens provided by patristic understandings of theosis. To understand Matthew's conception of divine-human relations, it is important to direct our attention to the OT because Matthew assumes the general understanding of the OT in articulating the divine-human relation, especially with respect to *the knowledge* of God. One important concept of knowledge in the OT has to do with an intimate relationship, such as that between husband and wife (ידע), so that "to know" points to union and oneness (e.g., Gen 4:1, 17; 1 Sam 1:19).[48] This relational dynamic is also found in Matthew, where Jesus says that "no one knows (ἐπιγινώσκει) the Father except the Son and anyone to whom the Son chooses to reveal the Father" (11:27). Thus, the knowledge of God can be understood in terms of our relationship with Jesus. While, according to Matthew, the knowledge of God is particularly revealed in Jesus, the hand of God that empowers human beings is already present in the OT. For instance, Moses's stretching out his hand over the sea becomes God's own hand that divides the waters (Exod 14:21). Moreover, God fills Bezalel and Oholiab with his spirit, knowledge, and skill to construct the tabernacle (Exod 31:2–6; 36:1–2). This shows how God in heaven already works toward and in human beings on earth in the OT. Being empowered by God's spirit and knowledge, Bezalel and Oholiab construct the *heavenly* designed tabernacle on earth.

Scholars such as Keating contend that the union of God and the human, theosis, is already grounded in Scripture, throughout "the entire narrative of the Bible from Adam to Christ."[49] Human beings are created in the *likeness* of God (Gen 1:26–27), such that they become like God and share in his life. Becoming like God thus implies that we have within us an element of the divine. Panayiotis Nellas calls this element "theological structure": "Having been made in the image of God, [the hu]man has a theological structure. And to be a true [hu]man, he [or she] must at every moment exist and live theocentrically."[50] Living theocentrically and reflecting God's life comprise "a noncompetitive participation" in God's life. This means that we remain creatures and human beings while sharing in God's life and certain of his attributes. While Adam and Eve attempted to become like God on their own terms, "in a competitive sense of being equal (and rival) to God" (cf. Gen 3:5), Jesus did "not count equality with God something to be grasped" (Phil 2:6).[51] The noncompetitive participation in God implies that the relationship between God and the human does not involve mingling supposedly alien natures or a union that threatens the distinction between divine and human natures. Rather, human nature is born to reflect divine nature in a noncompetitive sense, such that the distinction between them is itself a relation. In a similar vein, with respect to the oneness of Christ as divine and human, Dietrich Bonhoeffer observes that there is "one whole person" of the God-human.[52] For Bonhoeffer, divine and human natures are not "like two distinguishable entities, separated from each other until they came together in Jesus Christ."[53] That is, although Christ is the culmination of theosis as the full divine-human constitution is revealed in Christ, divine nature is already rooted in human beings from the beginning of Scripture (e.g., Gen 1:26–27; Lev 11:44; 19:2; 20:7).

Matthew assumes this understanding of the OT as he cites Isa 7:14 to depict Jesus as "God-with-us"—that is, as God's liberating presence *with* his people in Jesus (1:23).[54] The union of God and the human in Matthew's Gospel is particularly expressed in the language of "God-with-us" (1:23). Through God's indwelling presence, human beings do what God does. David D. Kupp observes that the language of God's presence with human beings frequently appears in the OT (e.g., Gen 21:20, 22; Exod 3:12; Jos 1:5; Ruth 2:4; 1 Kgs 11:38; 2 Chr 36:23). According to Kupp, God's presence with his people is "the promise, assertion and declaration of YHWH's distinctly personal company, activity and empowerment on behalf of his people in particular events of their individual and corporate human experience."[55] Kupp further observes that God's "I am with you" is "at the core of Israel's deliverance and restructuring in Deutero-Isaiah, [and] is constantly reiterated as Jeremiah's empowerment for his difficult commission."[56] As will be shown, Jesus's presence with his people is particularly revealed in his exercising of God's forgiveness (1:21). In this light, we should bear in mind that the OT offers illuminating background for divine-human action, such that this study is partly an attempt to recover a Jewish sensibility in the understanding of the divine-human relation, specifically with respect to forgiveness (cf. 2 Chr 36:22–23; Isa 53:4).[57]

The Use of Theosis in NT Scholarship

Paul M. Collins notes that although several texts of the NT were used as examples of theosis in the patristic period, the NT contains no explicit reference to theosis.[58] Byers similarly observes that the lexical repository related to theosis in patristic writings makes no appearance in NT writings.[59] Byers then points out that the absence of technical terminology does not prevent the application of theosis language to NT texts.[60] In this connection, Michael J. Gorman notes that the application of theosis language to NT texts should be seen not as "anachronistic" but as "retrospectively appropriate" and "accurate."[61] According to Gorman, the absence of words like "incarnation" or "Trinity" does not mean that "the concepts or realities they signify are missing from Scripture."[62] Thus, although terms like theosis or deification are absent from Matthew or "were unknown at the time it was written," this does "not invalidate the claim that its substance is there."[63] The literary critic Mikhail Bakhtin's observation is noteworthy in this connection: "Semantic phenomena can exist in concealed form, potentially, and be revealed only in semantic cultural contexts of subsequent epochs that are favorable for such disclosure."[64] M. David Litwa rightly notes that the question is not whether an NT author had a "doctrine" or "theory" or "idea" of theosis.[65] The question is whether *an* aspect of Matthew's theology can be called deification or theosis, by which I mean sharing in God's forgiving activity through Christ.[66] According to Collins, theosis is itself a "metaphor" that "arises from reflections on New Testament witnesses."[67] Building on these observations, this study articulates *an* aspect of Matthew's theology (i.e., Matthew's theology of forgiveness) that can be understood in terms of theosis. The focus of this study is thus not theosis per se, but theosis that is specifically Matthean.

In his work, *Inhabiting the Cruciform God*, Gorman notes the dynamic of theosis in relation to the enabling power of the Spirit: "believers experience the resurrection life and power of God as they are *enabled* by the Spirit to be conformed to the resurrected crucified Christ."[68] He notes further that "by the power of the Spirit of Father and Son," we as the church are "participating *now* in the life and mission of the triune cruciform God."[69] This suggests that the Spirit of God empowers us to participate in God's life.[70] That the Spirit of God empowers human beings is also resonant with patristic thought as it views theosis in a way that all human beings are "*filled with God's spirit* and perfected as creature[s]."[71] In this light, what perfects the human is God's power, the Spirit of God. Similarly, Matthew presents Jesus as an embodiment of the power of God as Jesus is conceived through the creative power of the Spirit (1:20). In John's baptism for the forgiveness of sins, Jesus is anointed with the Spirit (3:16). While the way John baptizes people (i.e., water, 3:11) is different from the way Jesus will baptize people (i.e., the Spirit, 3:11), the nature of their work is similar because they both work for the forgiveness of sins (3:6; 9:6; 20:28; 26:28). Since Jesus himself is anointed with the Spirit, the way God indwells and empowers Jesus is the power of the Spirit (3:16). That is to say, Matthew portrays the power of Jesus as the Spirit of God (e.g., 12:28). As bearer of the Spirit, Jesus saves his people by spreading God's forgiving power, empowering his people to embody the same power with which he was anointed (e.g., 10:1).[72] In this way, for Matthew, there is a transfer and an extension of power from God to Jesus and from Jesus to his people.

Regarding the use of theosis in the NT, Gorman proposes "missional theosis" in John's Gospel. Gorman thus provides a lens—mission—to understand John's construction of theosis.[73] He understands mission as participatory and cruciform, such that mission is a particular mode of theosis. According to Gorman, Johannine theosis consists in "the *mutual indwelling* of the Triune God (Father, Son, and Spirit) and Jesus' disciples" such that the disciples participate in the life of God.[74] Participation in the divine life effects transformation into the likeness of God, who is by nature missional. For Gorman, theosis is predicated on the experience of Christ's indwelling (e.g., 17:20–23). Also, while we are transformed, theosis is a "relational" participation in God rather than an ontological fusion, in line with patristic thought. John's Gospel has been a key source for the Christian doctrine of theosis (e.g., 1:12–13; 3:3–8; 10:34–35). Thus, Gorman's attention to theosis in John's Gospel is fitting. Also, Gorman's attention to the theme of mission is welcome because the language of "send" frequently appears in this Gospel. Gorman draws on a particular theme (i.e., mission) to construct a particular mode of Johannine theosis. In a fashion similar to Gorman, I assume one particular theme for articulating Matthean theosis, namely, forgiveness.

The line of questioning I wish to press is this: What does theosis add to interpretations of NT witnesses? What would be missed if we did not analyze mission, for example, in terms of theosis? How, then, might a theosis framework help us enhance our understanding of Matthew's Gospel in particular? More specifically, since forgiveness constitutes a noteworthy concurrence of divine and human action, how would forgiveness-as-theosis help us understand better what Matthew is saying about forgiveness?

In the interpretation of John, Gorman could draw even more deeply on the theological tradition of theosis, working, for example, with its key concepts of "knowledge" and "Spirit-empowered mission." Given that the concepts of knowledge and Spirit-empowered mission are key factors in interpreting John's Gospel, these concepts could be more fully explored by means of the framework of theosis. Otherwise, one may find it difficult to see how theosis clarifies and advances our reading of mission in John's Gospel. Based on these observations, what I want to develop from Gorman's articulation of theosis is exegesis that clarifies and advances our reading of forgiveness in

Matthew's Gospel through the framework of theosis, especially with respect to the transformative dynamics of heaven and earth.

Elsewhere in NT scholarship, theosis is indeed treated in relation to knowledge. James Starr observes with respect to 2 Peter, which may guide us on this point, that the cornerstone of 2 Peter's message is that "the knowledge of Christ" works out "a transformation in believers by giving them 'all things necessary for piety and life'" (1:3).[75] According to Starr, 2 Peter envisions that our participation in the divine nature is the "*result* of knowing Christ," not something we achieve by our "innate quality of human nature."[76] Starr also points out that the knowledge of Christ in 2 Peter is an expression of love and virtue. This means, as in the patristic tradition of theosis, that we share in the divine life by living virtuously; knowledge is not merely cognitive or even experiential as knowledge might suggest among English speakers today. The expectation is not moral perfection but continual growth in the virtue-forming knowledge of God (cf. "grow in Christ's grace," 3:18). Our participation in the divine life thus takes place in "the progressive moral transformation experienced by the one who knows Christ."[77]

The patristic concept of theosis as continual growth in the knowledge of God can be brought to Matthew's Gospel illustratively to show the value of a framework of theosis for interpreting it. Disciples' following Jesus as an embodied way of forgiveness is about "seeing and hearing" Jesus (e.g., 11:4). It is through seeing and hearing Jesus that the disciples continue to grow and participate in God's forgiving activity. By seeing how Jesus acts, the disciples learn what it means to do the will of the Father in heaven (7:21; 12:50). The will of the Father in heaven is manifested in Jesus's words and deeds. Throughout the narrative, Jesus desires mercy and forgiveness (e.g., 5:23–24, 43–47; 9:13; 12:7, 20; 18:27, 33; 20:34; 23:23; 26:28). Jesus sums up the entire law and the prophets through the hermeneutics of love (22:37–40). The will of the Father in heaven, then, is clearly manifest in the loving practice of mercy and forgiveness. Accordingly, the disciples participate in God's own will by seeing Jesus who embodies forgiveness as a way of life and learning from Jesus how to forgive, which is not a transaction but a transformation. Although the disciples often fail (e.g., playing the Satan and betraying Jesus), they gradually grow by virtue of seeing and hearing Jesus (e.g., 5:23–24; 9:9–13; 18:21–22; 26:28), as opposed to just a particular moment of belief (e.g., 16:16). As such, the disciples gradually learn to see the way Jesus sees, becoming Christ-like people who unfold God's own will, character, and power in their own, bodily life (28:19–20).

Similarly, regarding the knowledge of God, Jesus says that "no one knows the Father except the Son and anyone to whom the Son chooses to reveal the Father" (11:27). Jesus thus serves as God's unique way to reveal himself to human beings. For Matthew, God as Father is known not apart from the

Son, but in relation to the Son. In the Lord's Prayer, for instance, it is in and through Jesus that we participate in the Father-Son relation by addressing God as "our Father" (6:9). In particular, Jesus manifests God as the embodiment of the God of Israel, "God-with-us" (1:23). Thus, to know Jesus in Matthew's Gospel would mean understanding Jesus's relation to God as embodiment and presence of the God of Israel. To see Jesus, then, is to see God because Jesus serves as the very presence of God, not merely as the representative of God. Similarly, knowing God is not Jesus's privilege only but is shared with his people because of who God is, especially in Jesus, God-with-us. We as disciples of Jesus are empowered by Jesus's forgiving power to forgive others as we learn to see ourselves as sinners who have been forgiven. Because we have been forgiven, we are able to live as forgiving people, manifesting God's life that is in Jesus.

METHODOLOGY

This study employs a narrative approach to examine the literary, theological, and readerly concerns of Matthew's Gospel.[78] A narrative approach need not neglect the historical dimension of the text because Matthew's Gospel is a "cultural product," meaning that it is a narrative that speaks "both out of and over against the worlds within which [it was] written."[79] As Joel B. Green observes, works like Matthew's Gospel "participate in, legitimate, perpetuate, and criticize the worlds within which they were generated."[80] Michal Beth Dinkler similarly observes that "biblical literature embodies the cultural moment in which it arises."[81] She further notes that it is important to "situate literary texts within their historical contexts, while resisting 'old' historicism's positivist assumptions about objectivity."[82] In this sense, a narrative approach to Matthew's Gospel is not ahistorical but one that seeks to take seriously the narrative structure of Matthew's Gospel while being historically responsible about the emergence of the narrative itself.

As this study employs a narrative approach, I focus on important narratological elements like characterization (i.e., Jesus, the disciples, and opponents), rhetorical effect, and intertextuality within the text's socio-historical milieu. The main source for this project, then, is Matthew's Gospel, the canonical form of the text itself. Regarding characterization, I attend to how Jesus's character is built. John A. Darr observes that Jesus's character is built by his interaction with other characters: "Intermediate characters help the reader to construct the many images projected upon Jesus."[83] In Matthew's Gospel, Jesus is particularly characterized as "God-with-us" as Jesus touches and heals his people by drawing near to and being with them (e.g., 8:1–9:31). Further, Dinkler observes that Jesus is characterized by Jesus's interactions with other characters "within their broader narrative context."[84] For this reason, Dinkler points out that the beginning of a narrative is particularly important: "Because a narrative's linear order influences the audience's perceptions of its meanings, 'the perspectives established at the beginning, when we are seeking to orient ourselves in this new narrative world, will continue to operate until they are decisively challenged.'"[85] In Matthew's Gospel, Jesus is presented as God-with-us from the beginning of the narrative (1:23). Thus, Jesus's identity as God-with-us will help us to read later parts of the narrative, especially with respect to his interaction with other characters by sharing God's forgiving power. Regarding intertextuality, I examine Matthew's use of the OT because it provides the background for the divine-human relation, background that is both assumed and in some cases more directly mobilized in Matthew's presentation.[86]

This work is an exercise in theological interpretation of Scripture.[87] Rather than merely focusing on the world "behind," "of," or "in front of" the biblical text, theological interpretation considers the text in its canonical form. R. W. L. Moberly observes that "*theological interpretation is reading the Bible with a concern for the enduring truth of its witness to the nature of God and humanity, with a view to enabling the transformation of humanity into the likeness of God.*"[88] In this light, theological interpretation takes seriously the theological claim that the Bible is Scripture. As an instrument of divine communication, Scripture is the literary expression of God's revelation in history, especially for the life and practice of the church. In line with theological interpretation, this study has theological implications for the church, especially for the Korean church. The Korean church has suffered much from divisions throughout her history.[89] As Matthew invites *us* to embody God's forgiving power, we as the church need to listen to it and be shaped and transformed by its message.[90]

THE PLAN OF THE PRESENT STUDY

To establish my thesis by offering a plausible reading of forgiveness as theosis and to reinforce my arguments that theosis sheds light on forgiveness in Matthew's Gospel, the next four chapters examine how Matthew depicts forgiveness as theosis. To carry this out, passages from Matthew 6, 9, 18, and 26 will be examined for this study. This is not to say that other passages in Matthew lack the theme of forgiveness or repentance. But compared to other parts of the narrative, these four passages especially stand out because they unfold the transformative dynamics of heaven and earth (i.e., the transformative dynamics between the action of God and the action of human beings) in relation to the practice of forgiveness. Also, while the theme of forgiveness in these passages has been regularly discussed, no study has embarked on reading these passages through the framework of theosis. In particular, of these four passages, few studies anchor their exegesis in Matt 9, especially vv. 1–13, as an example of a forgiveness text. While Matthean scholars like Mbabazi emphasize the centrality of forgiveness in Matthew's Gospel, he mainly focuses on Matt 6 and 18.[91] In a similar vein, Todd Pokrifka-Joe directs his attention to Matt 6 and 18 as examples of forgiveness texts.[92] Matthew 9:1–13 unfolds the transformative dynamics of heaven and earth as specifically revealed in Jesus's forgiveness and healing. While Matthew briefly reports about Jesus's healing earlier in the narrative (4:23–24), the relation between Jesus's forgiving work and his healing are explicitly highlighted at this juncture in Matthew's narrative. Thus, the nature of Jesus's forgiveness as healing his people is concretely expressed in Matt 9. As will be shown in this study, Jesus's forgiveness of sins involves healing and repair of the inherited consequences of past sins over generations. The nature of forgiveness in Matthew, then, is a transformation of embodied life such that the consequences of past sins and corruptions are addressed and repaired. Forgiveness in this sense is healing participation in God's life. Accordingly, Matt 9, especially vv. 1–13, offers an inviting locus for considering Matthew's teaching of forgiveness through the lens of theosis.

Chapter 2 examines the dynamics of heaven and earth revealed in the Lord's Prayer, particularly through its words about embodying forgiveness prayerfully (6:12, 14–15). This prayer shows that to experience the life of the kingdom of heaven is not primarily about our afterlife beyond our deaths. The kingdom of heaven is what is coming to the earth, particularly as we embody forgiveness prayerfully. Thus, we unfold heavenly forgiving power through the practice of prayer and forgiveness. This chapter explores the nature of the Father and the language of *Father*, then discusses their significance in understanding theosis in Matthew's Gospel. It shows how our relation to God as Father expresses our participation in God's life rather than only our imitation of the Father. The Lord's Prayer unveils the message that Jesus is the fullness of the sonship that has already been Israel's life, as Jesus now teaches his people to pray to their Father as such. By sharing in Jesus's life of forgiveness, we come to participate in God's life as God's children (5:44–45; cf. 12:50). It is in and through sharing in Jesus's prayer, then, that we participate in the Son's relation to the Father, thereby experiencing God's life. This chapter also challenges the view that human forgiveness is the condition of God's forgiveness (6:12). I contend that what theosis allows us to see is that human forgiveness is not the condition of God's forgiveness but the mode of it, since human forgiveness embodies and extends God's own forgiveness. That is, God's act of forgiving is not simply based on our action of forgiveness; rather, our action becomes God's way of exercising forgiveness. Forgiveness in this sense is the process of transformation, one that may have a decisive beginning but is not simply a one-off transaction.

Chapter 3 examines the dynamics of heaven and earth revealed in Jesus's healing power (9:1–13). To understand Jesus's healing ministry, this study explores Matthew's presentation of Jesus as "God-with-us" (1:21), since Jesus's healing of his people is related to his presence with us (1:23; 8:1–9:38).[93] Because Jesus is with us, his healing power touches human beings so that they are transformed. Jesus's presence, then, is an ongoing means and empowerment of our life, transforming us. This study also explores the metaphor of God as healer, then examines the relation between healing and forgiveness. Given the connection between sickness and sin in Matthew's narrative world, Jesus's healing ministry can be thought of as "having saved people from their sins" through forgiveness of sins (1:21).[94] Sickness, in the concreteness of what it means for a person and in the community, is often viewed as one of the inherited consequences of past sins, as one outcome of a larger, intergenerational process of corruption. Thus, forgiveness involves repairing what that process has produced and setting the life of the people involved on a trajectory of health. In this light, forgiveness has to be understood as healing participation in God's transformative life. The nature of forgiveness, then, is a transformation of embodied life such that the consequences of past sins are confronted and repaired. In 9:1–13, Jesus as Son of Man heals a paralyzed person by forgiving him his sins. Thus, healing and forgiveness are juxtaposed and interrelated. Forgiveness enacts the heavenly healing power that makes one's life whole, restoring our relationship to God by the way it unites us with others. Additionally, this chapter shows that Jesus's authority to forgive sins given to human beings (9:8) is further confirmed in Jesus's mission discourse, where the disciples, now sharing in Jesus's authority, extend the forgiveness of sins by enacting God's heavenly power (10:1–7).

Chapter 4 continues to examine the transformative dynamics of heaven and earth revealed in our practice of forgiveness and prayer (18:15–35), now especially in 18:18–20. This chapter considers Matthew's presentation of the nature of the Father and its significance in understanding theosis, especially with respect to God's forgiveness (18:6, 10, 12–14, 19, 27) and the nature of our participation in God's forgiveness (18:35). I show how our way of exercising forgiveness as an extension of God's way of exercising forgiveness is grounded in embodied practice that reflects God's forgiving nature, presence, and activity (18:33, 35; cf. 5:23–24, 43–48; 7:21; 12:50). In my exegesis, I examine the ethic of forgiveness (18:15–17; 21–22) and challenge the excommunication reading. I contend that the church's discipline is aimed at the restoration and reconciliation of our relationship with God and with others. Next, I challenge the tendency to interpret heaven and earth as separate or conflicting realities. Jonathan T. Pennington contends that Matthew repeatedly sets up "a *contrast* between two realms—the heavenly and the earthly—which stand for God on the one hand, and humanity on the other."[95] While there is an important distinction between heaven and earth, that God's self in Jesus exercises the heavenly rule of God on earth points to a relational dynamic between heaven and earth. That is, earth is to be transformed by heaven. In God's self in Jesus, God participates fully in our earthly life so that we may participate in God's heavenly life. As such, the heavenly life becomes the reality of human life—the oneness of heaven and earth and of God and the human. To show this dynamic, I examine how the authority to forgive sins is given to the disciples through Jesus, particularly as community (18:18). By sharing in Jesus's authority as community, the disciples exercise God's own authority to bind and loose "on earth," manifesting God's forgiving power from heaven. Accordingly, our action of forgiveness as disciples of Jesus becomes what Jesus does. This chapter also explores Jesus's relation to the Spirit to challenge the scholarly tendency to disassociate the presence of Jesus from the presence of the Spirit as if they were not explicitly linked in Matthew's narrative (18:20). I suggest that theosis provides a lens that allows us to see the transfer and extension of power at work through the Spirit. Finally, I challenge the conditional view of God's forgiveness and demonstrate how forgiveness is the mode in which we extend God's own forgiveness (18:23–35). I also suggest that repentance is our relational mode of participating in God's gracious forgiveness, such that we embody God's forgiveness in repentance.

Chapter 5 examines the dynamics of heaven and earth revealed in Jesus's death, the culmination of God's forgiving power in the progress of Matthew's narrative (26:28). As the phrase, "for the forgiveness of sins," appears climactically at the end of the narrative (26:28), forming an *inclusio* with 1:21, this chapter shows how 26:28 expresses the culmination of God's forgiving power narratively. From the beginning of the narrative, Jesus's role is defined as delivering his people from their sins (1:21). Accordingly, Jesus's mission is oriented to delivering his people, specifically through forgiveness. This chapter also explores the nature of Jesus's table fellowship in 26:28 because Jesus's forgiveness is often expressed in his table fellowship (e.g., 9:9–13; 11:19; 26:20–29; cf. 21:31–32). I then examine how the nature of Jesus's death can be conceived in the framework of theosis, with respect to Jesus's shedding the blood of the covenant for the forgiveness of sins envisioned in the OT, discipleship, and the heaven-earth relation in Matthew. Jesus's forgiveness, which culminates in his death, empowers his followers to participate in Jesus's own life. Just as Jesus participates in God's life by embodying forgiveness, so he calls us to participate in God's own life by the way Jesus shares in our human life. Just as Jesus takes up his cross, so we are called to take up our own cross to share in his life. Just as we gather in Jesus's name in 18:20, so we are called to carry on Jesus's work in his name, God-with-us, "the name of the Father and of the Son and of the Holy Spirit" (28:19). We thus provide a faithful witness to the kingdom from heaven, embodying forgiveness wrought by Jesus in the Spirit.

NOTES

1. New Testament scholars concerned with theosis have focused their attention on the Johannine literature, Paul's letters, and 2 Peter. For instance, see, e.g., Michael J. Gorman, *Abide and Go: Missional Theosis in the Gospel of John*, The Didsbury Lectures 2016 (Eugene, OR: Cascade, 2018); idem, *Inhabiting the Cruciform God: Kenosis, Justification, and Theosis in Paul's Narrative Soteriology* (Grand Rapids: Eerdmans, 2009); Ben C. Blackwell, *Christosis: Engaging Paul's Soteriology with His Patristic Interpreters*, WUNT 2/314 (Tübingen: Mohr Siebeck, 2011; Grand Rapids: Eerdmans, 2016); Stephen Finlan, "Second Peter's Notion of Divine Participation," in *Theōsis: Deification in Christian Theology*, ed. Stephen Finlan and Vladimir Kharlamov, Princeton Theological Monograph Series 52 (Eugene, OR: Pickwick, 2006), 32–50. For the sake of convenience, I refer to the author of the Gospel of Matthew as "Matthew."

2. Stephen Finlan and Vladimir Kharlamov, "Introduction," in *Theōsis: Deification in Christian Theology*, ed. Stephen Finlan and Vladimir Kharlamov, Princeton Theological Monograph Series 52 (Eugene, OR: Pickwick, 2006), 2–4.

3. Isaac K. Mbabazi, *The Significance of Interpersonal Forgiveness in the Gospel of Matthew* (Eugene, OR: Pickwick, 2013), 7. See also John Nolland (*The Gospel of Matthew: A Commentary on the Greek Text*, NIGTC [Grand Rapids: Eerdmans, 2005], 505), who points out the "forgiveness project" of Matthew's Gospel; Anders Runesson, *Divine Wrath and Salvation in Matthew: The Narrative World of the First Gospel* (Minneapolis: Fortress, 2017), 121.

4. F. S. Spencer, "Forgiveness of Sins," in *DJG*, ed. Joel B. Green, Jeannine K. Brown, and Nicholas Perrin, 2nd ed. (Downers Grove, IL: InterVarsity Press, 2013), 285. Spencer notes that the term forgiveness is related to "freedom, release, letting go (*aphiēmi, aphesis, apolyō*)" and represents "less a static, juridical concept of expunging a record of transgression" than a dynamic "experience of being released from the deleterious effects of guilt and sinful behavior and restoring broken relations between human beings and God and among themselves" (284). In this sense, forgiveness is more than a one-off transaction but involves a relational dynamic between God and human beings. In Matthew, forgiveness also closely "aligns with liberation, salvation, reconciliation, and restoration" (284). The term σώζω refers to "preserve," "keep safe," "rescue," or "protect." See Franco Montanari, *The Brill Dictionary of Ancient Greek*, ed. Madeleine Goh and Chad Schroeder (Leiden: Brill, 2015), 2072. Salvation in Matthew refers to God's liberative acts for his people from their enemies or crisis (1:21). In the parallel formulated in 1:23, quoting Isa 7:14, Matthew shows who

Jesus is, Emmanuel, God-with-us (1:23). In the context of Isa 7:14, God protects and delivers his people from their enemies (7:14–25). For Matthew, the way God is with his people is thus the way God saves, liberates, and rescues his people, specifically through forgiveness. The concrete nature of Jesus as God-with-us and savior will be discussed more in chapter 3. Regarding the relation between salvation and forgiveness, Spencer notes that salvation or deliverance "no doubt includes forgiveness *as part* of a dynamic, holistic project of rescuing people from the ravages of sin and enabling them to flourish" (285; emphasis mine). Thus, God empowers forgiveness as one piece of his salvation.

5. In Matthew's narrative, our participation in God's forgiveness enables us to become his children and heirs (e.g., 5:44–45; 12:50; 28:18–20). The nature of our participation in God's forgiveness will be discussed in chapter 4.

6. In Matthew's narrative, these particulars are especially relational—that is, a healing unfolded by God's forgiving power in the human. Matthew's forgiveness is not merely transactional but involves the process of healing (cf. Jer 31:10–34). Forgiveness as healing participation in God's life will be discussed in chapter 3.

7. Grant Macaskill, *Union with Christ in the New Testament* (Oxford: Oxford University Press, 2013), 45.

8. Ibid. Similarly, see Norman Russell (*The Doctrine of Deification in the Greek Patristic Tradition* [Oxford: Oxford University Press, 2004], 262), who notes the observation of Maximus the Confessor: "deification is in the end the goal, the *skopos*, of the entire cosmos," the fulfillment of the entire created order.

9. Vladimir Kharlamov, "Introduction," in *Theōsis: Deification in Christian Theology*, ed. Vladimir Kharlamov, Princeton Theological Monograph Series 156 (Eugene, OR: Pickwick, 2011), 5. Kharlamov notes, "[Theosis] is a transformative experience that enables human beings" to participate in Christ (5).

10. Macaskill, *Union with Christ*, 45.

11. Norman Russell, *Fellow Workers with God: Orthodox Thinking on Theosis*, Foundations Series 5 (Crestwood, NY: St. Vladimir's Seminary Press, 2009), 36.

12. Stephen Finlan, "Deification in Jesus' Teaching," in *Theōsis: Deification in Christian Theology*, ed. Vladimir Kharlamov, Princeton Theological Monograph Series 156 (Eugene, OR: Pickwick, 2011), 21.

13. Gorman, *Inhabiting the Cruciform God*, 5. See Irenaeus of Lyons, *Against the Heresies* 5, preface 1; Athanasius, *On the Incarnation of the Word* 54.

14. Russell, *Doctrine of Deification*, 1–2.

15. Ibid., 14.

16. Daniel A. Keating, "Typologies of Deification," *International Journal of Systematic Theology* 17, no. 3 (2015): 273. Keating notes further, "Our deification is anchored in what God has done in Christ. . . . But deification also includes our graced response, the full cooperation of our mind and will and emotions" (282).

17. On the history of the concept of participation from Plato to the church fathers, see Daniel A. Keating, *Divinization in Cyril: The Appropriation of Divine Life* (Oxford: Oxford University Press, 2005), 147–55. In Neoplatonist thought, participation is understood as "the transference of what is essential of a thing to a subordinate." See Lucas Siorvanes, *Proclus: Neo-Platonic Philosophy and Science* (Edinburgh:

Edinburgh University Press, 1996), 76. Keating notes that the church fathers transposed the Neoplatonic concept of participation in "a specifically Christian theological context" (148).

18. Andrew J. Byers, *Ecclesiology and Theosis in the Gospel of John*, SNTSMS 166 (Cambridge: Cambridge University Press, 2017), 159 (emphasis original). See also Richard B. Hays (*The Faith of Jesus Christ: The Narrative Substructure of Galatians 3:1–4:11*, 2nd ed. [Grand Rapids: Eerdmans, 2002], xxxii), who points out the potential significance of "participation motifs" in the early patristic writings for NT study, though he does not explore this matter.

19. Russell, *Doctrine of Deification*, 203.

20. J. A. McGuckin, "The Strategic Adaptation of Deification in the Cappadocians," in *Partakers of the Divine Nature: The History and Development of Deification in the Christian Traditions*, ed. Michael J. Christensen and Jeffery A. Wittung (Grand Rapids: Baker Academic, 2007), 106.

21. Byers, *Ecclesiology and Theosis*, 171 (emphasis original). Hans Boersma calls it "Platonist-Christian synthesis" (*Heavenly Participation: The Weaving of a Sacramental Tapestry* [Grand Rapids: Eerdmans, 2011], 19–39).

22. Ibid.

23. In patristic thought, to share in God's character and to share in God's essence are distinguished. For instance, Irenaeus articulates this distinction that those who are in God's light do not themselves illuminate the light, but are illuminated by it (*Haer* 4.14). Thus, God can give God's own properties to human beings such that they are given but not innate by essence.

24. C. R. Strange, "Athanasius on Divinization," *StPatr* 16, no. 6 (1985): 343.

25. Macaskill, *Union with Christ*, 58.

26. Ibid., 60.

27. Russell, *Doctrine of Deification*, 266.

28. Ibid., 267.

29. Michael J. Christensen, "The Problem, Promise, and Process of *Theosis*," in *Partakers of the Divine Nature: The History and Development of Deification in the Christian Traditions*, ed. Michael J. Christensen and Jeffery A. Wittung (Grand Rapids: Baker Academic, 2007), 27.

30. Russell, *Doctrine of Deification*, 278. Russell notes that for Maximus, "The human and the divine begin to interpenetrate each other as we appropriate immortality, stability, and immutability" (294).

31. Ibid., 295 (emphasis original). Maximus maintains a Chalcedonian distinction between God and the human.

32. Christensen, "Problem, Promise, and Process," 29.

33. Ben C. Blackwell, "Immortal Glory and the Problem of Death in Romans 3.23," *JSNT* 32, no. 3 (2010): 304.

34. Ibid., 305.

35. Russell, *Fellow Workers with God*, 25–26. Russell aptly points out, "Through theosis we become *homotheoi*, one with God, not because we have become what God is in his essence, but because we have come to share in his attributes" (134).

36. Macaskill, *Union with Christ*, 43.

37. As Macaskill notes, "In Eastern Orthodox thought, *theosis* cannot be separated from a particular set of configurations of the relationship between God and his creation that are typically not shared by Western theology, even when there is a substantial common ground in terms of concepts of deification" (*Union with Christ*, 45).

38. Byers, *Ecclesiology and Theosis*, 183.

39. Robert W. Jenson, "Theosis," *Di* 32, no. 2 (1993): 110 (emphasis mine).

40. Byers, *Ecclesiology and Theosis*, 181.

41. Ibid. (emphasis original).

42. Ibid.

43. Myk Habets, "Reforming Theōsis," in *Theōsis: Deification in Christian Theology*, ed. Stephen Finlan and Vladimir Kharlamov, Princeton Theological Monograph Series 52 (Eugene, OR: Pickwick, 2006), 159. Macaskill points out that while "[m]uch has been made of the distinction between *koinōnia* and *methexis*," the terms can be used "interchangeably" at least in Paul because "the use of such vocabulary is governed by context" (*Union with Christ*, 72 n. 106). Macaskill goes on to say that when the patristic fathers speak of "kinship and participation, they operate with concepts of ontological distinction that require notions of *communication* and *communion*" (72; emphasis original).

44. Kharlamov, "Introduction," 7.

45. In a similar vein, Finlan and Kharlamov suggest that the terms "union" (ἕνωσις), "communion" (κοινωνία), and "participation" (μετουσία, μέθεξις, μετάληψις) are the language of theosis ("Introduction," 6).

46. This means that theosis does not present God's action and human action as separate, even as it maintains the distinction between creator and creation. They are on the same plane as God's own forgiveness of the human becomes humans' forgiving one another.

47. Unless otherwise specified, all NT translations are my own from NA^{28}. Warren Carter notes that "to be whole denotes the undivided heart which truly *knows* and loyally *does* God's will (Gen 6:9; Deut 18:13; 1 Kgs 8:61; 11:4; 15:3, 14; 1 Chr 28:9)" (*Matthew and the Margins: A Sociopolitical and Religious Reading*, The Bible & Liberation Series [Maryknoll, NY: Orbis Books, 2000], 157; emphasis mine).

48. See also Ezek 34:30, where the relationship between God and his people are framed in the language of knowledge (ידע): "They shall know (ידע) that I, the Lord their God, am with them, and that they, the house of Israel, are my people" (NRSV). Cf. The term ידע is also used to refer to observation (e.g., Gen 3:7; 15:13; Exod 2:4).

49. Keating, "Typologies of Deification," 281.

50. Panayiotis Nellas, *Deification in Christ: Orthodox Perspectives on the Nature of the Human Person*, trans. Norman Russell (Crestwood, NY: St Vladimir's Seminary Press, 1987), 42.

51. Keating, "Typologies of Deification," 282.

52. Dietrich Bonhoeffer, *Christ the Center*, trans. Edwin H. Robertson (New York: Harper & Row, 1978), 45. Bonhoeffer argues that the one God-human is "the starting point for Christology" (45).

53. Ibid., 101.

54. That Matthew assumes the general understanding of the OT is also attested in his narration of Jesus's genealogy. As Richard B. Hays observes, "Matthew anchors the story of Jesus in Israel's history by opening his Gospel with a genealogy" ("The Gospel of Matthew: Reconfigured Torah," *HTS* 61 [2005]: 169). According to Hays, Jesus is the "heir of a familial line that stretches back through forty-two generations to Abraham" (170). See also Margaret Hannan (*The Nature and Demands of God's Sovereign Rule in the Gospel of Matthew*, LNTS 308 [London: T&T Clark, 2006], 45): "the expression ὁ λαός (the people) is found fourteen times in Matthew and has clear reference in almost every case to Israel (cf. 1:21; 2:4, 6; 4:16, 23; 13:15; 15:8; 21:23; 26:3, 5, 47; 27:1, 25, 64)." Similarly, Ulrich Luz notes that "*Laos* ('people') is consistently applied to Israel" ("The Disciples in the Gospel according to Matthew," in *The Interpretation of Matthew*, ed. Graham N. Stanton [Edinburgh: T&T Clark, 1995], 132). J. G. van der Watt and D. S. du Toit note that in Matthew, the Hebrew meaning of Jesus's name ("God is savior") and his mission are related ("Salvation," in *DJG*, 828). In 1:21, Matthew assumes that "God as savior (cf. Deut 32:15; 1 Sam 10:19; Ps 23:5; Is 12:2; 43:4, 11–12) will save Israel from their sins through Jesus as instrument of salvation" (828). In the parallel formulated in 1:23, moreover, Matthew assumes that the way Jesus saves his people from their sins is made possible by his presence with us. This will be shown in detail in chapter 3.

55. David D. Kupp, *Matthew's Emmanuel: Divine Presence and God's People in the First Gospel*, SNTSMS 90 (Cambridge: Cambridge University Press, 1996), 144.

56. Ibid., 142–43.

57. God's forgiveness in the OT and Jesus's embodiment of God's forgiveness will be explored in the next section of this chapter ("The Lord's Prayer").

58. Paul M. Collins, *Partaking in Divine Nature: Deification and Communion* (London: T&T Clark, 2010), 38.

59. With regard to the vocabulary of participation, Keating points out two word groups—μετέχειν and κοινωνεῖν—found in the NT (e.g., Rom 15:27; 1 Cor 10:14–22; Heb 2:14–15; 6:4; 12:10; Phil 2:1; 2 Pet 1:4). While there is no explicit language of theosis in the NT, the church fathers like Irenaeus employed the terms κοινωνία, μεταλαμβάνειν, and μετέχειν to express the idea of participation in God's life (Keating, *Divinization in Cyril*, 151).

60. Byers, *Ecclesiology and Theosis*, 157.

61. Michael J. Gorman, "Romans: The First Christian Treatise on Theosis," *JTI* 5, no. 1 (2011): 18.

62. Ibid.

63. Ibid.

64. Mikhail M. Bakhtin, "Response to a Question from the *Novy Mir* Editorial Staff," in *Speech Genres and Other Late Essays*, trans. Vern M. McGee, ed. Caryl Emerson and Michael Holquist, 2nd ed. (Austin: University of Texas Press, 1986), 5.

65. M. David Litwa, "2 Corinthians 3:18 and Its Implications for Theosis," *JTI* 2, no. 1 (2008): 117.

66. As noted at the outset, this study does not mean to claim that forgiveness is the sum total of theosis in Matthew, but one aspect of theosis.

67. Collins, *Partaking in Divine Nature*, 38.

68. Gorman, *Inhabiting the Cruciform God*, 167 (emphasis mine).

69. Ibid., 173 (emphasis original).

70. The Spirit of God as a source of power is attested in the OT (e.g., Judg 14:6; 1 Sam 16:13, 23).

71. Christensen, "The Problem, Promise, and Process," 29 (emphasis mine). Jenson also writes, "It is the church which is filled by the Holy Spirit and it is precisely for this reason that every human person has the possibility of becoming a partaker of the divine nature" ("Theosis," 108).

72. In Matthew's narrative, Jesus himself unfolds God's forgiving power by being empowered by the Spirit (12:28; cf. 9:2, 6). It is no coincidence that the Spirit is particularly presented as the forgiving power of God (12:24–32). Jesus warns that to blaspheme the power of the Spirit is not forgivable because to blaspheme the power of the Spirit is to speak directly against the very forgiving power of God that touches and heals God's own people. It is to name God's forgiving power of the Spirit itself the satanic power that tears people apart from one another (12:24). In this sense, Jesus's power is none other than the power of the Spirit. It is plausible, then, that the way Jesus empowers the disciples is by means of the same power of the Spirit he receives (10:1). Further, when Jesus says he is "in the midst" of his people (18:20), Jesus's presence implies the presence of the Spirit, the forgiving power of God. Jesus's presence is related to God's forgiving power because 18:20 is given in the literary context, where the process of reconciling forgiveness between the community members is discussed. In this reconciling process, the church, empowered by the presence of Jesus, exercises an authority to bind and loose, unfolding God's forgiving power from heaven (18:18–20). Jesus's relation to the Spirit will be discussed further in chapter 4.

73. In his *Inhabiting the Cruciform God*, Gorman provides a lens—cruciformity—to understand Paul's construction of theosis. While the theme of cruciform God is not a new idea, he spells out how cruciformity is an expression of Pauline theosis.

74. Gorman, *Abide and Go*, 179 (emphasis original). Gorman notes that "Spirit-enabled transformative participation in the life and character of God revealed in the crucified and resurrected Messiah Jesus" is "the *starting point* of mission" and is "its *proper theological framework*" (190; emphasis original).

75. James Starr, "Does 2 Peter 1:4 Speak of Deification?," in *Partakers of the Divine Nature: The History and Development of Deification in the Christian Traditions*, ed. Michael J. Christensen and Jeffery A. Wittung (Grand Rapids: Baker Academic, 2007), 87–88.

76. Ibid., 88 (emphasis mine).

77. Ibid., 85.

78. Michal Beth Dinkler, *Literary Theory and the New Testament* (New Haven: Yale University Press, 2019); Joel B. Green, "Narrative Criticism," in *Methods for Luke*, ed. Joel B. Green, Methods in Biblical Interpretation (Cambridge: Cambridge University Press, 2010), 74–112. See also Sookgoo Shin (*Ethics in the Gospel of John: Discipleship as Moral Progress*, BibInt 168 [Leiden: Brill, 2019], 23): "The reader is not to remain neutral but is encouraged to either identify or disidentify with characters by sharing their experiences and reflecting on the ethical dimensions of character's actions." The reader thus actively engages with the text's theological

vision, thereby being shaped by its vision. Shin notes further, "Such a transformative power of narrative enables readers to engage the story not as passive spectators but as active participants who are expected to align themselves with the view of the narrator and the worldview presented by the narratives" (122).

79. Joel B. Green, "Rethinking 'History' for Theological Interpretation," *JTI* 5, no. 2 (2011): 171.

80. Ibid.

81. Dinkler, *Literary Theory*, 193.

82. Ibid., 141. Regarding the "old historicism's positivist assumptions about objectivity," Dinkler notes that objectivity is not possible because all historical accounts are "partial" and "selective" (142).

83. John A. Darr, *On Character Building: The Reader and the Rhetoric of Characterization in Luke-Acts*, Literary Currents in Biblical Interpretation (Louisville: Westminster John Knox, 1992), 41.

84. Dinkler, *Literary Theory*, 143.

85. Ibid. Dinkler's quotation is from Robert C. Tannehill, "Beginning to Study 'How Gospels Begin,'" *Semeia* 52 (1990): 188.

86. Regarding Matthew's use of the OT, see Richard B. Hays, *Echoes of Scripture in the Gospels* (Waco, TX: Baylor University Press, 2016); idem, "The Gospel of Matthew," 165–90; Craig L. Blomberg, "Matthew," in *Commentary on the New Testament Use of the Old Testament*, ed. G. K. Beale and D. A. Carson (Grand Rapids: Baker Academic, 2007), 1–109; Richard Beaton, *Isaiah's Christ in Matthew's Gospel*, SNTSMS 123 (Cambridge: Cambridge University Press, 2002), 14–34; Donald Senior, *What Are They Saying About Matthew?*, rev. ed. (New York: Paulist, 1996), 51–61; Eugene Eung-Chun Park, "Rachel's Cry for Her Children: Matthew's Treatment of the Infanticide by Herod," *CBQ* 75, no. 3 (2013): 473–85; Dale C. Allison Jr., *Studies in Matthew: Interpretation Past and Present* (Grand Rapids: Baker Academic, 2005); Woojin Chung, *Translation Theory and the Old Testament in Matthew: The Possibilities of Skopos Theory*, Linguistic Biblical Studies 15 (Leiden: Brill, 2017). Chung argues that "Matthew not only renders the OT materials linguistically, but also translates their cultural and theological realities into his Christological narrative to communicate purposefully their significance to his audience" (14). That is, "the NT writers attempted to translate the meaning of particular OT texts into the world of the NT for their purposes of which the old passage is interpreted anew" (14). Also, on the features of intertextuality, see Steve Moyise, "Intertextuality and the Study of the Old Testament in the New Testament," in *The Old Testament in the New Testament: Essays in Honour of J. L. North*, ed. Steve Moyise (Sheffield: Sheffield Academic, 2000), 14–41; Stanley E. Porter, "Further Comments on the Use of the Old Testament in the New Testament," in *The Intertextuality of the Epistles: Explorations of Theory and Practice*, ed. Thomas L. Brodie, Dennis R. MacDonald, and Stanley E. Porter (Sheffield: Sheffield Phoenix, 2007), 98–110.

87. Joel B. Green, "Practicing the Gospel in a Post-Critical World: The Promise of Theological Exegesis," *JETS* 47, no. 3 (2004): 387–97; Kevin J. Vanhoozer, "What Is Theological Interpretation of the Bible?," in *Dictionary for Theological Interpretation of the Bible*, ed. Kevin J. Vanhoozer (Grand Rapids: Baker Academic, 2005),

19–25. See also Marianne Meye Thompson ("On Writing a Commentary," *JTI* 15, no. 2 [2021]: 344): "for those who consider these texts to be Scripture, these texts are not merely or even primarily documents of antiquarian interest. Throughout time, the people of God who wrote, preserved, canonized, and read Scripture have borne witness that these texts are about God, and that God addresses us in them. . . . We hear the Scriptures addressed to us not merely because there are analogies between the people of the past and us, not only because we have similar problems and face similar challenges, not because we are *like* those who were originally addressed in Scripture, but because we are *one* with them" (emphasis original).

88. R. W. L. Moberly, "What Is Theological Interpretation of Scripture?" *JTI* 3, no. 2 (2009): 163 (emphasis original).

89. See, e.g., In Soo Kim, *History of Christianity in Korea* (Seoul: Qumran Publishing House, 2011), 503; Sebastian C. H. Kim and Kirsteen Kim, *A History of Korean Christianity* (Cambridge: Cambridge University Press, 2015), 159–61; 197–206. Kim and Kim note, "The denomination most affected by division was the largest, the Presbyterian Church, which by 1960 had fractured into four different denominations in the South" (197). This study's theological implication for the church will be revisited in its concluding chapter.

90. As Joel B. Green observes, as "model readers," we hear the text's own voice "from within its own various contextual horizons. At the same time, we remain open to God's challenge of developing those habits of life that make us receptive to God's vision, God's character, and God's project," such that we allow "the terms of these texts to address us: to critique, to encourage, to motivate, to instruct, to redirect—that is, to shape us" (*Practicing Theological Interpretation: Engaging Biblical Texts for Faith and Formation*, Theological Explorations for the Church Catholic [Grand Rapids: Baker Academic, 2011], 20).

91. See Mbabzi, *Significance of Interpersonal Forgiveness*, 117–89.

92. Todd Pokrifka-Joe, "Probing the Relationship between Divine and Human Forgiveness in Matthew," in *Forgiveness and Truth: Explorations in Contemporary Theology*, ed. Alistair I. McFadyen, Marcel Sarot, and Anthony Thiselton (Edinburgh: T&T Clark, 2001), 165–72.

93. In Matthew's narrative, Jesus's being God-with-us is particularly paired with his calling as deliverer of his people from their sins (1:21, 23). Named God-with-us, Jesus saves his people, especially through forgiveness of sins. Chapter 3 will discuss that Jesus's forgiveness is expressed in his healing.

94. W. D. Davies and Dale C. Allison Jr., *Matthew 1–7: A Critical and Exegetical Commentary on the Gospel according to Saint Matthew*, ICC (London: T&T Clark, 2004), 602.

95. Jonathan T. Pennington, "The Kingdom of Heaven in the Gospel of Matthew," *Southern Baptist Journal of Theology* 12, no. 1 (2008): 47 (emphasis original). According to Pennington, Matthew urges us to sense that there is "a great disjunction between heaven and earth, between God's way of doing things and ours" (47). See also idem, *Heaven and Earth in the Gospel of Matthew* (Grand Rapids: Baker Academic, 2007).

Chapter 2

The Lord's Prayer

Embodying Forgiveness as Participation in the Father in Heaven

The Lord's Prayer is significant for this study because, particularly through its words about embodying forgiveness prayerfully (6:12, 14–15), it epitomizes the Father-Son relation and the transformative dynamics of heaven and earth in Matthew.[1] While this part of the Lord's Prayer has regularly been read as an example of a forgiveness text in Matthean scholarship, what will be usefully explored is the particular way theosis sheds light on the concept of forgiveness in the Lord's Prayer.[2] What theosis allows us to see is that practicing forgiveness prayerfully is not merely following Jesus and imitating what Jesus does. We are not only to imitate the Father's forgiving life. We receive forgiving life from the Father, thereby embodying on the earth God's own heavenly forgiveness. That is what it means to participate in the Son's relation to the Father in the context of the Lord's Prayer. As such, one important element of this chapter is to demonstrate how our relation to God as Father expresses our participation in God's own life, as opposed to merely our imitation of God's character.[3] Another important element of this chapter is to shed light on the relational dynamics of heaven and earth through the framework of theosis. Finally, this chapter challenges the view that human forgiveness is the condition of God's forgiveness. I contend that what theosis allows us to see is that human forgiveness is not the condition of God's forgiveness but the mode of it, since human forgiveness embodies and extends God's own forgiveness. Thus, God's act of forgiving is not simply based on our action of forgiveness, but rather our action becomes God's way of exercising forgiveness. Forgiveness in this sense is a process of transformation, often with a decisive beginning, not simply a one-off transaction.

To make my argument, I first examine the theological and literary contexts of the Lord's Prayer to grasp its position and significance in Matthew's narrative.[4] I then consider Matthew's presentation of the nature of the Father and its significance in understanding theosis, especially with respect to God's forgiving nature and activity. When Jesus teaches that God is merciful, the underlying assumption is that just as God mercifully forgives, so God's children are called to embody merciful forgiveness. I also briefly examine the language of *Father* because Matthew's distinctive use of Father language accentuates the nuance of the familial relation of belonging between God and his children. I then offer an exegesis of portions of 6:9–15 in three steps. Each step has its own distinct emphasis, but together they contribute to an understanding of how a focus on theosis sheds light on forgiveness in Matthew's Gospel. First, I focus on the phrase "our Father" in 6:9 to show how our relation to God as Father expresses our participation in God's life rather than only our imitation of the Father. Furthermore, the character of the Father reveals the character of Jesus as the Son. By sharing in Jesus's life of prayer, we grow as God's own children rather than merely imitating what the Father does. Second, I focus on 6:9–10 to examine the transformative dynamics of heaven and earth through the framework of theosis. This shows how the action of God and the action of human beings converge through Jesus, who exercises the heavenly rule of God on earth. Finally, I focus on 6:12 and 14–15 to examine how our embodying forgiveness prayerfully is not a conditional dynamic but indeed a relational one between God and the human.

THE THEOLOGICAL AND LITERARY CONTEXTS OF THE LORD'S PRAYER

The Lord's Prayer is located in a theological context marked by what we might call kingdom ethics, namely, the Sermon on the Mount (5:1–7:29). Allen Verhey notes that the kingdom ethic is "an ethic of response to the coming kingdom of God."[5] The proper response to the kingdom in Matthew is "a way of life marked by compassionate concern for the other."[6] This is later developed by Jesus's recurrent teachings on caring for the hungry and the least (e.g., 18:5; 25:35–45). That is, Jesus continues to invite his people to show mercy to others (e.g., 9:13; 12:7; 20:34; 22:37–40; 23:23). The kingdom ethic Matthew envisions, then, is a call for each of us to learn a way of life of loving others, not least through embodying forgiveness.

In the Sermon on the Mount, in the section leading up to that in which he teaches his prayer (5:21–48), Jesus first touches on the issue of anger in our relationships (5:21–26). Anger can prevent us from reconciling with God and with others. Thus, Jesus urges his people to reconcile with others before they bring their offering to God (5:23–24). Embodying reconciling forgiveness is therefore the proper mode of worshipping God. It is in this mode that our relationship to God is restored by the way it unites us with others. Similarly, Jesus continues to teach the disciples to embody God's love by loving one another, even their enemies (5:43–48). The Lord's Prayer will then express the concern for Jesus's followers to embody God's heavenly forgiving power (6:12, 14–15; cf. 5:7, 9, 21–26, 38–42, 43–48).

The Lord's Prayer is also located among the pillar practices of the community—almsgiving (6:1–4), prayer (6:5–15), and fasting (6:16–18). Jesus presents his prayer in contrast with the prayer of the hypocrites: "When you pray, do not be like the hypocrites" (6:5).[7] The hypocrites are those who misconstrue the will of the Father, with the result that their inner person does not match their outward behavior.[8] They focus on their outward appearance and "trumpet their deeds to receive honor from others (6:2)."[9] Jesus teaches that "when you pray," the prayer is not to be aimed at impressing others (6:5) or being verbose and meaningless like the prayer of gentiles (6:7). The principle of not being showy like the hypocrites also applies to almsgiving (6:2) and fasting (6:16). This is in line, as a theosis sensibility would recognize, with the character of the Father in heaven who sees in secret and rewards those who do good works in secret (6:4, 6, 18).[10] Thus, God's children are invited to help others "without concern for show and only for God's viewing (6:3–4)."[11] The Lord's Prayer is given in this context to invite God's children to discern and embody God's heavenly will on earth (cf. 7:21; 12:50), as opposed to misconstruing God's will as a basis for hypocritical self-righteousness.

THE NATURE OF THE FATHER AND *FATHER* LANGUAGE IN MATTHEW'S GOSPEL

The Nature of the Father in Matthew's Gospel

It is important to consider Matthew's own terms for describing the nature of the Father. When Jesus blesses those who are merciful (5:7), the underlying assumption is that just as God is merciful, so his children are to be merciful. When Jesus defines "peacemakers" as children of God (5:9), the underlying assumption is that just as God is the God of peace and reconciliation, so we are to be. When Jesus encourages his followers to love their enemies (5:44), the underlying assumption, which Jesus makes explicit, is that just as the Father is generous with human enemies, finally in the love for enemies the Father's Son embodies on a cross (this will be discussed in chapter 5), so his children are expected to care for their enemies (5:44–48). Thus, God's children are called to reflect the nature of the Father "who is whole and loves his enemies (5:45)."[12] By loving our enemies, we reflect God's loving character, who sends rain on both the righteous and the unrighteous (5:45). Also, just as the Father feeds the birds of the air and cares for his children (6:11, 6:25–34; 7:11), so his people are expected to embody the Father's mercy.[13] Thus, God's love and mercy serve as both a model and a kind of intergenerational power for how God's people are to understand and practice our vocation as the kingdom family. As the concept of theosis emphasizes, we are to participate in God's merciful character as the children of that God. To embody forgiveness, then, is grounded in God's character as our Father. According to Isaac K. Mbabazi, "God's mercy and forgiveness exemplified in Jesus's life" provide a paradigm for us to embody.[14] But, as I will emphasize, it is also a flow of power, from the Father, in Jesus the Son, to us as the children of the Father. For Matthew, the central mark of God's family is doing the will of the heavenly Father (7:21; 12:50), especially embodying with others God's own generous love (5:44–45), which can take the form of forgiving them.[15] This means that we should leave our former ways and patterns of feeling, thinking, and behaving, insofar as these refuse to be like our Father, and follow the new pattern of life revealed and conveyed to us through Jesus's teaching on forgiveness, including his example. As Matthew portrays God as a merciful God who forgives, our action of forgiveness reflects God's merciful character. Accordingly, embodying forgiveness is our participation in the Father's loving character in Matthew's Gospel.[16]

The Language of *Father* in Matthew's Gospel

Compared to Mark and Luke, Matthew has a distinctive interest in *Father* language. Jonathan T. Pennington notes that Jesus refers to God as Father forty-four times in Matthew, whereas this reference is found only four times in Mark and seventeen times in Luke. Pennington goes on to note that while Matthew refers to God as Father more often than he refers to human fathers, both Mark and Luke refer to "human fathers more often than God as Father."[17] Matthew's distinctive interest in the language of Father is also expressed in his preference of possessive formulations like "my Father," "our Father," and "your Father." The expression "my Father" appears fifteen times in Matthew, whereas this formulation appears four times in Luke and never in Mark.[18] Moreover, the formulation "your Father" appears fifteen times in Matthew, whereas it appears three times in Luke and once in Mark. The frequent appearance of the possessive formulations in Matthew accentuates the nuance of the character of our relation to the Father as an intimate, kinship relationship of belonging and mutual sharing (e.g., 12:50).[19]

THE LORD'S PRAYER: FORGIVENESS AS PARTICIPATION IN THE FATHER IN HEAVEN

The Lord's Prayer shows that to experience the life of the kingdom of heaven is not primarily about our afterlife.[20] In Matthew, that the kingdom of heaven is not primarily about our afterlife or a future destination is confirmed by the rule of Israel's God in history and his continued rule "that runs from John (3:2), to Jesus (4:17, 23; 9:35), to the mission of the twelve (10:7), to the ongoing mission of Jesus's followers (24:14), to the eschaton itself (25:1, 34; 26:29)."[21] Joel B. Green notes that "the introduction of Jesus as king is set within a birth narrative accentuating God's past activity on behalf of God's people and shows Jesus' continuity with and consummation of that history."[22] In Matthew's conception, therefore, the kingdom of heaven is not something to wait for until the end, for the kingdom "has come near" (ἤγγικεν) in Jesus (3:2; 4:17; 10:7).[23] Matthew portrays Jesus's message as "the good news of the kingdom" (4:23; 9:35), indicating that Jesus embodies the heavenly kingdom in his message and now ushers this in us through prayer at this juncture of the narrative (6:10). The coming of the rule of Israel's God is further enacted by our prayer here and now ("Your kingdom come," 6:10), as it anticipates the action of forgiveness requested later in the prayer (6:12, 14–15). The kingdom of heaven is thus what is coming to the earth, particularly, per the concluding lines of the prayer (6:12, 14–15), as we embody forgiveness prayerfully. This prayer thus specifies that the kingdom comes through, among other things, the practices of prayer and forgiveness. This is not to say that the kingdom comes only through prayer and forgiveness. The practices of prayer and forgiveness are particular acts that can enact the rule of Israel's God on the earth. Elsewhere in Matthew's narrative, embodying forgiveness prayerfully manifests the will of the Father in heaven (e.g., 18:18–20; cf. 5:23–24, 44–45; 18:33–35; 22:37–40). Thus, it is through embodying forgiveness prayerfully that we come to live the kingdom life on the earth. In this sense, the coming of the kingdom and the doing of God's will in this particular way—the practices of prayer and forgiveness—are tied together. The Lord's Prayer is also more than a matter of imitating of Jesus's life. By considering the prayer through the lens of theosis, we will see that embodying forgiveness prayerfully is about exercising God's own heavenly forgiving power; Jesus does this and, by extension, other human beings do this in relation to him. Given that the Lord's Prayer addresses "our Father" (6:9), this prayer presumes the presence of the Father. Thus, prayer empowers us and others to participate in God's presence. Further, as Jesus shows later in his Gethsemane prayer which empowers his forgiveness (26:39–42), prayer can empower our act of forgiveness, such that we participate in God's forgiving life.[24] Thus, our forgiveness of others through prayer becomes an expression of the forgiving power of God. We express God's own heavenly forgiving power through the related practices of prayer and forgiveness. In this way, Jesus teaches how human beings participate in God's own forgiving life and action, thereby becoming God-at-work in us. It is in and through sharing in Jesus's prayer, then, that we participate in the Son's relation to the Father, thereby experiencing and conveying God's life.

This section particularly attends to the Father-Son relation as Jesus introduces it (6:9), because this expresses our participation in the Father's life rather than merely our imitation of the Father's life. I then examine the heaven-earth relation (6:9–10) because theosis provides the framework in which the relational dynamics of heaven and earth can be understood. Finally, I contend that in the framework of theosis, human beings' forgiveness of one another is better understood as the mode of God's own forgiveness rather than a condition that human beings meet in order to receive forgiveness from God (6:12, 14–15). Each element of this section contributes to understanding how a focus on theosis clarifies the nature of forgiveness in Matthew's Gospel.

The Father-Son Relation in Matt 6:9

At this point in Matthew's narrative, Jesus does not teach anything about himself specifically as the Son. But Matthew already presented Jesus as the Son in John's baptism (3:13–17). The voice from heaven characterizes who Jesus is: "This is my beloved Son" (οὗτός ἐστιν ὁ υἱός μου ὁ ἀγαπητός, 3:17; cf. Ps 2:7). Thus, Jesus's identity as the Son determines his steps in the subsequent narrative, such that the sonship of Jesus is operative in the Lord's Prayer. Moreover, as the narrative bears out, Jesus explicitly reveals himself as "the Son" (ὁ υἱός, 11:27) and addresses God as "my Father" (πατρός μου, 7:21; 12:50), indicating his identity as the Son. In responding to Jesus's question about his identity, Peter confesses Jesus as "the Son of God" (ὁ υἱὸς τοῦ θεοῦ, 16:16). In his Gethsemane prayer, Jesus also affirms this relationship by addressing God as "my Father" (26:39). This later development of Jesus as the Son also enriches what Jesus teaches in the Lord's Prayer because earlier passages in the narrative like the Lord's Prayer are "implicitly understood to provide the grounds for" what Matthew wants to develop later in the narrative.[25] In light of both the earlier and later narrative presentation of Jesus as the Son, the language of the Lord's Prayer already connotes the sonship of Jesus, even though it is not explicitly expressed by Jesus at this point. Through the Son, his people are invited to pray to God as "our Father" (Πάτερ ἡμῶν, 6:9). This inclusive language of "our Father" suggests that the people of Israel *and* Jesus together pray to God as our Father. Thus, the address to God as Father is not something to be protected from the people of Israel.

The address to God as Father is rather shared with and extends to his people through Jesus.[26] This is further expressed and confirmed by the later narrative that Jesus's unique knowledge of God is shared with and extends to his people (11:25–27; cf. 9:8; 10:1). Thus, in the Lord's Prayer, Jesus teaches his people to relate to God as their Father in a way Jesus will fulfill as the Son in the rest of Matthew's narrative.

The Father-Son relation is an important locus for considering the concept of theosis in Matthew's Gospel because it expresses a particular participation in God's life rather than mere imitation of God's life. In Matthew, Jesus frequently addresses God as "my Father," implying Jesus's unique filial relation to the Father. Jesus's relation to God as Father reveals the character of Jesus as Son. The character of Jesus as Son is also what defines God as Father. But this character of the Father-Son relation is already in place in God's relation to Israel. Thus, theosis is already anticipated in Israel's covenant history, and that history is fulfilled in Jesus, who is God's presence in the flesh, "God-with-us" (1:21, 23). In the beginning of the narrative, Matthew quotes the Hebrew text of Hos 11:1 to describe the situation of infant Jesus in 2:15: "When Israel [was] a child, I loved him and out of Egypt I called my son."[27] In Hosea, Israel is depicted as God's child and son. Just as Hosea narrates the infant stage of Israel ("When Israel was a child"), so Matthew narrates the infant stage of Jesus. The language of sonship applied to the God-Israel relation is now applied to the God-Jesus relation.[28] In this way, Jesus becomes the very embodiment of the people of Israel. This sonship of Jesus does not replace Israel's sonship but consists in the gathering and saving of Israel as God's son. The sonship of Jesus and the sonship of Israel, then, are not competitive but characterized by mutuality, Jesus as a son and heir of Israel who, as Son of God, saves God's son, Israel, from their sins (1:21).

The Lord's Prayer confirms the message that Jesus is the fullness of the sonship that has already been Israel's life, as Jesus now teaches his people to pray to their Father as such (6:9–15).[29] The fatherhood of God is explicit in the address: "our Father" (6:9).[30] Matthew depicts God as Father by alluding to Isaiah's language and imagery of the fatherhood of God (6:9). Addressing God as our Father ties the audience of Jesus's words to the witness of Scripture, especially with respect to the relation between God and Israel. In Isa 63:16 LXX, the fatherhood of God is invoked: "For you are our Father . . . you Lord, our Father."[31] In the context of Isa 63:16, it is the people of Israel who address God as "our Father." Israel is regarded as God's child and "holy people" who will inherit God's heritage (63:17–18). The fatherhood of God is thus anchored in the story and people of Israel. This is further confirmed in the Hebrew text of Jeremiah, where God hopes for Israel to call upon him as "my Father" and sees Israel as "the beautiful heritage of nations" (3:19).[32] Jeremiah also states that God is depicted as the Father of Israel: "for I am a

Father to Israel" (31:9). Israel is God's child and, as such, is God's heir. As Marianne Meye Thompson puts it, "God is the Father of Israel as the one who called it into being and would give it its inheritance as his heir."[33]

While Matthew invites us to address God as "our" Father rather than as "my" Father in the Lord's Prayer (6:9), scholars like Thompson point out that Matthew "retains the singularity of Jesus' address to God as 'my Father' and his admonitions to his disciples regarding obedience to 'your Father'" (e.g., 6:4, 8).[34] This may indicate that the way Jesus relates to God as Father is distinct from the way the disciples relate to God as Father (cf. John 20:17).[35] According to Thompson, although Israel is often characterized as God's child (e.g., Exod 4:22–23; Hos 11:1; Jer 31:9), there is no other "Son" like Jesus.[36] Thus, Thompson contends that Matthew singles out Jesus's relation to the Father as "an exceptional instance of the Father/Son relationship."[37] The distinctive character of Jesus's sonship is also evidenced by the mutual, intimate knowledge between Father and Son (11:27): "No one knows the Son except the Father (εἰ μὴ ὁ πατήρ) and no one knows the Father except the Son (εἰ μὴ ὁ υἱὸς)."[38] However, the seemingly unique, exclusive knowledge between the Father and the Son is shared with Jesus's followers: "anyone to whom (ᾧ ἐὰν) the Son wishes to reveal the Father" (11:27). Likewise, the expression "our Father" in 6:9 rather suggests that Jesus is teaching his disciples and others to address the God of Israel as Father together and with him, not laying claim to a sonship that is unique to him.[39] The expression "our Father" points to our communal, corporate participation in God as God shapes the community as Father through Jesus.[40] By sharing in Jesus's prayer, we as the church of his disciples become participants in the Son's intimate relation to the Father. In this light, Jesus's address to God as "your Father" also suggests that Jesus's unique filial relation is shared with his followers, as his Father is the same Father we know as such. This public character of the Lord's Prayer shows that our participation in God's life, theosis, entails a communal and corporate reality.

Thompson rightly notes that while the fatherhood of God can be specifically applied "in terms of his relationship to the Son," the fatherhood of God "can also be explicated more broadly beginning with God's relationship to Israel and culminating in the fulfillment of God's promises to be a Father to his people."[41] This means that we become heirs and sharers of God's revelation and inheritance *in* and *through* Jesus who is God's unique revealer and heir.[42] Thus, both Jesus's distinct relationship with the Father and the divine relationship that is passed along to us through Jesus can be true at once. In becoming God's heirs through Jesus, we receive God's life, thereby participating in God's own life. The Lord's Prayer unpacks this relational dynamic of God and the human through Jesus, who invites his followers to address God as "our Father" (6:9).[43] Jesus shares what he uniquely knows of the

Father with his followers, who are to share it with others. This means that Jesus's sonship is *for* the sonship of Israel rather than something to be simply set apart from the sonship of Israel. Thus, the intimate, familial relationship between Father and Son extends to his people through Jesus, especially as his disciples learn and share his ways. It is through Jesus, then, that we become God's own children, the heirs and sharers of God's inheritance, as opposed to mere imitators of God's life. Thus, God's familial life is the ambit of the God-human relation and our participation in God's life by inheritance in Matthew (5:44–45; 6:9; 12:50). That is what it means to be the children of God in Matthew, namely, sharers in the Father's nature and life.

The Heaven-Earth Relation in Matt 6:9–10

Another important element of this study is to shed light on the relational dynamics of heaven and earth through the framework of theosis. Matthew's distinctive connection of references to God as Father with heaven signals the transformative dynamics of heaven and earth, as in "Father in heaven" (6:9). Throughout the narrative, Matthew frequently depicts God as the "Father in heaven" and the "heavenly Father," phrases that occur thirteen and seven times respectively.[44] As the narrative bears out, for something to have been loosed or bound in heaven is for it to be done by Jesus's Father in heaven (18:18). Thus, that the terms "Father" and "heaven" are frequently intertwined in Matthew suggests that they are closely related realities. The idea that heaven is God's dwelling place is qualified by the use of the preposition ἐν (6:9).[45] For Matthew, heaven is not primarily a static place. Heaven is the realm that is the source of the Father's action, his "place" of rule over the earth. The Father exercises his dominion over life on earth as well as in heaven, such that the heavenly realm is not a matter of spatial limits such as the sky but a domain of divine power.[46] Gerhard Schneider confirms this point by describing heaven and earth in terms of the domain of God's rule: "Himmel und Erde sind von Gott geschaffen. Sie bilden zusammen den Herrschaftsbereich Gottes."[47] Indeed, Matthew presents God as "the Lord of heaven and earth" (11:25), heaven being "the throne of God" and earth being God's "footstool" (5:34–35). The heavenly realm, then, is characterized by the exertion of God's own rule and authority. That God's self in Jesus exercises the heavenly rule of God on earth indicates that earth is to be transformed by heaven. In Jesus, earth comes to participate in heavenly life, such that the relation between heaven and earth can also be better understood in terms of theosis. The heavenly life, then, becomes the reality of human life. There is thus no spatial distinction between heaven and earth as these converge, through God's self, in Jesus (28:18). Accordingly, earth is to be filled with heaven (cf. Hab 2:14). The heaven-earth relation, then, is one of perfection, heaven being a dominion of the Father's perfect will in operation,[48] whereas earth names the habitation of the human and other creatures where the will of the Father in heaven is working toward perfect expression.[49]

The transformative dynamics of heaven and earth is unpacked by Jesus's petition: "Your *name* be hallowed. Your *kingdom* come. Your *will* be done, on earth, as it is in heaven (ὡς ἐν οὐρανῷ)" (6:9–10). The phrase ὡς ἐν οὐρανῷ in 6:10 suggests that for Matthew, heaven is a place where God's name is already holy and God's heavenly rule and will are fully exercised. Through praying and embodying Jesus's prayer, the full reality of the heavenly realm is to become fully so on the earth: "on earth as it is in heaven." Thus, this petition indicates that our prayer enacts the dynamics of heaven and earth. The sanctification of God's name, specifically by God's people, is to express the holy presence of God in and as God's heir.[50] We participate in God's presence by hallowing God's name with our prayer and lives. As such, the sanctification of God's name is a matter of expressing on the earth the divine, ruling power of God in heaven, through the way that Israel prays and lives, which is how God's name takes shape on the earth. New Testament commentators like Dale C. Allison Jr. and W. D. Davies view the passive verbs ἁγιασθήτω (6:9) and γενηθήτω (6:10) as the divine passive.[51] But this may obscure the expected human response and involvement in the fulfillment of what is prayed. Isaiah 29:23 LXX points to human action: "They will sanctify my name."[52] Thus, honoring God's name involves the human response. At the same time, Ezek 36:23 LXX points to God's action: "I will sanctify my great name" (cf. Lev 18:21; 22:32; Isa 9:7; Jer 33:2; Ezek 36:20; 38:23; John 12:28).[53] Thus, human beings can join in serving and honoring God's name. The subject of hallowing God's name, then, is both God and human beings. This is also consistent with Matthew's emphasis on our *doing* the will of God (7:21; 12:50). Accordingly, we hallow God's name and embody God's will with our lives as theosis, in the expectation that the full reality of the heavenly realm will fully become the reality of the earth.

In the Jewish practices of Jesus's day, God's name is not pronounced because God's name is holy.[54] On the significance of God's name, John A. Wilson notes that "to the ancient[s], the name was an element of personality and of power."[55] Since God's name indicates his presence, personality, and power, God's name holds the highest honor and thus is to be hallowed. In line with this Jewish practice, Jesus prays that God's name be hallowed (6:9; cf. Exod 20:7; Lev 19:12; 22:2; Pss 74:18; 139:20; Mal 1:6). Also, the name of God is closely related to the presence of God (Num 6:27; Deut 12:5; 1 Kgs 8:16; Neh 1:9). When God is present in the burning bush, God is made known to Moses by revealing his name as "I am who I am" (Exod 3:14; cf. Ps 111:9; Isa 12:4).[56] Moreover, the presence of God is identified as God's name in places like the Mercy Seat (Deut 12:11; 1 Chr 22:19). God's name, then, is a crucial mode of God's presence on the earth. In Matthew's narrative, the name of Israel's God becomes God's presence with us through Jesus, whose own name is "God-with-us" (1:23; cf. Isa 7:14). Jesus thus becomes the very embodiment of God's name. The name of God is a particular form of God's presence, and Jesus corresponds to that particular presence of God in Matthew. Named God-with-us, what Jesus does from the beginning to the end of Matthew is to save people from their sins by forgiving them (e.g., 1:21; 4:17; 9:2; 20:28; 26:28).[57] The way Jesus embodies the name of God, then, is particularly expressed in Jesus's unfolding of God's forgiving power. In Matthew, Jesus is God-with-us not only in his own name but in what he does and what his people do through him. Thus, just as the name of God operates in Jesus, whose name is God-with-us, so the name of God operates in his people who share in Jesus's prayer and life of forgiveness, thus hallowing God's name.

Regarding the kingdom of Israel's God (6:10), it originates from God as Father and "draws its character from the Father's domain."[58] Given that the Father is depicted as the heavenly Father, God's kingdom is of heavenly origin.[59] Schneider notes that God's heavenly kingdom, expressed on earth even in John's baptism, is "Herrschaft, die vom Himmel her kommt und in diese Welt eintritt. Die Stimme aus den Himmeln (3:17), das Zeichen vom Himmel (16:1), die Taufe des Johannes (21:25) gehen von Gott aus."[60] Accordingly, "Your kingdom come" is a prayer that God's heavenly rule be reflected on earth. In particular, the eschatological kingship of God envisioned in the OT is now being fulfilled in and through Jesus, who embodies God's liberating power by touching and healing the lives of people in the subsequent narrative (e.g., 8:1–9:38; 11:4–6).[61] God's heavenly kingdom is thus present in Jesus's touching and healing of his people.[62] In this light, God's heavenly kingdom is not merely a future development in Matthew (cf. 4:17; 5:3, 10). Heaven becomes a present reality on the earth in and through Jesus, who delivers God's heavenly forgiveness on earth. As such, God the Father of Israel is present now in and through Jesus who exercises the heavenly rule of God on earth. That God's heavenly rule is present now is also evidenced by Jesus's injunction to pray for "today" (σήμερον) rather than tomorrow (6:11; cf. 6:34). Accordingly, God's people come to participate in God's heavenly presence now on the earth. It is not only in the future but today that we come to receive life from the Father, thereby participating in God's heavenly life.

Regarding the will of God (6:10), "Your will be done" is a prayer that God's will as done in heaven be reflected on the earth. In the prayer, this will be expressed immediately as the provision of daily bread and forgiveness. In the narrative beyond the prayer, which the prayer anticipates, the will of the Father in heaven is manifest in Jesus's words and deeds. This is because Jesus serves as the Father's unique revealer. Jesus is the unique revealer of the Father's will because the Father has given "all things" (πάντα) to Jesus (11:26). Jesus shares uniquely in the Father's will because no one knows the Father except the Son, and no one knows the Son except the Father (11:27). Jesus is thus *one* with God; what Jesus does is what the Father does. This oneness shared between God and Jesus is then shared with whomever Jesus chooses to reveal the Father (11:27). Matthew's Jesus tells us that the Father's will is especially revealed to children (11:25). It is no coincidence that Jesus aligns himself with children and the least (18:5; 19:14; 25:40). To receive children and the least is to receive him (18:5; 25:40). It is with them that the Father's will is shared. Elsewhere in Matthew's narrative, Jesus calls *us* to do the will of God so that we act as God's family (e.g., 7:21; 12:50; cf. Ps 103:21). Jesus says that not everyone who says to him "Lord, Lord" but only the one who does the will of the Father in heaven will enter the kingdom of heaven (7:21). This will of the Father in heaven is manifest in Jesus's words and deeds. Throughout Matthew's narrative, Jesus desires love and mercy (5:44–47; 9:13; 12:7, 20; 20:34; 23:23). Thus, Jesus reads the entire law and the prophets, as the written testimony to God's will, through the hermeneutics of love (22:37–40). Jesus himself also submits his own will to the Father's will in his Gethsemane prayer (26:39, 42), on his way to shedding the blood of the covenant for the forgiveness of sins (26:28).[63] To do the will the Father in Matthew, then, is to practice love and mercy.[64] As the prayer continues, this is what we do by forgiveness and thus enjoy and extend God's forgiveness: "Forgive us our debts as we have forgiven our debtors" (6:12). Through embodying forgiveness, we participate in the heavenly Father's will on earth. It is through doing the Father's will, then, that heaven is coming to the earth in Matthew and, as theosis, we participate in and enflesh God's life on the earth.

Forgiveness as Mode in Matt 6:12 and 14–15

Forgiveness in Matthew is one way of Jesus's saving his people from their sins (1:21; 26:28).[65] For Matthew, sins are not only the current patterns of injustice and disobedience in Jesus's generation but the inherited consequences of corruption over generations, accumulated "debts" (e.g., 23:29–24:2).[66] A key way Jesus saves his people from their sins, then, is the way Jesus ends those inherited patterns of injustice, which is to exercise God's forgiveness. The relation between Jesus's saving his people from their sins and the forgiveness he empowers as one piece of that salvation would involve what Jesus does himself, especially in his death, but also what he teaches and empowers us to do, not least through his death.

God's salvation and God's forgiveness in Matthew involve the transformation of the fabric of Israel's bodily life on the earth, as opposed to taking place primarily in a realm of legal abstractions or individuals' relationship with God independent of their bonds to one another and to land. Thus, forgiveness in Matthew is not merely transactional but involves the process of transformation. As shown in my analysis of the Fatherhood of God, the hallowing of God's name, the coming of the kingdom, and the doing of God's will, this prayer concerns the ways God acts as the Father of Israel on the earth, as opposed to a fatherhood or hallowedness or a kingdom that remained aloof from the drama of earthly life. Jesus's petition, "Give us this day our daily bread" (6:11), only confirms and advances this, so that what comes next, "Forgive us our debts as we have forgiven our debtors" (6:12) concerns not merely a change in status with God but a change in the conditions of indebted human lives in relation to one another, land, and the rest of the creation that shapes their life together in relation to God as their Father. That forgiveness is the process of transformation in Matthew is anticipated in the language of Jeremiah. In Jer 31, God's forgiveness involves the concrete process of change as God calls his people to turn away from their inherited patterns of sins and transforms their hearts, relationships, and land (31:9–40). In Matthew's narrative, Jesus touches and heals the fabric of Israel's bodily life on the earth, transforming their relationships with God and with others (8:1–9:31). In particular, Jesus's healing of the paralyzed person shows the transformative dynamic of God's forgiveness in Israel's life (9:1–9).[67] That is, Jesus's forgiveness of sins involves healing and repair of the inherited consequences of past sins over generations. The nature of forgiveness in Matthew, then, is a transformation of embodied life such that the consequences of past sins and corruptions are addressed and repaired. In this light, the prayer for forgiveness is not a prayer for a change of status or abstract relationship with God but for a change in the concrete conditions of the prayers' lives.

In 6:12, Jesus invites us to ask our Father in heaven to forgive our "debts" (ὀφειλήματα) the way we forgive our debtors (6:12; cf. 18:28, 30, 32; Sir 28:2–7). This petition implies that human beings are sinners who need God's forgiving power (cf. 7:11). Ulrich Luz points out that the forgiveness petition is a "central theme of Jewish praying."[68] Jesus's way of relating God's forgiveness of human beings with human beings' forgiveness of one another indicates that prayer implies human action, the human action involved in forgiveness. In interpreting 6:12, scholars like R. T. France offer a conditional interpretation that human forgiveness is the condition of God's forgiveness. France claims that "the conditional element which was apparently implicit in 6:12 becomes quite explicit" in 6:14–15.[69] Luz also contends that 6:12 "does mean a condition in the sense of 5:23–24; 6:14–15; 7:1."[70] While this conditional understanding seems plain enough in the Lord's Prayer, it does not reflect well God's forgiving nature as found within the rest of Matthew's Gospel.[71] Jesus characterizes the Father as the giver of gifts, one who gives not only to those who do right but also to those who do evil (6:26–31; 7:9–11). As shown, the Father is depicted as forgiving and merciful in Matthew. This suggests that God's forgiveness is based on the Father's forgiving character rather than on our action, such that his forgiveness is not merely dependent on our meeting a condition of forgiving one another.

The conditional interpretation also struggles to fit into Matthew's larger narrative flow. Regarding the conditional element in Matthew's narrative, France points out that in 25:31–46, the salvation of the "righteous" is dependent on their behavior toward the needy.[72] France links this with the parable of the wedding feast (22:1–14), where the properly dressed are accepted in the feast (22:11, 14). As France puts it, "Salvation according to that parable may be undeserved and unexpected, but it is not without conditions."[73] But this is only part of the picture and neglects to consider the gracious action of God that underlies the conditions in which human forgiveness is needed. While God indeed rewards our action toward the needy (e.g., 10:42; 18:5; 25:40, 45), God's saving action is not merely dependent on the merit of meeting certain conditions. This is evidenced by the parable of the laborers in the vineyard (20:1–15), where their wages are not in proportion to their differing amounts of work. Further, God's unconditional grace toward his debtor in the parable of the unforgiving servant points to this reality (18:27). France suggests that "like the debtor of 18:23–35, one of the recipients of grace turns out not to meet the expectations on which the continuation of that salvation depends."[74] In other words, France points to a conditional aspect of God's forgiveness in this parable as the servant is not forgiven because he does not forgive his debtor. But the emphasis in this parable lies in God's forgiving of his servant's enormous debt without his meeting a prior condition (18:26–27, 33) and signals to the disciples the appropriate reflection of God's lavish forgiveness between human beings. The parable tells us that the lord does not wait to see whether his servant will forgive others before he forgives him, even as his servant's subsequent failure to forgive complicates his ability to enjoy the forgiveness his master had given him. The servant is punished because of his failure to manifest "forgiven-ness" in "his relations with those who are indebted to him" (18:33).[75] In this light, forgiveness in Matthew is not conceived as a legal transaction as if human forgiveness and God's forgiveness were simply successive movements, one following the other (this transactional view is what allows for an interpretation like France's). Instead, forgiveness in Matthew describes the material circumstances and quality of people's relationships; any need for human forgiveness arises in a context in which God's forgiveness has already been operative, not least through the good that human beings have previously done. Thus, human forgiveness becomes a matter of continuing and extending the forgiveness of God that human beings have already enjoyed. On the other hand, not forgiving opposes the forgiveness of God that has already been at work. This keeps human beings from enjoying God's forgiveness, which takes shape in the life of human beings and their treatment of one another as theosis. Accordingly, by forgiving one another, human beings come to participate in the forgiving activity of God as opposed to operating in some sphere separate from God in their forgiving one another. This is made possible finally through Jesus, who is the fullness of the shared forgiving activity of God and human beings attested in Israel and thus the power by which his followers embody together God's forgiveness of their debts. Jesus acts to save his people from their sins, shedding the blood of the covenant irrespective of the unfaithfulness of his people, including his disciples, who desert him and betray him (26:26–56). Thus, we come to embody the forgiveness that Jesus teaches us to practice according to his prayer in the wake of his work for our forgiveness, even as that work is yet to be revealed narratively when he teaches his prayer for his disciples in the hearing of the crowd in the Sermon on the Mount.

In his exposition of gift giving in the ancient Greco-Roman world, John M. G. Barclay views "the Christ-event" as "incongruous" (i.e., "the distribution of the gift without regard to the worth of the recipient") or "unconditioned" gift.[76] Barclay observes that in antiquity, gifts can "operate in both equal and unequal relationships, both among the poor (e.g., food and services exchanged by those living at subsistence level) and between the powerful and their clients (e.g., public benefactions to citizens)."[77] In the latter case, "some 'return' is expected—not in material terms, but in honor or public praise."[78] Thus, the "circulation of benefits and counterbenefits was generally regarded as the glue that kept ancient societies together."[79] Barclay notes that "a gift may be incongruous but not noncircular, that is, it may be a 'pure gift' in the sense of being unconditioned, but not in the sense that it carries no expectations."[80] He then notes that in the Greco-Roman world, "gifts normally are understood to create and cement social ties, and reciprocity is integral to their purpose."[81] According to Barclay, the fulfillment of gifts takes place "not primarily in one-way gifts but in the reciprocity."[82] While this gift is "not conditioned by previous criteria of worth, ethnic, social, or moral," he opines that gift giving in the Greco-Roman world is "unconditioned, but not unconditional."[83]

While Barclay adequately articulates the view that God's gift elicits our response and accountability, a theosis framework suggests a more nuanced understanding of God's unconditional gift, with respect to forgiveness. When forgiveness is conceived with the lens of theosis, human forgiveness is not a condition of receiving God's forgiveness, but it is the theater of and proper response to God's merciful forgiveness already given. This does not imply that God's forgiving grace is based on our action or worth but that our forgiveness becomes God's way of extending forgiveness. In other words, human forgiveness is itself a way God forgives human beings.[84] It is through embodying forgiveness that we embrace and manifest God's own forgiveness toward us. Thus, embodying forgiveness is more than a one-off transaction, which as a condition met, God then reciprocates by forgiving those who have forgiven others. This is further evidenced by Jesus's exhortation to love our enemies without condition (5:46–47). As Warren Carter rightly observes, "The emphasis on indiscriminate rather than reciprocal love continues" in 5:46–47.[85] According to Carter, "Reciprocity was a common behavior, binding parties in obligations and securing the patron-client status of each. Indiscriminate loving, part of the greater righteousness required of disciples (5:20), is a countercultural practice, undermining, not securing, social hierarchies and obligations."[86] The God-human relation in Matthew's Gospel is thus more than one of reciprocal, patron-client relation.[87] In addressing "a deeper righteousness" (5:20), Jesus is concerned to address hypocrisy and inadequate righteousness, where people, following current and influential authorities, imagine that they can enjoy God's righteousness while they treat one another unrighteously (e.g., 5:23–26). Jesus's answer to this tendency is not that we have to be righteous first if we expect to enjoy God's blessings but that God's righteousness is expressed in the way we treat one another. Thus, we cannot pretend to enjoy God's blessings while acting hypocritically and treating others unrighteously. God has already acted to forgive us, since God is merciful upon all (5:45), and we are to reflect and extend the gracious forgiveness that God has already given to us to be able to enjoy that gracious forgiveness ourselves. In brief, God's gracious forgiveness is not expressed by human ungraciousness but by human graciousness toward one another. The problem with some of the authorities in Jesus's context is not that they are teaching their people wrongly (cf. 23:3), neglecting to model and meet the conditions that God requires for them to receive blessing in response to human obedience. The problem is that they do not teach the covenant nearness of Israel's God to the people, that God lives and moves through the way his people treat one another, not only in rewards for showy and well-measured acts of obedience. There may be a kind of conditionality at work here, but it is not that of human beings on one side, meeting conditions, so that God acts from the other side. It is the conditionality that arises from God's unconditional and merciful gifts and then seeks the extension of those gifts in the way the human recipients treat one another.

Elsewhere in Matthew's narrative, Jesus continues to teach that the lord in the parable of the vineyard gives the same wage to all workers, even though their working hours are significantly different (20:12, 15). The differences in our work, then, are "not sufficient to explain God's gracious act" of forgiveness.[88] Moreover, in light of Jesus's response to Peter's questions about how often to forgive—"until seventy-seven times" (18:21–22)—the underlying assumption of Jesus's response is that just as God's forgiveness is limitless and gracious, so ours is to be. This is also the mode in which Jesus participates in table fellowship with the disciples. Regardless of their denial and betrayal, Jesus unconditionally embodies God's forgiveness by sharing with all of them the covenant blood for the forgiveness of sins (26:28). Forgiveness in this sense becomes the particular way Jesus embodies the Father's will prayerfully: "Your will be done" (26:42; cf. 6:10). By sharing in Jesus's life of forgiveness, then, according to the prayer Jesus teaches us, we manifest God's own will. By sharing in Jesus's life of forgiveness, we come to participate in God's life as those who love and forgive their enemies are called God's children (5:44–45). Accordingly, taking Matthew's characterization of the Father as forgiver and his larger narrative presentation into account, human forgiveness is not a condition human beings meet in order to receive God's forgiveness but the very mode and manifestation of God's exercising of God's own forgiveness.[89]

In this light, Matt 6:12 expresses the ongoing dynamics of the God-human relation rather than a one-off transaction. Thus, the Lord's Prayer is not primarily given to those who have previously done good. J. C. O'Neill notes, "If [Jesus's followers] have been ready to forgive [their debtors] and have already forgiven them, then they need not pray for something that has already happened."[90] They would pray this prayer to seek God's grace and forgiveness rather than proving that they have already met the condition of forgiving others and thus are eligible to receive God's forgiveness. Davies and Allison similarly observe that implicit "in the Lord's Prayer is the fundamental obligation to recognize the need of God's forgiveness."[91] Accordingly, the aorist form ἀφήκαμεν in 6:12 should not be read as something that strengthens our conditional action. If we take ἀφήκαμεν to mean an action that is previously done ("we forgave"), our forgiveness of others becomes prior to God's forgiveness of our debts.[92] God's forgiveness would be something earned by human beings, as if God waits to forgive us until we have forgiven others. But God's forgiveness of us "cannot be merited, [but] must be received."[93] God's forgiveness is being received by those who are embodying God's forgiveness in the way they forgive others. That is, God's forgiveness can be "received by or become effective in" those who forgive others,[94] not as a condition they meet but as their expression of God's own forgiveness. God's forgiveness is thus already operative in our will and desire to forgive rather than being occasioned as entirely subsequent to our action of forgiveness, as if human beings had met a prior condition independently of God's forgiveness that supposedly operates on a different plane of reality.[95]

The brief appendix to the Lord's prayer (6:14–15) elaborates what Jesus prays in 6:12: Forgive us our debts as we forgive our debtors. Jesus teaches that "if (ἐάν) you forgive people their trespasses, your heavenly Father will also forgive you. But if (ἐάν) you do not forgive people, neither will your Father forgive your trespasses" (6:14–15). As it stands, it appears that if (ἐάν) we fail to participate in God's own forgiveness to others, God will potentially withdraw his original gift of forgiveness to us. While there may be a kind of conditionality at work here, what theosis allows us to see is that the seemingly conditional phrase in 6:14–15 does not indicate God's conditional forgiveness that depends entirely on our forgiving action. Instead, consistent with 6:12, Matt 6:14–15 indicates how God's forgiveness takes shape in our forgiving one another, in the language of theosis, how we participate in the forgiving activity of God. Our action of forgiveness becomes the way God's forgiveness unfolds. It is not a matter of independent and entirely sequential agencies, human and then divine. Our forgiving action rather becomes the way God continues to act as forgiver. Our forgiveness manifests God's own forgiveness, such that if (ἐάν) we are not forgiving others, we will not be enjoying God's forgiveness ourselves. Thus, the dynamic is not condition in the usual sense, but there is a contingency to God's forgiveness in that it is enacted in human forgiveness and thus is not enacted where human forgiveness is lacking. This is how we can read our action of forgiveness as theosis in the Lord's Prayer. In this way, the Lord's Prayer becomes the way to practice and participate in the kingdom of heaven on the earth, which is the promised, eschatological coming of God's presence.

SUMMARY

This chapter has shown how the dynamics of heaven and earth operate, partly through the activity of God's people, especially as we embody forgiveness prayerfully. God's people participate in the forgiving activity of God rather than acting in some sphere separate from God. By sharing in Jesus's life and prayer of forgiveness, we receive forgiving life from the Father, thereby participating in the Father's forgiving life in the way we relate to others. Thus, our relation to God as Father expresses our participation in God's own life rather than merely our imitation of the Father's character. This chapter also examined the transformative dynamics of heaven and earth through our hallowing God's name, doing God's will, and praying that God's kingdom be reflected on the earth. Finally, this chapter challenged the conditional interpretation of God's forgiveness. I demonstrated that human forgiveness is the mode of God's own forgiveness rather than a prior condition we meet independently by forgiving one another. Thus, forgiveness is more than a one-off transaction. It is in embodying forgiveness continually that we live God's forgiving life, reflecting God's forgiving nature as revealed in and by Jesus.

NOTES

1. The way the Lord's Prayer closes suggests that forgiveness is programmatic in this prayer. This study will discuss part of the Lord's Prayer (i.e., 6:9–10, 12, 14–15) rather than discussing the whole.

2. On the thematic importance of forgiveness in the Lord's Prayer, see Todd Pokrifka-Joe, "Probing the Relationship between Divine and Human Forgiveness in Matthew," in *Forgiveness and Truth: Explorations in Contemporary Theology*, ed. Alistair I. McFadyen, Marcel Sarot, and Anthony Thiselton (Edinburgh: T&T Clark, 2001), 165–72; Isaac K. Mbabazi, *The Significance of Interpersonal Forgiveness in the Gospel of Matthew* (Eugene, OR: Pickwick, 2013).

3. In exploring Matthew's kinship language (7:21; 12:50), Mbabazi observes that "the concept of fictive kinship of Christians with God is embedded in the notions of fatherhood of God and the *imitatio* Dei/Christi" (*Significance of Interpersonal Forgiveness*, 49; emphasis mine). Mbabazi points to the imitation motif of Matthew to describe the relation between God and his children. On the further discussion of the concept of imitation, see Cornelis Bennema, *Mimesis in the Johannine Literature: A Study in Johannine Ethics*, LNTS 498 (London: Bloomsbury T&T Clark, 2017), 35–38. Bennema defines mimesis as "a creative, cognitive and mnemonic process that directs the believer's conduct and character" rather than mere replication (cloning) or "a list of do's and don'ts" (201). He notes that mimesis "needs an action from both persons involved—one person performs an act or displays a state that serves as an *example* for the other person to emulate" (35; emphasis original). He distinguishes mimesis from reciprocity, though they are in some ways overlapped: "with mimesis, person A upholds an *example* for person B to follow or emulate," whereas "with reciprocity, person A bestows a *gift* on person B, who returns the favour in the form of other goods or services" (37; emphasis original). Also, Bennema notes that the relationship between mimesis and theosis needs refinement and distinguishes imitation from theosis, though they may be overlapped in some ways: "both performative mimesis and existential mimesis seem to indicate that believers do not only imitate Jesus' example but also his very being" (204). Regarding the concept of imitation in the Greco-Roman world, Teresa Morgan observes, imitation is "more than learning to do what is done before you. . . . a habit of mind or body is established in the pupil until he [or she] is able to behave and think *independently* in the manner of his [or her] teacher" (*Literate Education in the Hellenistic and Roman Worlds* [Cambridge: Cambridge University Press, 1998], 253; emphasis mine). While theosis in Matthew's Gospel may involve some aspects of emulation or mimesis, it is more than our imitation of Christ. Theosis is divinely empowered human life, such that God exercises God's own power in us. We thus reflect God's own life. God and human beings do not act independently as our relationship with God is not one of independence. So with our bodily relationship with others (e.g., 9:7). Theosis in Matthew is concerned with the result of God's forgiving power working itself out in the lives of Jesus's followers. Cf. A good example of theosis is found in Exodus, where Moses's radiant face manifests God's own presence in him rather than his imitation of God (34:29). Consider also Bezalel and Oholiab's construction of a heavenly-designed tabernacle

(31:2–6; 36:1–2). The design of a tabernacle is downloaded from heaven. That is to say, God fills them with his knowledge and wisdom to construct the tabernacle on earth (cf. 1 Chr 28:12, 19).

4. Regarding the significance of the Lord's Prayer in Matthew's narrative, Tertullian calls this prayer an "abridgment of the entire Gospel" (*Or.* 1), and Cyprian calls it a "compendium of heavenly doctrine" (*Dom. or.* 9). See Ulrich Luz, *Matthew 1–7: A Commentary*, trans. James E. Crouch, Hermeneia (Minneapolis: Fortress, 2007), 312. This suggests that the Lord's Prayer can be a lens through which other parts of Matthew can be read, especially with respect to forgiveness. It is also noteworthy that no virtue or practice other than the practice of forgiveness appears in this model prayer. That is, Jesus's request after this Lord's Prayer is not to go and do something good but to forgive (6:14–15). Forgiveness is the first act of love in our relationship with God and with others (e.g., 5:23–24). Further, the act of love Jesus shows on a cross is forgiveness (26:28).

5. Allen Verhey, *The Great Reversal: Ethics and the New Testament* (Grand Rapids: Eerdmans, 1984), 24. See also Brian K. Blount (*Then the Whisper Put on Flesh: New Testament Ethics in an African American Context* [Nashville: Abingdon, 2001], 68), who notes that the kingdom ethic is "an imperative call to kingdom responsive behavior."

6. Margaret Hannan, *The Nature and Demands of God's Sovereign Rule in the Gospel of Matthew*, LNTS 308 (London: T&T Clark, 2006), 57.

7. For Jewish people, three times a day were set for prayer—morning, afternoon, and evening (e.g., Dan 6:10; Acts 3:1; 10:30; Did. 8:3).

8. Jonathan T. Pennington, *The Sermon on the Mount and Human Flourishing: A Theological Commentary* (Grand Rapids: Baker Academic, 2017), 79. Jeannine K. Brown and Kyle Roberts also note that "hypocrisy is a misalignment between outward and inward (6:2, 5, 16)" (*Matthew*, THNTC [Grand Rapids: Eerdmans, 2018], 69). Paul J. Achtemeier, Joel B. Green, and Marianne Meye Thompson observe that the charge of hypocrisy against the Pharisees in Matthew's Gospel is not akin to deceit but instead would mean "a misconstrual of the divine will" (*Introducing the New Testament: Its Literature and Theology* [Grand Rapids: Eerdmans, 2001], 114).

9. Brown and Roberts, *Matthew*, 69.

10. This does not mean that public prayer does not count. Jesus confirms that the public temple is a place of prayer (21:13; cf. 1 Kgs 8). Jesus also urges his disciples to pray together (18:19–20). Further, the Lord's prayer is given as a public and communal prayer ("our Father," 6:9). This suggests that all true prayer is not purely private and personal. See R. T. France, *The Gospel of Matthew*, NICNT (Grand Rapids: Eerdmans, 2007), 244. Jesus's point is not that we abandon public prayer but that our prayer should be addressed solely to God rather than "to those looking on." As Brown and Roberts write, "Prayer, of all pious actions, should happen with only the true recipient, God, in focus" (*Matthew*, 69).

11. Brown and Roberts, *Matthew*, 69.

12. Pennington notes that the call to wholeness or "*teleios*-ity" in 5:48 is "not moral perfection but wholehearted orientation [or dedication] toward God" (*Sermon on the Mount*, 78). Enemies in Matthew's Gospel include the opponents of Jesus's followers

(5:10–12), personal foes (5:38–42), "one's household (10:36), and those who cause economic havoc with sabotage (13:25, 28)." See Warren Carter, *Matthew and the Margins: A Sociopolitical and Religious Reading*, The Bible & Liberation Series (Maryknoll, NY: Orbis Books, 2000), 154–55.

13. God's provision appears in 6:11, where Jesus invites us to pray for God's "daily bread" (6:11). The phrase "daily bread" evokes Israel's manna in the wilderness (Exod 16:4, 31–32; Num 21:5; cf. Pss 78:23–25; 104:14–15; 132:15; Prov 30:8). The exodus narrative shows that the God of Israel feeds his people by providing daily manna. Likewise, Matthew's narrative unfolds that the Father in heaven cares for our need, even for the birds of the air (6:25–34). Just as the Father provides our daily needs, so God's children are called to live generously.

14. Mbabazi, *Significance of Interpersonal Forgiveness*, 210.

15. Mbabazi adequately observes that the theme of forgiveness in Matthew is closely related to the themes of "mercy, reconciliation, love, and non-retaliation" (*Significance of Interpersonal Forgiveness*, 27). According to Mbabazi, these are all related concepts of forgiveness because forgiveness is an expression of love, mercy, and reconciliation (e.g., 5:7, 21–26, 38–42, 43–48; 6:12, 14–15; 7:1–2, 12; 9:2–6; 18:15–17, 21–35).

16. Quoting Roger Mohrlang (*Matthew and Paul: A Comparison of Ethical Perspectives*, SNTSMS 48 [Cambridge: Cambridge University Press, 1984], 80), Mbabazi notes that of all the Synoptic writers, Matthew "draws the most winsome picture of God as a kind and caring heavenly Father" (*Significance of Interpersonal Forgiveness*, 201).

17. Jonathan T. Pennington, *Heaven and Earth in the Gospel of Matthew* (Grand Rapids: Baker Academic, 2007), 231–32. Matthew employs the term πατήρ forty-four times in reference to God (cf. Mark 4x; Luke 17x) and nineteen times in reference to human fathers (cf. Mark 14x; Luke 39x).

18. Marianne Meye Thompson, *The Promise of the Father: Jesus and God in the New Testament* (Louisville: Westminster John Knox, 2000), 105. Regarding the significance of Father language in Matthew, Thompson notes that "the increase of language for God as Father is coupled with the increased emphasis on the shape of discipleship. God is Father of the community gathered around Jesus; and this relationship creates and shapes the commitment that those in the community owe not only to God but also to each other" (115).

19. This is not to say that other Gospels lack the view of the intimate relationship between God and the human. Matthew's particular possessive formulations distinctly nuance the character of the God-human relationship.

20. Scholars such as J. Weiss contended that Jesus views God's kingdom as utterly future and transcendent. See Weiss, *Jesus' Proclamation of the Kingdom of God*, ed. R. H. Hiers and D. L. Holland (Philadelphia: Fortress, 1971). On the temporality of the kingdom of God in scholarship, see, e.g., A. Schweitzer, *The Quest of the Historical Jesus: A Critical Study of Its Progress from Reimarus to Wrede*, trans. F. C. Burkitt (London: A & C Black, 1910); C. H. Dodd, *The Parables of the Kingdom*, rev. ed. (London: Collins, 1961); G. E. Ladd, *The Presence of the Future: The Eschatology of Biblical Realism* (Grand Rapids: Eerdmans, 1974); G. R. Beasley-Murray, *Jesus and*

the Kingdom of God (Grand Rapids: Eerdmans, 1986). For Schweitzer, the coming of God's kingdom is imminent in Jesus. Dodd argued for a "realized eschatology," that is, the kingdom is present in the ministry of Jesus. Ladd and Beasley-Murray articulated "inaugurated eschatology," that is, the coming of God's kingdom is now and not yet.

21. Joel B. Green, "Kingdom of God/Heaven," in *DJG*, 474.

22. Ibid.

23. In a similar vein, John Nolland observes, "Jesus' own ministry represented the present stirrings of the coming kingdom (see at 4:17)" (*The Gospel of Matthew*, NIGTC [Grand Rapids: Eerdmans, 2005], 287).

24. The relation between Jesus's Gethsemane prayer and his forgiveness will be discussed in chapter 5.

25. Joel B. Green, "Narrative Criticism," in *Methods for Luke*, ed. Joel B. Green, Methods in Biblical Interpretation (Cambridge: Cambridge University Press, 2010), 95. Green notes that "retrospectively, we sometimes venture to say that event X led to event Y, or event Z was the probable outcome of event A" (95). Thus, audiences experience narratives "as a progression of events with the next understood in light of the preceding" (95).

26. While Jesus is primarily addressing his disciples in the Sermon: "his disciples came to him" (προσῆλθαν αὐτῷ οἱ μαθηταὶ αὐτοῦ, 5:1), its closing shows that the crowd is also part of the audience (7:28).

27. In 2:15, Matthew seems to use the MT ("my child," Hos 11:1) rather than the LXX ("his children," Hos 11:1). Scripture translations are mine unless noted otherwise. Regarding the influence of the MT on Matthew, see Sherman E. Johnson, "The Biblical Quotations in Matthew," *HTR* 36, no. 2 (1943): 135–53.

28. See also Exod 4:22–23 and Deut 8:5, where the sonship of Israel is depicted.

29. Regarding the Jewish sensibility of the Lord's Prayer, see Otto Betz, *Jesus der Messias Israels: Aufsätze zur biblischen Theologie*, WUNT 42 (Tübingen: Mohr Siebeck, 1987), 185–91. Betz points out the close relation between Ps 103 and the Lord's Prayer. For instance, just as the psalmist proclaims God's holy name (103:1), so Jesus calls on God's holy name (6:9). Just as the psalmist proclaims that God's kingdom rules over all (103:19), so Jesus hopes for God's kingdom to come (6:10). Just as the psalmist thanks God for his provision (103:5), so Jesus prays for our daily bread (6:11). More importantly, just as the psalmist names God who forgives our iniquity and heals our diseases (103:3), so Jesus prays for God's forgiveness (6:12). Just as the psalmist proclaims that God redeems us from the pit (103:4), so Jesus prays for God to deliver us from the evil one (6:13). This similar construction leads Betz to assert that the Lord's Prayer is influenced by Ps 103: "Unsere Untersuchung hat gezeigt, dass sich der Einfluß von Psalm 103 nicht etwa nur auf die sogenannten 'redaktionellen' Abschnitte in den Evangelien erstreckt, sondern gerade auch in der unbestritten echten Jesusüberlieferung vorhanden ist, so etwa im 'Vater Unser'" ("Our study has shown that the influence of Ps 103 does not only extend to the so-called 'redactional' portions in the Gospels, but is also present in the undisputed authentic Jesus tradition, such as in the 'Our Father' [the Lord's Prayer]" [199; All the German translations are mine]). Didache 8:3 also reads: "Pray like this three times a day" (cf. Sir 28:2–5). The

content of the Lord's Prayer is also similar to the Kaddish prayer prayed in Jewish synagogues. For more discussion on the Jewish sensibilities of the Lord's Prayer, see Dale C. Allison Jr., *The Sermon on the Mount: Inspiring the Moral Imagination* (New York: Crossroad, 1999), 121–23; Luz, *Matthew 1–7*, 324: The Lord's Prayer "bears the imprint of Jesus the man and messenger of God, and it does so both where it is characteristically Jewish as well as where it has distinctive features within Judaism."

30. The expression πατήρ is the translation from the Aramaic term ἀββά. Jesus refers to God as ἀββά to refer to his intimate relationship with God (cf. 11:25–26; Mark 14:36; Rom 8:15; Gal 4:6). As Luz writes, "The Lord's Prayer was *Aramaic*, while most extant Jewish prayers are Hebrew" (*Matthew 1–7*, 324). According to Thompson, Jesus's understanding of God as Father is not concerned with "males or distinctive of human fathers. Rather, in the biblical narratives it is the father's role as head of the family in the sense of 'founder' of the family line and guardian of its heritage, rather than as controlling or sovereign, that shapes the presentation of God" (*Promise of the Father*, 183). Thus, the emphasis falls on "the Father as the source and giver of life" (183). In trusting God as one who is the source and giver of life, Jesus addresses God as Father. As Thompson writes, "[T]he God who is confessed as trustworthy is properly known as the one designated by Jesus as *abba*" (184). Although no prayer in the OT begins with this address, Jesus's address to God as Father is a typical Jewish expression for God (e.g., Exod 15:2; Deut 14:1; 32:6; Isa 63:16; 64:8; Jer 3:19; 31:9, 20; Hos 11:1–4; Mal 2:10; Sir 23:1, 4). Allison notes that the Mishnah uses the phrase "Our Father in heaven" (*Sermon on the Mount*, 117). He also points out that "extrabiblical Jewish prayers do have invocations with 'Father'" (e.g., 3 Macc 6:3; Wis 14:3; Taʿan. 23b), especially in the Qumran texts (e.g., 4Q372; 4Q460).

31. The cross-reference in the margin of 6:9 in NA[28] points to Isa 63:16 LXX. In this passage, the MT is almost identical and runs as follows: "For you [are] our Father . . . you YHWH, our Father."

32. Jeremiah 3:19 LXX simply reads "Father," lacking the personal pronoun "my."

33. Thompson, *Promise of the Father*, 87.

34. Ibid., 111.

35. Similarly, Andrew J. Byers notes that "the juxtaposition of the singular first person possessive ('my') alongside the plural second person possessive ('your') preserves a subtle, yet significant, degree of distinction between Jesus' relationship to God and that of his disciples" (*Ecclesiology and Theosis in the Gospel of John*, SNTSMS 166 [Cambridge: Cambridge University Press, 2017], 182–83). France observes, "[Matthew] posits a unique filial relationship for Jesus and a derivative relationship for God's other 'children' into which Jesus introduces them (cf. 11:27)" (*Gospel of Matthew*, 245).

36. Marianne Meye Thompson, *John: A Commentary*, NTL (Westminster: John Knox, 2015), 55.

37. Thompson, *Promise of the Father*, 88.

38. As Thompson observes, "regarding the mutual knowledge of Father and Son, the emphasis falls not on the metaphysical relationship of Father and Son . . . but rather on the way in which God's hiding and revealing are effected *through* and *in* the ministry of Jesus" (*Promise of the Father*, 112; emphasis mine).

39. It should be noted that although the Sermon on the Mount is addressed to Jesus's disciples, the hearing of the crowd (per 5:1 and 7:28–29) implies that Jesus is teaching his disciples, who are joining him in teaching their people (the next discourse, Matt 10, is that of Jesus's sending the twelve to his people in the land). Thus, it is indeed all the people of the God of Israel who are invited to learn Jesus's prayer as their own.

40. Luke's version reads "Father" (11:2) instead of "my Father" or "our Father."

41. Thompson, *Promise of the Father*, 185. Thompson aptly points out, "To speak of God as Father is to acknowledge that God gives to his people their inheritance in Christ, the heir through whom God's promises are guaranteed and received" (185).

42. As noted earlier, sonship is not a matter simply of status but of the intergenerational flow of life and power. In that sense, son means heir and thus sonship denotes inheritance.

43. Elsewhere in Matthew's narrative, Jesus reveals the Father's knowledge and will through his reading of the law in terms of love and mercy (22:37–40; cf. 5:43–48; 7:21; 9:13; 12:7, 50).

44. For the phrase "Father in heaven," see 5:16, 45; 6:1, 9; 7:11, 21; 10:32, 33; 12:50; 16:17; 18:10, 14, 19. For the phrase "heavenly Father," see 5:48; 6:14, 26, 32; 15:13; 18:35; 23:9.

45. See also 5:34 and 23:22, where heaven is referred to as the throne of God (cf. Ps 103:19).

46. The God of Israel is not contained in the spatial dimension (e.g., 1 Kgs 8:27; Isa 66:1).

47. Gerhard Schneider, "'Im Himmel—auf Erden': Eine Perspektive matthäischer Theologie," in *Studien zum Matthäusevangelium: Festschrift für Wilhelm Pesch*, ed. Ludger Schenke (Stuttgart: Katholisches Bibelwerk, 1988), 288: "Heaven and earth are created by God. They together build the domain of God."

48. Paul envisions that there are "spiritual forces of evil" in the heavenly realm (e.g., Eph 6:12). By contrast, heaven has positive connotations in Matthew (e.g., 6:10; 18:14; 22:30).

49. In the OT, God fills Bezalel and Oholiab with his Spirit, knowledge, wisdom, and skill to construct the tabernacle (Exod 31:2–6; 36:1–2). This shows how God in heaven works toward the human on earth. Being empowered by God's Spirit and wisdom, Bezalel and Oholiab construct the *heavenly* designed tabernacle on earth.

50. In Matthew, God's name is concerned with the Fatherhood of God in Matthew. The cross-reference in the margin of 6:9 in NA[28] points to Isa 63:16 LXX, where the Fatherhood of God and the name of God are juxtaposed: "You, Lord, are our father, our Redeemer from beginning is your name." Thus, the name of God and the Fatherhood of God are closely related. But this is not to say that Father is a name for God. Thompson notes one analogy that "'Mom' or 'Dad' functions like a nickname, indicating what it is appropriate for the children of a family to call a parent" (Thompson, *Promise of the Father*, 177). By "nickname," Thompson means a nickname that "signals what someone with a particular or special relationship may call another" (177). Just as "'Mom' and 'Dad' are not the 'public names' of these individuals but the way in which they are known and the name to which they respond within a particular

family unit" (178). Likewise, "the designation Father functions within the Christian family to speak of the one to whom the community owes its life and being and to remind them of their collective identity as the people called out by God" (178).

51. W. D. Davies and Dale C. Allison Jr., *Matthew 1–7: A Critical and Exegetical Commentary on the Gospel according to Saint Matthew*, ICC (London: T&T Clark, 2004), 602; cf. Allison, *The Sermon on the Mount*, 120; Donald A. Hagner, *Matthew 1–13*, WBC 33A (Waco, TX: Word, 1993), 144. In line with my observation, see France (*Gospel of Matthew*, 246), who observes that while God's name is already holy (e.g., Pss 30:4; 97:12; 103:1; 111:9), "it is that people may recognize and acknowledge its holiness by giving God the reverence which is his due." This suggests that God's holy name "should not be profaned as a result of his people's sinful behavior and its punishment (Ezek 20:8–9; 36:20–23; cf. Isa 48:11; 52:5–6)." France further writes that this petition is "itself an expression of that reverence which his holiness requires" (246). In giving ten commandments, the God of Israel declares that "you shall not make wrongful use of the name of the Lord your God, for the Lord will not acquit anyone who misuses his name" (Exod 20:7). See also Schneider ("Im Himmel—auf Erden," 294): "es wird auch gewünscht, dass Gottes Wille von den Menschen treu erfüllt werden möge" ("it is also desired that God's will be faithfully fulfilled by people").

52. The cross-reference in the margin of 6:9 in NA[28] points to Isa 29:23 LXX.

53. Another cross-reference in the margin of 6:9 in NA[28] points to Ezek 36:23 LXX.

54. God, when asked his name, tells us that it does not concern us (e.g., Gen 32:29).

55. John A. Wilson, "The God and His Unknown Name of Power," in *Ancient Near Eastern Texts Relating to the Old Testament*, ed. James B. Pritchard (Princeton: Princeton University Press, 1969), 12. Regarding the significance of God's name, Terence E. Fretheim notes that naming admits "a certain intimacy in relationship. . . . Naming makes true encounter and communication possible. Naming entails availability. By giving the name, God becomes accessible to people" (*Exodus*, IBC [Louisville: Westminster John Knox, 1991], 65). God reveals his name to Moses to become accessible to his people. Fretheim further notes that "naming also entails vulnerability. In becoming so available to the world, God is to some degree at the disposal of those who can name the name. God's name may be misused and abused as well as honored. . . . Naming entails the likelihood of divine suffering" (65). Thus, the act of name-giving is closely related to God's knowledge of his people's suffering: "I know their sufferings" (Exod 3:7). In Matthew's narrative, Jesus bears the name of God and thus suffers and dies for his people for the forgiveness of sins (1:21; 26:28).

56. The hiphil form, אֶהְיֶה (Exod 3:14), is a causative verb that takes action to cause others. Thus, "I am who I am" can be rendered as "I cause you to be."

57. God's name and God's forgiveness are often closely related in the OT. God forgives because of his name (e.g., Exod 15:26; 23:20–22; Pss 78:38; 79:9; 103:3; Isa 48:9; Ezek 20:9–10). The psalmist proclaims that "For your name's sake, O Lord, pardon my guilt" (25:11 NRSV), "O God of our salvation . . . forgive our sins, for your name's sake" (79:9 NRSV). The prophet Isaiah also writes, "For my name's sake I [God] defer my anger" (48:9 NRSV). In Exod 23:20–22, moreover, God's name dwells in an angel with the theme of forgiveness ("for my name is in him"). In

the midrashic tradition, the angel in Exod 23:20–22 is particularly linked with Son of Man in Dan 7. Regarding the connection between Exod 23:20–22 and Dan 7, see Joel Marcus, "Authority to Forgive Sins upon the Earth: The Shema in the Gospel of Mark," in *The Gospels and the Scriptures of Israel*, ed. W. Richard Stegner and Craig A. Evans, JSNTSup 104 (Sheffield: Sheffield Academic, 1994), 205–206. As Matthew's narrative bears out, Jesus is also presented as Son of Man (9:6; 24:30; 26:64). What Jesus does as Son of Man is unfolding God's heavenly healing power so that the lives of his people can be repaired and transformed (8:1–9:38). This is how Jesus, particularly as God-with-us, embodies God's presence among his people.

58. Green, "Kingdom of God/Heaven," 474.

59. In parsing the relationship between βασιλεία and τῶν οὐρανῶν, Pennington suggests a genitive of source or origin (i.e., heaven is the origin of the kingdom) and an attributive genitive (i.e., the essential quality of the kingdom). See Pennington, *Heaven and Earth*, 294–95. In a similar vein, Green points out that the phrase "kingdom of heaven" emphasizes "the heavenly origin and nature of the kingdom" ("Kingdom of God/Heaven," 474).

60. Schneider, "Im Himmel—auf Erden," 289; "dominion that comes from heaven and enters this world. The voice from heavens (3:17), the sign from heaven (16:1), John's baptism (21:25) come from God."

61. The cross-reference in the margin of Matt 11:4–6 in NA[28] points to Isa 26:19; 29:18–19, where God's liberation unfolds for the dead body and the sick. Cf. Isa 52:7–10; Ezek 20:33–34.

62. Jesus's healing of his people's lives will be discussed in chapter 3.

63. To do the Father's will on earth in Matthew is to submit one's will to God as shown in Jesus's prayer in Gethsemane (26:39; cf. Abot 2:4): "Not my will but your will be done." Avot 2:4 is as follows: "Set aside your will in the face of his will."

64. For instance, Jesus rebukes the Pharisees and the scribes for not enacting justice, mercy, and faithfulness (23:23).

65. Regarding the concept of forgiveness and its relation to salvation, see chapter 1, n. 4. Matthew assumes the picture of salvation envisioned in the OT. Salvation is understood as the language of exodus and liberation. In the exodus story, God saves his people by liberating his people from Egypt (e.g., Exod 3:8). God's liberating power is also revealed in Israel's return from exile, a fulfillment of the exodus (e.g., 2 Chr 36:22–23). That is, God empowers King Cyrus of Persia to send the people of Israel back to Judah to build God's house. In Matthew's narrative, Jesus himself experiences exile (2:13–18; cf. Hos 11:1; Exod 20:2; Deut 24:18), such that the language of exile initially applied to Israel is now applied to Jesus.

66. The nature of inherited sins over generations in Matthew's narrative will be discussed in chapter 3.

67. This will be developed exegetically in chapter 3.

68. Luz, *Matthew 1–7*, 322.

69. France, *Gospel of Matthew*, 252.

70. Luz, *Matthew 1–7*, 322.

71. In the OT, the God of Israel does not deal with us according to our sins (Ps 103:10). God has rather compassion for his children for he knows how we were made (Ps 103:13–14).

72. France, *Gospel of Matthew*, 253.

73. Ibid.

74. Ibid.

75. Jones, *Embodying Forgiveness*, 195.

76. For the notion of "six perfections of gift," see John M. G. Barclay, *Paul and the Gift* (Grand Rapids: Eerdmans, 2015), 66–78. For more recent discussion, see John M. G. Barclay, "The Gift Perspective on Paul," in *Perspectives on Paul: Five Views*, ed. Scot McKnight and B. J. Oropeza (Grand Rapids: Baker Academic, 2020), 219–36; idem, *Paul & the Power of Grace* (Grand Rapids: Eerdmans, 2020).

77. Barclay, "Gift Perspective on Paul," 222.

78. Ibid.

79. Ibid.

80. Ibid., 223. For an extensive discussion on the relation between gifts and expectations/costs in the Greco-Roman world and Second Temple Judaism, see Barclay, *Paul and the Gift*, 79–188.

81. Barclay, "Gift Perspective on Paul," 232.

82. Ibid., 234.

83. Ibid., 227, 232. Barclay notes that "Jewish practices (the 'works of the law') are by no means wrong or misguided, but they are not the criteria of worth in the Christ-economy" (227). All "systems of worth" and "the usual antitheses of ethnicity, gender, or social status" are not erased but "they are no longer what counts, what gives value" (226, 229).

84. In articulating the divine-human relationship, Barclay notes that "it is better to talk of 'energism' (cf. Phil 2:12–13) than to use the traditional alternatives of 'monergism' and 'synergism'" ("Gift Perspective on Paul," 233). Regarding the nature of "energism," he emphasizes the role of the Spirit: "the Spirit works to create a congruity between the life of the believer and the life of God. . . . This congruity arises from the transformative work of the Spirit. . . . It is the new self, sourced in and activated by the gift of God in Christ" (233). For further detail, see also Barclay, *Paul and the Gift*, 439–42. While Barclay does not use the term "theosis," he points out that "the 'Gift Perspective' connects well with analyses of Pauline theology that elucidate salvation as 'participation in Christ' or 'union with Christ'" (233).

85. Carter, *Matthew and the Margins*, 156.

86. Ibid.

87. Andrew Wallace-Hadrill observes that patronage in the Greco-Roman world is characterized by "the manipulation of scarce resources: where all need resources that are in short supply, it is easier for the patrons to secure control of the route of access. . . . Here food may stand as the symbol of the resources a patron distributes: his [or her] power over the client derives not from generous and regular distribution, but from keeping him [or her] on tenterhooks with the prospect of access to resources which is in fact never fully granted" ("Patronage in Roman Society: From Republic to Empire," in *Patronage in Ancient Society*, ed. Andrew Wallace-Hadrill,

Leicester-Nottingham Studies in Ancient Society 1 [London; New York: Routledge, 1989], 73). But, for Matthew, God's resource is unlimited and generously distributed to his people (e.g., 14:20; 15:37). In this regard, Matthew's metaphor for God is not patron but *Father*. For further discussion on the elements characteristic of patronage in the Greco-Roman world, see Jerome H. Neyrey, "God, Benefactor and Patron: The Major Cultural Model for Interpreting the Deity in Greco-Roman Antiquity," *JSNT* 27, no. 4 (2005): 467–68.

88. Pokrifka-Joe, "Divine and Human Forgiveness," 171.

89. Psalm 18:25–28 conveys a similar idea that our way of life is the very mode in which we participate in God's character.

90. J. C. O'Neill, "The Lord's Prayer," *JSNT* 51 (1993): 16. O'Neill suggests that 6:12 should be read as "we pray forgiveness for our debtors" (16).

91. Davies and Allison, *Matthew 1–7*, 612.

92. M. Zerwick and M. Grosvenor notes that the aorist ἀφήκαμεν could be "a Semitic perfect which in certain circumstances may have present sense" (*A Grammatical Analysis of the Greek New Testament*, SubBi 39, 5th ed. [Rome: Gregorian & Biblical Press, 2013], 16). That is, the aorist ἀφήκαμεν can be taken as an Aramaic perfect, meaning "as herewith we forgive" (J. Jeremias, *New Testament Theology: The Proclamation of Jesus* [London: SCM, 1971], 201).

93. Davies and Allison, *Matthew 1–7*, 611. In the OT, when people plea for forgiveness, God's forgiveness of us does not wait for or depend on our forgiveness of others (e.g., Exod 32:32; Ps 25:18).

94. As Allison observes, "Matthew 6:12 is not about some worthiness earned through our pale imitation of divine forgiveness; it is about our desire" (*Sermon on the Mount*, 127).

95. Brown and Roberts similarly point out that "God's forgiveness is tied to their own willingness to forgive a wrong" (*Matthew*, 71).

Chapter 3

Forgiveness as Transformative Healing Participation in God's Life

Matthew 9:1–13 is significant for this study because it epitomizes the concrete nature of Jesus as "God-with-us" (1:23), depicting the transformative dynamics of heaven and earth revealed in Jesus's forgiveness and healing. While Matthean scholars like Isaac K. Mbabazi emphasize the thematic importance of forgiveness in Matthew's Gospel, he mainly focuses on Matt 6 and 18.[1] In a similar vein, Todd Pokrifka-Joe directs his attention to Matt 6 and 18 as examples of forgiveness texts in Matthew's Gospel.[2] Thus, the examination of forgiveness in Matt 9:1–13 has not received adequate attention in NT scholarship. More importantly, theosis provides a theological lens that allows the meaning of forgiveness to come into sharper focus, especially with respect to healing in Matthew's Gospel as presented in Matt 9:1–13.

Matthew briefly reports Jesus's healing activity earlier in the narrative (4:23–24), but the relation between Jesus's forgiving work and his healing is explicitly highlighted at this juncture in Matthew's narrative (9:1–13). In 4:23, Jesus announces the good news of the kingdom and heals every disease and sickness among the people, and 8:1–9:38 shows *how* he heals his people, especially through forgiveness (9:2, 6). Thus, the nature of Jesus's forgiveness as healing his people is concretely expressed in Matt 9. As will be shown in this study, Jesus's forgiveness of sins involves healing and repair of the inherited consequences of past sins over generations. The nature of forgiveness in Matthew, then, is a transformation of embodied life such that the consequences of past sins and corruptions are addressed and repaired. Forgiveness in this sense is our transformative, healing participation in God's life. Accordingly, Matt 9:1–13 offers an inviting locus for considering Matthew's teaching on forgiveness through the lens of theosis.

To make my argument, I first examine Matthew's presentation of Jesus as God-with us because Jesus's healing of his people is related to his being with us (1:23; 8:1–9:38). The way God's self in Jesus is with his people is the way he saves, heals, and rescues his people. I then examine the metaphor of Israel's God as healer in the OT because Matthew presents Jesus's healing ministry as continuing and embodying God's healing action in our midst. Finally, I offer an exegesis of 9:1–13 in five steps. First, I explore sickness in Matthew's narrative because sickness is one of the important features of the segment, 8:1–9:38, where Jesus encounters various kinds of sick and suffering people. Second, I consider the nature of Jesus's healing in Matthew's narrative in relation to forgiveness. Since Jesus's forgiveness and healing take place in Capernaum (9:1; cf. 8:5–13), I also attend to the significance of Capernaum, where Jesus's presence and healing save and liberate the people in the land (4:13–16; cf. Isa 8:23–9:2 LXX). Third, I focus on Jesus's forgiveness and healing in 9:2–5, where the paralyzed person is healed by the power of Jesus's forgiveness. This shows that Jesus's forgiving the paralyzed person makes his life whole, restoring his relationship to God by the way it unites him with others. Jesus's forgiveness thus enacts healing that repairs our brokenness, which we variously share with others. Fourth, I interpret Jesus's healing and the heaven-earth relation in 9:6–8 through the lens of theosis. This shows how Jesus's authority to forgive sins entails God's heavenly healing on earth (9:6). I examine how Jesus's authority to forgive sins, given to him as a human being, is extended to the disciples in Jesus's mission discourse, where the disciples, now sharing in Jesus's authority, extend the forgiveness of sins by enacting God's heavenly forgiving power (10:1–7). Thus, I briefly address how God's own forgiveness, given to Jesus, is extended by Jesus's followers later in the narrative. In this way, we as disciples embody and express God's forgiveness through healing in our own, bodily life. Finally, I briefly consider Jesus's table fellowship and healing in 9:9–13. At this juncture of the narrative, Jesus presents himself as a physician (9:12), and, as such, he embodies God's merciful forgiveness through healing (9:13). Each step has its own distinct emphasis, but together all the steps contribute to understanding how a focus on theosis sheds light on the dynamics of forgiveness and healing in Matthew's narrative.

JESUS AS HEALER

Jesus as God-with-Us and Healer

In Matthew's narrative, Jesus's being God-with-us is paired with his calling as savior of his people from their sins (1:21, 23).[3] Generally in Matthew, the term σώζω means to "preserve," "keep safe," "rescue," or "protect."[4] Joel B. Green notes that "in the ancient world, the language of *saviour* or *salvation* often had a medical sense, occurring in references to healing, health, and human flourishing. Physicians are called *saviours* and people speak of restoration to health as *being saved*."[5] J. G. van der Watt and D. S. du Toit similarly note that Jesus's healing is "signified by the term *sōzō* (8:25; 9:21–22; 14:30)," portraying "Jesus's presence in Israel as salvational presence."[6] In this light, it is no coincidence that the Hebrew meaning of Jesus's name is "God is savior" (*yēšūaʿ*, 1:21).[7] As implied in his name, Jesus's mission is oriented to delivering his people from their sins, healing their infirmities, where empowering forgiveness is a key piece of that salvation (e.g., 4:17; 9:2; 20:28; 26:28).[8]

With this in mind, we can see that the significance of Jesus's encounter with various kinds of people in Matthew's narrative (8:1–9:38) is to reveal *who* Jesus is as savior, particularly as God-with-us (1:23). Quoting Isa 7:14, Matthew tells us Jesus is God-with-us (1:23). The force of Matthew's quotation of Isa 7:14 about the significance of the name "Jesus" lies with the name *Emmanuel* in the context of Isaiah's prophecy, that is, God's promise to save and thus be with his people. Isaiah 7:14 is originally addressed to king Ahaz: "God's protection will soon intervene to carry Judah past its present crisis. Isaiah 7:14–25 thus points to deliverance."[9] By drawing on Isa 7:14, Matthew suggests that the way Jesus is God's presence with his people is the way he saves his people from their crisis, which, in Jesus's generation, reflects the crises they have inherited from their past, from the days of Ahaz and before. In line with Isaiah's imagery of Emmanuel, salvation in Matthew's narrative refers to God's liberative acts for his people from their enemies or crisis (1:21). Further, given that Jesus's being God-with-us is paired with his name "God is savior" (*yēšūaʿ*) and his calling as deliverer of his people from their sins in Matthew's narrative (1:21, 23), this parallel construction of Jesus's name and calling suggests that God's forgiveness of sins through God's saving presence is a focal point of Jesus's existence. Named *God-with-us*, Jesus embodies God's saving power in the midst of his people (1:21).[10] For Matthew, the way God is with his people is thus the way God saves, liberates, and rescues his people through Jesus, specifically through forgiveness. That is, God gives forgiveness to human beings, who forgive one another, as one piece of his salvation.

In Israel's history, God's liberative presence is especially revealed in Israel's return from exile, a fulfillment of the exodus (e.g., Exod 20:2; Deut 24:18; 2 Chr 36:22–23; Hos 11:1). For instance, 2 Chr 36:22–23 LXX indicates that the restoration of God's presence is Israel's return from exile. God empowers King Cyrus of Persia to declare God's presence with the people of Israel and to send them back to Judah to build God's house.[11] Similarly, the memory of exile appears in Matthew's narrative as Jesus himself experiences exile (2:13–18). As in 2 Chr 36:23 LXX ("God will be with him or her"),

God promises his presence with his people that leads them out of exile in the person of Jesus (2:19–21). More importantly, Matthew quotes Hos 11:1 to indicate God's liberative presence in Jesus who will embody God's healing in the lives of the people of Israel (2:15).[12] God's liberative presence in Hos 11:1 is given in the context of God's healing and mercy: "they [Israel] did not know that I have healed (ἰάομαι) them" (11:3). Hosea 11:8 narrates that God's heart recoils within him and God's mercy is stirred for Israel. By drawing on Hos 11:1 in relation to Jesus's return from Egypt to the promised land, Matthew signals that Jesus continues and embodies God's merciful healing in the midst of his people, participating in their plight, and this mercy is manifest as the forgiveness and healing of his people (9:13; 12:7). Jesus has the Father's compassion, which he communicates to the people such that they are forgiven and healed (e.g., 9:36; 14:14; 15:32; 20:34). Thus, for example, Jesus heals the sick on the sabbath because of his mercy (12:7–13). In this way, Jesus becomes God's saving presence at work in his people (1:21). He embodies God's mercy, protection, liberation, accompaniment, and empowerment for his people as found within the Jewish Scriptures (e.g., Exod 3:12; Deut 2:7; 20:1; Jer 1:8, 17, 19; 15:20; 42:11; 46:28).

In Matthew's narrative, Jesus saves and heals his people not by rising above their infirmities but by drawing near to *us*. Thus, quoting Isa 53:4, Matthew describes Jesus's healing ministry as follows: "the thing spoken through Isaiah the prophet was fulfilled, saying, he took our weaknesses and bore [our] diseases" (8:17). Scholars often do not adequately attend to the nature of Jesus's healing in relation to the suffering of his people.[13] But as envisioned in Isa 53:4, Jesus's healing ministry deals with his people's sins and infirmities and makes their suffering and sins his own by suffering himself (e.g., 16:21; 17:22–23; 20:18–19), with the result that he fulfills the eschatological vision of the bodily transformation of Israel. Jesus's delivering of his people from their sins and suffering, then, involves his interacting with them bodily and directly (e.g., 8:3, 15). This suggests that for Matthew, Jesus's healing presence is especially revealed in our weakness as he takes on our infirmities (8:17). Although Jesus does not take on our infirmities and diseases by becoming sick himself, he takes them on by healing them in us. This resonates with Matthew's portrayal of Jesus's joining in John's baptism for the forgiveness of sins (3:13–17). Jesus identifies himself with his people in John's baptism by knowing their sins as his own. Just as Isaiah knows Israel's sins as his own (Isa 6:5), so Jesus assumes his people's sins as his own (cf. 2 Cor 5:21). As the narrative bears out, because Jesus is with us rather than far away from us (e.g., 18:20; 28:20), he is able to touch and embrace our infirmities (8:1–9:38). Because Jesus is with us, his healing power reaches and embraces human beings through word and touch so that they are transformed (e.g., 8:3, 8–9; 9:6–8). Jesus's presence, then, is an ongoing means of our transformed life in Matthew's narrative.

The Metaphor of Israel's God as Healer in the OT

To understand Jesus's healing ministry in Matthew's Gospel, it is important to consider how Jesus continues and manifests the presence of the God of Israel. Immediately following the scene of Jesus's healing that we will consider below (9:2–9), Matthew draws on Hos 6:6 LXX to connect the God of Israel with Jesus to signal who Jesus is, particularly as "physician" (ἰατρός, 9:12–13). In the context of Hos 6, God will heal his people and bind them up: "He [God] will heal you" (ἰάσεται ἡμᾶς, 6:1 LXX).[14] In drawing on Hos 6:6, Matthew delivers the message that Jesus's action of healing continues and embodies in Israel God's action of healing. The way Jesus acts as healer, then, is the way the God of Israel acts as healer.[15] Hosea's context further reveals that God promises restoration even in the midst of his people's wickedness (6:10–11).

On the nature of Israel's God's healing and restoration, Chong-Hyon Sung notes that the actions of Yahweh as doctor ("das Arzt-Handeln Jahwes") are especially revealed in the context of God's promise of eschatological salvation (e.g., Isa 30:26; 33:24; 57:19; Jer 30:17; 33:6; Mal 4:2–3).[16] For instance, the prophet Isaiah declares that God binds up the injuries of his people and heals their wounds in the days of the Lord's salvation (30:26). The prophet Jeremiah also declares that God will restore his people's health and heal their wounds in the day of the Lord (30:8, 17), and God's healing is given in the context of God's promise for Israel's return to the land from exile (30:3). The prophet Malachi harmonizes with Isaiah and Jeremiah, proclaiming God's healing in the day of the Lord (4:1–2). Matthew's Jesus also experiences exile and returns to his land (2:13–23; cf. Hos 11:1), embodying Israel's exile and return to their land. Thus, Jesus, who inherits the sonship of Israel's God (e.g., 3:17; 6:9; 7:21; 11:27; 12:50; 16:16; 26:39), and is as such heir to God's rule and promises, fulfills God's promise of deliverance through healing.[17]

FORGIVENESS AS HEALING PARTICIPATION IN GOD'S LIFE

Sickness in Matthew's Narrative

Matthew 9:1–13 is located in the context of Jesus's healing of his wounded people.[18] In its larger literary context, Jesus spreads and unfolds God's forgiving power as he heals his people's wounded life in the land. Sickness is thus one of the important features of the narrative of 8:1–9:38. In Matthew's narrative world, sickness and sin are closely related as Jesus issues the forgiveness of sins to the paralyzed person (9:2), which culminates in his healing.[19] Given this connection, Jesus's healing ministry can be understood as "saving [his] people from their sins" through the forgiveness of sins.[20] God's healing power revealed in Jesus is also God's forgiving power.[21] But we should bear in mind that the relation between sickness and sin is complex, as opposed to a relation that is only punitive or transactional (i.e., people sin, so God punishes them with sickness).[22] Sickness, in the concreteness of what it means for a person and in the community, is conceived as one of the inherited consequences of past sins, as one outcome of a larger, intergenerational process of corruption that is not altogether traceable. For instance, Matthew narrates the intergenerational and accumulated injustice "resulting from all the shedding of righteous individual's blood, from Abel to Zechariah" (23:35).[23] Anders Runesson observes that the concept of inherited guilt is found in Exod 20:5–6, where it states that God punishes children for the iniquity of parents: "punishment for sins committed by others in history may befall later generations within the people."[24] The implication is not necessarily that this "punishment" is retributive but that later generations find themselves enduring the consequences of what their forebears have done, and in some cases what they themselves have continued to do. For Matthew, the scope of inherited injustice is not limited to but goes beyond the biological family as Matthew portrays those who killed the prophets as the "fathers" (πατέρων) of the scribes and Pharisees (23:31–32; cf. 12:50).[25] Thus, there is no "predestining gene" in Matthew.[26] The concept of inherited guilt also appears in 27:25, where the crowds call the blood of Jesus down on themselves and their children. For Matthew, therefore, Jesus's forgiveness involves repairing what the intergenerational process of Israel's life among other peoples has produced and setting the life of the people involved on a trajectory of health. As will be shown, Jesus's forgiveness of sins conveys healing (9:2) that restores and transforms one's life with God and with others (9:6–7). For Matthew, this is how Jesus as God-with-us is present with his people, especially at this juncture of the narrative. To forgive sins is to heal people of the intergenerational consequences of sins. Thus, as we will see further below, forgiveness can be understood as healing participation in God's transformative life. The nature of forgiveness is a transformation of embodied life, such that the consequences of past sins are addressed and repaired.

Another significant element for understanding sickness in Matthew's narrative is related to the historical context in the first century CE. Matthew's Gospel is written in a historical context where the socioeconomic structure is divided into "elites and non-elites."[27] While elites largely benefit from the imperial system, non-elites live in poverty, "marked by squalor, garbage, human excrement, animals, disease . . . and unstable dwellings" under the Roman empire.[28] As Warren Carter points out, "The lethal quality of this imperial existence is evident in short life spans and high mortality rates."[29] In this light, it is no coincidence that Matthew's narrative highlights the sick and the suffering. Thus, Matthew's narrative in some ways reflects the destructive reality of the imperial structure. It is in this context that Jesus's healing power unfolds, manifesting God's liberating power and God's presence among the sick and suffering of God's people.

The Nature of Jesus's Healing in Matthew's Gospel

In the segment of the narrative (8:1–9:38) that includes the healing of a paralyzed person (9:1–8), Jesus encounters various kinds of needy people, such as a leprous person (8:1–4), a centurion with a suffering slave-boy (8:5–13), the demon-possessed (8:16–17, 28–34; 9:32–34), a scribe (8:19), a hemorrhaging woman (9:20–22), and a ruler with a dying daughter (9:18–19, 23–25). Jesus's encounter with various groups of people implies that forgiveness is concerned with our "bodily and relational transformation."[30] For instance, in Jesus's time, the person with leprosy in 8:1–4 is restricted from contacting others by the law (e.g., Lev 13–14).[31] But Jesus touches that person to heal his body and to restore his relationship with others. As such, Jesus's healing affects not only the person with leprosy in isolation but the person in relationship to others, thereby affecting those others.[32] Jesus's healing also affects the meaning of leprosy wherever it is known because its limit has now been revealed in Jesus. As the prophet Isaiah envisions (53:4), Jesus fulfills the eschatological vision of transformation by touching the weak, the blind, and the needy (Matt 8:17). The significance of Jesus's encounters with various kinds of people is to reveal who Jesus is, particularly as God-with-us who heals his people along the particular lines of their disease (4:23; 8:1–17). That is, Jesus saves his people by drawing near to them. Jesus's healing power is thus revealed in our weakness. It is revealed in Jesus's transformative intimacy with vulnerable people and his being a vulnerable person, and, as such, a powerful member of his people (cf. 3:13–17).[33]

In 9:1, Jesus is now back in Capernaum (cf. 4:13; 8:5), having come "to [his] own city" (εἰς τὴν ἰδίαν πόλιν).[34] The significance of Capernaum depends partly on its connection with the tribes of Israel—Zebulun and Naphtali (Matt 4:15; cf. Isa 8:23–9:2 LXX). In Israel's history, Capernaum was in the territory of Naphtali (cf. Josh 19:32–39). Naphtali was one of the first tribes of Israel to be taken captive when the Assyrians invaded the northern kingdom of Israel (2 Kgs 15:29). In this historical context, Matthew narrates that Jesus goes to Capernaum, in the ancient territory of Naphtali, as the central base of his ministry to exercise the heavenly rule of God in the place where historical wounds and traumas had invaded his people from the north and east (4:13–16). Drawing on Isa 8:23–9:2 LXX, Matthew relates that with the presence of Jesus (4:13), light has shined on those who live in this land of darkness (σκότος). J. J. M. Roberts notes that "darkness is used here as a metaphor for political oppression and injustice, and light is the contrasting metaphor for political release from such oppression. This imagery was traditional in the ancient Near East."[35] This darkness first came by the encroachment of the Assyrians and later by the Romans. But as the prophet Isaiah envisions, there will be no more gloom (σκότος) for those who live in the land because Israel's God will make a way for his people (Isa 8:23 LXX). The presence of the Romans, like the Assyrians, will thus no longer hold the people in darkness in the land because the people come to see light (φῶς) through Jesus whose presence brings the healing of the people (4:14–16; 8:1–9:38), not least by bringing healing to the enemy of Israel in the land. This is confirmed by Jesus's healing of a Roman centurion's slave in Capernaum (8:5–13).[36] The slave's need and healing draw his gentile lord to serve the lordship of Jesus (8:6, 8). The Roman centurion says that he is "under power" (ὑπὸ ἐξουσίαν) and has people under his power and that as such he submits to Jesus's power (ἐξουσία). Jesus's power is apparently greater than the power of Rome, which orders the relations between the centurion and his superiors and inferiors especially by the power of their words, that of military command. This is a key way in which Rome has power to extend its reach across great distances and yet is not powerful enough to reach the body of the centurion's slave. But Jesus's presence and power bring light, healing the slave's body by his word. Saving his people from their sins must address, among other things, their oppression under foreign rule. Thus, Jesus's power in relation to the centurion is a picture of the healing that is coming to Israel, gathering the broken and scattered people, bringing gentiles with them: "from the east and west" (8:11; cf. Isa 43:5–6; 49:12; Matt 28:19–20). For Matthew, this is how Jesus's presence and healing touch liberate his people in the land.

Jesus's Forgiveness and Healing in Matt 9:2–5

Jesus now encounters the paralyzed person (παραλυτικός) in a house in Capernaum,[37] declaring that "your sins are forgiven" (ἀφίενταί σου αἱ ἁμαρτίαι, 9:2; cf. 1:21).[38] Carter observes that Jesus's declaration is "strange when the man's sins have not been mentioned." This implies that "Jesus assumes the common link between sickness and sin" (e.g., Lev 26:14–16; Deut 28:21–22; 2 Chr 21:15, 18–19).[39] In Matthew's larger literary context, when Jesus says, "your sins" (9:2), it is not merely confined to a matter of individual guilt but involves their social environments. Green observes that for people in the world of the Bible, "the source of sickness rested not only in the bodies of the sick but also and sometimes especially in their social environments and in the larger universe."[40] This is because the fabric of the lives of Israel is inextricably bound up with others as a web in the land. Matthew thus narrates that parents' guilt is bound up with their children (27:25; cf. 23:35–36). The narrative of Matthew assumes these social and intergenerational realities, such that the people suffer from sickness as one outcome of a larger, intergenerational process of corruption. Thus, narratively, Jesus's forgiveness of sins entails the healing of the paralyzed person's body. It repairs and transforms the fabric of the lives of Israel in the land in and from that body, healing the web of relations of the paralyzed person as it heals his body. It should be noted that Jesus's healing is not merely limited spatially to the physical body but involves the transformation of the web of relations of the paralyzed person.[41] Once the paralyzed person is healed and raised up, he is able to join his community (9:7). Likewise, cleansing of leprosy allows the person with leprosy to access his community (8:3–4). Thus, healing effects the restoration of persons to community. Healing in this sense should be understood in "*wholistic* ways," involving "the embodied lives of persons in community."[42] In the OT, Exodus captures this holistic view of healing. God presents himself as "I am the Lord who heals you" (15:26 NRSV). In context, God's liberative work for Israel has just been celebrated (15:21). This suggests that God's saving action for Israel—his rule over Israel's enemies—is "epitomized in the metaphor of healing."[43] That is, God's healing encompasses his powerful intervention and liberative action for his people. The interweaving of healing and liberation speaks to the wholly integrated vision of Yahweh the healer.

Jesus's healing enables those who question him to know that the Son of Man has power on the earth to forgive sins.[44] Jesus asks those who question him which might be easier—to forgive sins or to make the paralyzed person walk (9:5). The underlying logic of Jesus's question is that it seems easier to proclaim forgiveness of sins than to command the paralyzed person to walk. Perhaps this is because "only the latter can be objectively verified."[45] Jesus thus seems to confront the implicit charge of the authorities that he has spoken an easy word. By doing with his word what the authorities assume is harder (i.e., to heal the person), Jesus shows that his word of forgiveness is not cheap or easy but in fact the greater exercise of power, that is, the power of God to forgive sins embodied and spoken by Jesus as a human being. Healing of the paralyzed person thus becomes a witness to the greater power of forgiveness of which his healing is only a sign. Accordingly, healing embodies forgiveness, such that the other healing in Matthew's narrative, including that done by the disciples and others (e.g., 10:1), is enacting God's forgiveness from heaven.

Also, it should be noted that it is when Jesus sees the "faith" (πίστις) of those who bring the paralyzed person to him, the act of faith whereby they place him before Jesus, that he says to the person that his sins are forgiven (9:2; cf. Mark 2:1–5).[46] R. T. France notes that the phrase "their faith" (πίστιν αὐτῶν) implies that "the mere act of bringing the man to Jesus was enough to demonstrate their faith."[47] Here, as with the Roman centurion (8:10) and the many who bring their sick to Jesus, faith occasions Jesus's healing (e.g., 8:13; 9:22, 28–29; 15:28). In particular, the faith of the paralyzed person's helpers and the Roman centurion is expressed by their bold, longing, even humiliating trust in Jesus for the care of others. In the language of theosis, God's forgiveness revealed in Jesus is expressed by the way they treat one another, thereby participating in God's healing presence. It is in that mode of faith, caring for others, that Jesus's forgiveness and healing are activated.

Their faith moves Jesus to speak forgiveness and healing. This suggests that healing comes not only from outside but also from among human beings—that is, through faith. Human beings, then, mediate God's heavenly healing among them (cf. 9:8). It is the faith of human beings that occasions the heavenly power of God's forgiveness on earth. The faith of human beings, in and through Jesus, enacts the power of God's forgiveness in their own, bodily life (cf. 9:22).[48] To put it another way, being able to forgive is a Christ-like dimension of faith. But the authorities accuse Jesus of blasphemy because Jesus claims for himself power that is uniquely God's (9:3). Jesus shows, then, that he is indeed embodying God's forgiving power and doing so as a human being—Son of Man. Matthew 9:8, the narrator's report of the crowds' response to God's giving such power to "human beings" (ἀνθρώποις), indicates that Jesus embodies God's forgiving power not as a human being set apart from others but as one human being among others, who together have been given forgiving and healing power by God. We can see this in the faith of others that occasions Jesus's forgiveness and healing but also the healing power that Jesus gives to others, starting with his disciples (10:1). Insofar as healing embodies the forgiveness of sins, and the forgiveness of sins is the activity of God's own power, then Jesus empowers others to activate their faith and participate in God's own activity of forgiveness, thereby bringing bodily healing. Through activating faith, therefore, we come to enact God's own healing and transform our past and memories in hope rather than despair.[49]

Jesus's Healing and the Heaven-Earth Relation in Matt 9:6–8

The pericope under consideration offers a telling witness to the relational dynamics between heaven and earth and thus between God and the human, which can be seen more clearly through the lens of theosis. The narrative depicts Jesus not only as uttering forgiving words but also as conveying power to make the paralyzed person walk. Jesus declares that the "Son of Man" (apparently he himself) has power (ἐξουσία) "to forgive" (ἀφιέναι) sins "on earth" (ἐπί τῆς γῆς, 9:6).[50] As evident in Matt 26:64 ("the Son of Man sitting at the right hand of God and coming on the clouds of heaven"),[51] but not clarified narratively until then, the Son of Man is linked to a figure of unique authority in Dan 7.[52] In Dan 7:13–14, "one like a son of man," a human figure, is given the power of the Ancient Days and rules over all peoples and nations. In its context, the identification of this human figure is tied to the holy people of the Most High (7:27). By alluding to Danielic language, Matthew presents Jesus as the Son of Man who is "enthroned in heaven to share God's sovereignty over all peoples" and "authorized to dispense God's forgiveness."[53] Insofar as Dan 7 anticipates what Daniel reports and prays for in Dan 9, which deals explicitly with forgiveness, the enthronement scene of Dan 7 is indeed a vision of the forgiveness of Israel's sins.[54] In this regard, Matthew brings together Dan 7–8 with Dan 9 to show that just as the forgiving power of one like a son of man in Dan 7:13–14 is exercised over all peoples on the earth from his heavenly throne ("all peoples, nations, and languages should serve him"), so Jesus as the Son of Man exercises God's heavenly forgiving power as a human being among others on the earth. In Matthew's narrative, Jesus embodies and enacts this power especially by extending God's healing forgiveness to human life rather than bypassing or inflicting bodily infirmities as beastly human kingdoms have done.[55]

That Jesus is characterized as Son of Man, the heir of the human, at this juncture of the narrative reveals that the way Jesus is with his people is realized by Jesus's touching and healing the life of human beings as a human being himself (9:6). As the prophet Isaiah envisions the coming of God in history to bring salvation and healing (e.g., Isa 30:26; 35:4–6), in Jesus's bodily healing, the scriptural portrait of God the healer is extended. The significance of Jesus's healing, then, lies in the extension of God's healing in Jesus's presence. To put it another way, that Jesus embodies and extends God's healing points to Matthew's way of presenting the oneness of God and Jesus. In this relational dynamic, it is more than a matter of imitating God but one of theosis, the extension of God's own forgiving power working itself out in and through Jesus's action of forgiveness. We should bear in mind that in Matthew, Jesus is presented as God-with-us (1:23), such that Jesus is *theosis* itself, a union of God and the human in which other human beings are enabled to participate. Jesus's action of forgiveness and healing is thus the expression of God's own forgiveness. In this way, Matthew shows how Jesus embodies God's forgiving power as a human being, who empowers others to participate in God's forgiving power. The oneness of God and the human in Jesus, then, is a reality in which Jesus empowers others to participate, and that is the dynamic of theosis.

Being healed by Jesus, the paralyzed person "stands up" (ἐγείρω) and joins communion with family and other neighbors by returning "to his house" (εἰς τὸν οἶκον αὐτοῦ, 9:7). In the OT, those who are paralyzed or lame are excluded from the priesthood (e.g., Lev 21:18), but they receive God's promise for healing (Isa 35:6).[56] That the paralyzed person is reconnected to his family and other neighbors indicates that Jesus touches wounds that tear people apart from one another, thereby fulfilling the promised healing of the condition of the people of Israel (e.g., Isa 35:4–10). Given that paralysis makes parts of the body unable to move, as with those who are lame, and thus affects the function of the whole body (cf. 1 Cor 12:26), the healing of paralysis suggests the restoration of the condition of the whole body, which results in restoring one's relationship with others (9:7). Jesus's forgiveness here thus entails bodily transformation that unites us with God and with others, with God by the way it unites us with others. In other words, forgiveness delivers the power of the kingdom from heaven that makes one's life whole, restoring their relationship to God and to others, since their relationship with God is not independent of their bodily relationship with others. God's forgiving power is thus not merely absolution from abstract guilt but the restoration of communion with God and with others.

Jesus exercises the authority to forgive sins as a human person who embodies God's heavenly, forgiving power on earth. Jesus does not deny what some of the scribes imply (i.e., forgiving sins is a power of God). Instead, Jesus says that such divine power is power he has, as Son of Man. Jesus claims as a human being to be exercising the forgiving power that is God's own power. That is, Jesus does what only God can do (9:3), so Jesus must share in who God is. God is now acting on earth through Jesus who embodies and extends God's heavenly power. Matthew reports the reaction of the crowds as praising God not because of the miracle itself but because God "has given 'people' (ἀνθρώποις) the power to forgive sins" (9:8).[57] The plural noun ἀνθρώποις is surprising because it is Jesus rather than other human beings who heals here. The unexpected use of the plural suggests that God's power is extended to human beings through Jesus as himself a human being.[58] That is, the power to forgive sins given to Jesus is understood to be available to other human beings. The dative construction τοῖς ἀνθρώποις could function as an indirect object ("to human beings") here with an accusative (ἐξουσίαν) as the direct object.[59] That human beings are given the power to forgive sins is confirmed in the church's authority to forgive sins later in Matthew's narrative (18:18–20), where the community of Jesus comes to participate in the power demonstrated here by Jesus (9:6). As Jacques Dupont puts it with respect to the narrator's report of the crowd's reaction in 9:8, "Sa manière de décrire la réaction de la foule juive veut suggérer à la communauté chrétienne l'action de grâces qu'elle doit rendre à Dieu pour le pouvoir qui, départi à Jésus en sa qualité de Fils de l'homme, reste présent dans l'Eglise par les hommes auxquels Jésus a communiqué ce pouvoir."[60] In the discourse on Jesus's discipline of the church, the power to forgive sins is given to the church through Jesus (18:18). Jesus teaches about binding and loosing in the context of a sheep of the community that has been led astray (i.e., sinned against the disciples Jesus is addressing) and the forgiveness of that person and therefore the healing of the community, as confirmed by Peter's question and Jesus's response (18:21–22), and in the parable of the unforgiving servant (18:23–35).[61] Jesus's power (ἐξουσία) in 9:6 is concerned with forgiveness of sins as delivered by Jesus as Son of Man. Then, by sharing in Jesus's power, the church comes to exercise God's own power (ἐξουσία) to bind and loose "on earth," thus manifesting God's heavenly forgiving power (18:18). Accordingly, our action of forgiveness as disciples becomes what Jesus has empowered us to do and what he does through us. We participate in the fullness of heaven and earth revealed in Jesus who has all power (ἐξουσία) in heaven and on earth (cf. 11:27; 28:18).[62] Thus, what generates and energizes the church is power (ἐξουσία), especially God's forgiving power. It is the power of the Son of Man who empowers the church to forgive sins. Jesus is Son of Man not as an isolated individual but in what he does for others and what his people do through him. Just as the power (ἐξουσία) of God operates in Jesus, who is God's human heir, so the power of God operates in his people who share in the power of Jesus.[63] Thus, just as Jesus shares in God's heavenly power to rule on earth, so his people become sharers of this heavenly power through Jesus.[64]

That Jesus's power to forgive sins is given to human beings per 9:8 is clarified in what follows Matt 8–9: Jesus calls twelve (δώδεκα) of his disciples and gives them power (ἐξουσία) to heal (10:1).[65] Luz notes that the term "twelve" appears three times (10:1, 2, 5) and "twelve disciples correspond to the twelve tribes of Israel (19:28)."[66] The specific number twelve thus indicates that Jesus's healing is directed to the whole people of Israel, especially those that are gathered in the promised land in his generation. The phrase "[the] house of Israel" (οἴκου Ἰσραήλ) in 10:6 also specifically refers to the people of Israel in the OT (e.g., Lev 17:8, 10; 1 Kgs 20:31; Isa 46:3; 63:7; Jer 2:4; 11:10; 23:8; 31:31; 48:13; Hos 6:10). Taken together, the number twelve and the phrase "the house of Israel" indicate who Jesus is; Jesus is the savior of all Israel from their sins and thus the full embodiment of the life of Israel (cf. 1:1–17). In its larger literary context, Jesus's healing power for Israel is eventually extended to all peoples through his disciples (e.g., 10:1–8; 28:18–20; cf. 2:6; 10:6; 15:24).[67]

To heal his people, Jesus empowers the disciples to share in his authority to spread God's healing power: "He [Jesus] gave them authority" (ἔδωκεν αὐτοῖς ἐξουσίαν, 10:1). The nature of exercising God's heavenly healing power is derivative of the authority of Son of Man envisioned in Dan 7, such that people glorify God when this power is exercised (9:8).[68] Jesus now shares his heaven-derived power with his disciples by commissioning them to carry on his work of healing the sick and casting out demons (10:1), work that the pericope about the healing of the paralyzed person shows to involve the forgiveness of sins. The disciples make use of the power given them to proclaim the kingdom from heaven (10:7). By sharing in Jesus's authority, the disciples embody and extend God's heavenly healing power. Just as Jesus heals every disease, unfolding forgiving power from heaven (9:35), so the disciples are empowered to do so (4:24; 9:6, 35; 10:1). Just as Jesus is meant primarily to preach to Jewish communities in Israel, so the disciples are sent primarily to those communities in Israel (9:35; 10:5–6; 15:24), though Jesus's last commission broadens their vocation (28:18–20). Jesus says that those who welcome his disciples welcome him, and anyone who welcomes Jesus welcomes the one who sent him (10:40). This chain of authority shows the sequence of power by which we come to have the full authority of God in and through Jesus. The dynamic power relation between God and the human in Jesus leads Tommy Givens to assert, "Jesus is the human body where that power is unfolding and spreading, such that with him we human beings are made participants in this healing power of God, the power of forgiving sins."[69] Jesus as God-with-us, then, provides a way to conceive of Jesus's action in and through us as our participation in God's life. Thus, in Matthew we find that discipleship is not a matter of merely imitating Christ but one of theosis, the extension of God's own power working itself out through Jesus in our lives. God exercises God's own forgiving power in human beings by extending God's power to us through others and through us to others. In this way, human forgiveness becomes an expression of God's own forgiving power, which brings bodily healing.

Jesus's Table Fellowship and Healing in Matt 9:9–13

Jesus's forgiving power continues as he calls a tax collector, Matthew (9:9–13). We are invited to see Jesus's forgiving power in this pericope by the forgiveness of the paralyzed person in the previous scene. Tax collectors in Jesus's time were "associated with the Roman soldier camps," thus collecting their own people's taxes for Rome.[70] Also, in Matthew's narrative world, tax collectors are coupled with "sinners" (ἁμαρτωλοὶ, 9:10–11; 11:19) and "prostitutes" (πόρναι, 21:31–32). The juxtaposition of tax collectors with sinners and prostitutes shows "the paradigmatic nature of that occupation as representing immorality and treason against Israel."[71] Thus, as a tax collector, Matthew would have been regarded as a sinner and traitor (9:9). Jesus's injunction to follow him in 9:9 is about discipleship because the expression, "follow me" (ἀκολούθει μοι), is used only when Jesus is calling disciples (e.g., 8:19, 22–23; 9:9).[72] In its larger literary context, the nature of Jesus's discipleship involves "repentance" as Jesus calls his people including the tax collectors and the prostitutes to repentance in light of the coming kingdom from heaven (4:17; 11:20, 23; 12:38–42; 21:32, cf. 3:3; 9:12–13).[73] For Matthew, repentance is linked to "a corresponding way of living" (3:7–9), which entails "believing in the context of the proximity of the kingdom" (21:32).[74] Thus, to align oneself with another way of living revealed in Jesus is what it means to repent in Matthew.[75] In this light, although Jesus does not explicitly call Matthew to repent, Jesus's injunction to follow him as his disciple involves repentance as it requires Matthew to align himself with a new pattern of life revealed in Jesus.

Repentance is not just an attitude or a feeling. It must be practiced and embodied in response to God's forgiveness and as an expression of God's forgiveness. As in John's baptism of forgiveness of sins, forgiveness entails repentance (3:6, 11).[76] While repentance is not a condition to earn God's forgiveness, we participate in God's forgiveness in repentance. This means that God's forgiveness entails our accountability through the practices of prayer and repentance. When discipleship as an embodied practice of repentance is conceived in the framework of theosis, it is more than our repenting of sins to follow Jesus. It goes further by emphasizing our participating in God's own, forgiving life through our repentance. It is what the presence of Jesus that abides with us enables us to do. Repentance as an embodied way of forgiveness is the way we appropriate and extend God's forgiveness. It is in this way that we become pure in heart and "see God" (5:8), thereby participating in and reflecting God's own life.[77]

In this pericope, Jesus presents his role as a physician (ἰατρός), who comes to heal his people by embodying and spreading God's forgiving power (9:12; cf. 1:21). That is, God's forgiveness revealed in Jesus entails bodily, relational restoration. After calling Matthew, Jesus welcomes sinners and tax collectors with table fellowship (9:10; cf. 11:19). This time, the Pharisees come to ask Jesus's disciples why he shares the table with those sinners. Quoting Hos 6:6, Jesus responds to the Pharisees that God desires "mercy" (ἔλεος, 9:13). Elsewhere in the narrative, Matthew draws on Isaiah's imagery to depict Jesus as a compassionate and merciful healer: "he will not break a reed being crushed and extinguish a smoking lamp wick" (12:20; Isa 42:3). Margaret Hannan contends that in the hands of the Pharisees as Matthew portrays them, the Holiness Code can create "oppressive barriers between the righteous and sinners," "the observant and the non-observant."[78] Jesus thus quotes Hos 6:6

to "contrast the Pharisees' narrow understanding of God's holiness" with Jesus's image of God as one who is "gracious and merciful . . . forgiving iniquity and transgression" (Exod 34:6–7).[79] This view may, however, obscure the Pharisees' legal policy.[80] Yair Furstenberg argues that the Pharisees take a lenient approach which "contradicted the priestly concern to separate impure from pure."[81] For instance, the Pharisees "wiped the impure liquids from the exterior and continued using the vessel, while the priests removed it for immersion" (e.g., 23:25–26).[82] Thus, the Pharisees are blamed for not observing the basic principle of the priestly code. As such, they rather "promoted a policy of compromise even to the degree that it undermined the Levitical system of holiness and purity," "making room for an alternative non-priestly purity by endorsing a less restrictive form of observance oriented toward the human circumstances with an impure environment."[83] In this light, Jesus's quotation of Hos 6:6 is not likely to complain against the Pharisees' narrow understanding of God's holiness, as though they create the oppressive barriers between the righteous and sinners. The primary purpose of Jesus's use of Hos 6:6 is to reveal who God is. Thus, that Jesus characterizes what he is doing by virtue of table fellowship with tax collectors and sinners as "calling sinners" (9:13) indicates that he shares in who God is, with the result that he is engaged in conveying forgiveness to sinners. This is not to imply, however, that Jesus excludes the righteous and reaches out to sinners.[84] In Matthew, God's forgiving power touches both the righteous and sinners, neighbors who are enemies and neighbors who are not. This fits the image of God's bestowing benefaction on both the good and the bad (5:45). In 9:13, that God desires mercy "more than" (καὶ οὐ) compliance with a law prescribing sacrifice reveals God's character.[85] That is, God is gracious and merciful.[86] In the Sermon on the Mount, when Jesus blesses those who are merciful (5:7), the underlying assumption is that just as God is merciful, so we are to be. When Jesus exhorts us to love our enemies (5:44), the underlying assumption is that just as God is the God of love and forgiveness, so we are to be. Being merciful, then, we reflect God's own character. It is in embodying God's merciful, forgiving nature that we participate in God's own life as it moves to fill the world. With Jesus who spreads God's forgiving power, here by sharing a table with tax collectors and sinners, being with them as the one who is God-with-us, we participate in this merciful, forgiving character of God.

Jesus's table fellowship with sinners recurs on his way to the cross. Although Jesus knows that the disciples will deny him, betray him, and flee, he shares table fellowship with them. In this table fellowship, Jesus not only welcomes the disciples but also takes their sins as his own: "for the forgiveness of sins" (26:28).[87] It is in Jesus's taking our sins and infirmities as his own, enduring their consequences of sins in his own body, that he is able to forgive our sins (cf. 3:13–17; 8:17). This is also hinted at in the parable of the unforgiving servant, where the lord forgives his servant's enormous debt by canceling the entire debt of his servant (18:26–27). Thus, Jesus comes to fulfill Isaiah's vision of transformation by taking our enormous debt and infirmities as his own, finally on a cross (8:17; Isa 53:4).

SUMMARY

This chapter has shown how the dynamics of heaven and earth unfold, specifically through Jesus's forgiveness and healing. I have shown that Jesus embodies the healing presence and action of the God of Israel. Matthew presents Jesus's healing ministry as continuing and embodying God's healing action in our midst. Thus, named God-with-us, Jesus's forgiving power delivers the bodies of the people of Israel, thereby touching and healing the brokenness that divides them from one another. Further, in Matthew's narrative, Jesus's healing of his people particularly is related to his being with us (1:23; 8:1–9:38). The way Jesus is with his people is thus the way he saves, heals, and rescues his people.

This chapter also examined that Jesus's healing of the paralyzed person makes one's life whole, restoring our relationship to God by the way it unites us with others (9:2–7). Thus, Jesus's forgiveness enacts healing that repairs our brokenness, which we variously share with others. I then attended to Jesus's healing and the heaven-earth relation specifically in 9:6–8. When Jesus's healing is conceived in the framework of theosis, we can clearly see that Jesus's authority to forgive sins involves God's heavenly healing on earth (9:6). Further, Jesus's healing power from heaven is extended to his disciples in the later development of the narrative (10:1). By sharing in Jesus's authority, the disciples come to exercise God's forgiving power from heaven. Just as Jesus touches and heals the brokenness of his people's lives, so his disciples are made participants in this healing power of God, embodying God's forgiveness of sins. Finally, I considered Jesus's table fellowship and healing in 9:9–13, where Jesus presents himself as a physician (9:12) and embodies God's merciful forgiveness through healing the broken bonds of his people (9:13).

NOTES

1. See Isaac K. Mbabazi, *The Significance of Interpersonal Forgiveness in the Gospel of Matthew* (Eugene, OR: Pickwick, 2013), 117–89.

2. Todd Pokrifka-Joe, "Probing the Relationship between Divine and Human Forgiveness in Matthew," in *Forgiveness and Truth: Explorations in Contemporary*

Theology, ed. Alistair I. McFadyen, Marcel Sarot, and Anthony Thiselton (Edinburgh: T&T Clark, 2001), 165–72.

3. Jesus's name as God-with-us is one of Matthew's "programmatic statements for Jesus" through which we can read other parts of the narrative, where we find Jesus providing this deliverance through forgiveness. See David D. Kupp, *Matthew's Emmanuel: Divine Presence and God's People in the First Gospel*, SNTSMS 90 (Cambridge: Cambridge University Press, 1996), 56. The terms of 1:21–23 ("God-with-us" and "salvation from sins") are thematic for the following reasons. First, the God-with-us motif forms for Matthew's Gospel an *inclusio*. The narrative begins by introducing Jesus's name as God-with-us (1:23), and it ends by promising Jesus's everlasting presence with us (28:20). Second, as implied in Jesus's calling as savior of his people from their sins (1:21), Jesus's mission is oriented to save his people from their sins, specifically through forgiveness (e.g., 4:17; 9:2; 20:28; 26:28).

4. See Franco Montanari, *The Brill Dictionary of Ancient Greek*, ed. Madeleine Goh and Chad Schroeder (Leiden: Brill, 2015), 2072.

5. Joel B. Green, *Discovering Luke: Content, Interpretation, Reception*, Discovering Biblical Texts (Grand Rapids: Eerdmans, 2021), 133; emphasis original. See also idem (*Why Salvation?*, Reframing New Testament Theology [Nashville: Abingdon, 2013], 32): "the Greek terms associated with 'salvation'—σώζω (*sōzō*, 'to save'), σωτήρ (*sōtēr*, 'savior'), σωτήρια (*sōtēria*, 'salvation'), and σωτήριον (*sōtērion*, 'saving')—related generally to rescue from misfortune of all kinds: shipwreck, the ravages of a journey, enemies in times of conflict, and so on. By far, however, the most common use of these terms in the larger Greco-Roman world was medical. 'To save' was to 'to heal.'"

6. J. G. van der Watt and D. S. du Toit, "Salvation," in *DJG*, 828.

7. Van der Watt and du Toit observe, "Matthew 1:21 assumes that God as Israel's savior (cf. Deut 32:15; 1 Sam 10:19; Ps 23:15; Is 12:2; 43:3, 11–12) will save Israel from its sins through Jesus as instrument of salvation" ("Salvation," 828).

8. As Paul Kunjanayil observes, "In the biblical background, the proper names are noteworthy. The name denotes the person, establishes his identity, defines his mission, and is a part of him [or her]" ("The Interconnection between the Emmanuel Theme and the Forgiveness of Sins Theme in the Gospel of Matthew," *Studia Biblica Slovaca* 13, no. 1 [2021]: 21). Cf. Gen 3:20; 4:1; 5:29; 25:25–26; 1 Sam 25:25. Jesus's name and mission as deliverer culminates in his declaration of "for the forgiveness of sins" (26:28).

9. Kupp, *Matthew's Emmanuel*, 164. Van der Watt and du Toit similarly observe that Emmanuel is associated with the presence of God that "save[s] from imminent judgment (Isa 7:17–25; 8:6–8, 14–15)" ("Salvation," 828).

10. In Israel's faith, God is the God of "Befreier." See Chong-Hyon Sung (*Vergebung der Sünden: Jesu Praxis der Sündenvergebung nach den Synoptikern und ihre Voraussetzungen im Alten Testament und frühen Judentum*, WUNT 2/57 [Tübingen: Mohr Siebeck, 1993], 40), who notes that "erfährt Israel seine Existenz in der Weltgeschichte von Anfang an als 'Immanuel-Existenz,' die allein durch Gottes rettende Gnadentaten und sein Erbarmen bestehen kann" ("Israel experiences her existence in world history from the beginning as an 'Emmanuel existence,' which can exist

only through God's saving acts of grace and his mercy"). The people of Israel thus experience God's saving work as God's Emmanuel presence. Sung further notes that this exodus-experience became "für den Glauben Israels fundamentale Bedeutung, und das Volk Israel wurde durch Höhen und Tiefen seiner Lebensgeschichte hindurch von dieser hoffnungsvollen Gotteserfahrung getragen" ("Fundamental to the faith of Israel, and the people of Israel were carried by this hopeful experience of God through the ups and downs of their life story," 40).

11. In particular, 2 Chr 36:23 LXX runs as follows: "my Lord, the God of heaven, gave me all the kingdoms of the earth, and he commanded me to build him a house at Jerusalem, [which] is in Judah. Whoever is among you of all his people, God will be with him or her! Let him or her go up."

12. Richard B. Hays observes that "the effect of the juxtaposition" of the two stories of Israel's exodus and Jesus's story is "to hint that Jesus now will carry the destiny of the people Israel, and that the outcome will be the rescue and vindication of Israel" ("The Gospel of Matthew: Reconfigured Torah," *HTS* 61 [2005]: 174). According to Hays, Israel's exodus story functions as "a narrative template" for God's liberating his people, "a template that can be applied to subsequent historical circumstances—whether God's mercy to disobedient Israel in Hosea's day or God's climatic rescue of his people Israel in the person of the Messiah Jesus" (174). Thus, the language of exile initially applied to Israel is now applied to Jesus.

13. For instance, John Nolland contends, "Matthew is well attuned to the significance of the suffering of Jesus, but he makes no particular link between that and the healing ministry of Jesus" (*The Gospel of Matthew*, NIGTC [Grand Rapids: Eerdmans, 2005], 362).

14. The image of God as healer is also attested in other OT passages. God as healer brings diseases on his people or keeps them away from his people (Exod 15:26). God wounds but God also binds up and heals (Job 5:18). God is the lord of the life and death of people in every situation: "I kill and I make alive, I wound and I heal" (Deut 32:39; cf. Hos 6:1; 14:5).

15. There are various metaphors for God, such as creator (e.g., Gen 1:1; Ps 136:5; Isa 43:1; Ezek 37:1–14), shepherd (e.g., Pss 23:1; 80:1; Jer 31:10), king (e.g., Dan 7:9), and Father (Exod 4:22; Jer 3:19; 31:9).

16. Sung, *Vergebung der Sünden*, 45.

17. In Matthew, "sonship" is a matter of the transmission of power and authority from ruling fathers, that is, authority to their sons, who are their disciples, heirs to their promises in Israel. This is especially clear in Matthew's use of υἱός in 12:27 and 17:25–26, where sonship is presented in terms of the transmission of power and authority. Similarly, the terms like "Son of David," "Son of Abraham," "Son of Man," and "Son of God" in Matthew indicate that Jesus is not Son to these fathers as merely a matter of ancestry but as heir to their power and promises. Similarly, W. D. Davies and D. C. Allison Jr. observe that the phrase "the sons of the kingdom" indicates "natural or rightful heirs of the kingdom" in 13:38 (*Matthew 8–18: A Critical and Exegetical Commentary on the Gospel according to Saint Matthew*, ICC [London: T&T Clark, 2004], 92). But they do not emphasize "heirs" enough as a term of rule and promise.

18. While Matt 9:1–13 is to be read in light of its larger rhetorical flow of 8:1–9:38, this pericope is an appropriate unit of this study because it is unified by the theme of forgiveness (9:2, 5–6, 8, 13). Moreover, geographical shift happens between 8:34 and 9:1. The discourse marker "then" or "at the time" (τότε) in 9:14 also signals the minute shift from the discussion of forgiveness itself.

19. On the possible connection between sickness and sin in the OT, see Exod 20:5; Lev 26:14–33; Deut 28:15–68; 2 Chr 21:15. In the Second Temple Jewish texts, see, e.g., 1 En. 10:7; 4 Ezra. Green nuances the relation between sickness and sin: "Although one could never argue that health is necessarily the direct result of God's favor, nor that sickness is necessarily the direct result of divine punishment, it is nevertheless true that for ancient Israel there could be a causal link from sin to sickness (For example, see Deut 28; 1 Kgs 13:1–25; Prov 3:28–35; 11:19; 13:13–23; 1 Cor 11:29–30)" (*Why Salvation?*, 38).

20. W. D. Davies and Dale C. Allison Jr., *Matthew 1–7: A Critical and Exegetical Commentary on the Gospel according to Saint Matthew*, ICC (London: T&T Clark, 2004), 210. For a discussion on the causes of sin in Matthew's narrative, see Judith V. Stack, *Metaphor and the Portrayal of the Cause(s) of Sin and Evil in the Gospel of Matthew*, BibInt 182 (Leiden: Brill, 2020), 113–200. Stack observes that the cause of sin is depicted by way of metaphor in Matthew, and these metaphors display a significant diversity "that spans a spectrum from those that indicate essentially external causes to those that indicate causes that are so internal to the human" (201). In particular, he views one part of the person (e.g., the eye, 5:28–30; 18:9), the heart—"one's whole inner person" (e.g., 12:34–37; 15:17–19)—and Satan (e.g., in the parable of the wheat and the tares, 13:24–30) as the causes of sin. Stack observes that one's heart is not merely a single organ of the body but represents one's inner self (165–70).

21. Matthew's juxtaposition of healing and forgiveness is reminiscent of several OT passages. For instance, the psalmist proclaims that God forgives all our iniquities and heals all our diseases (103:3). The psalmist prays for God's healing and forgiveness: "Heal my soul because I have sinned against you" (41:4; cf. 107:17). The prophet Isaiah directly links God's healing and God's forgiveness: "And no inhabitant will say, 'I am sick,' the people who dwell in it [will be] forgiven [their] iniquity" (33:24). These OT passages show that healing and forgiveness go hand in hand (e.g., Isa 38:16–17). See also Jas 5:16, where healing and forgiveness are juxtaposed.

22. Ulrich Luz contends that sins are "the cause of sickness" (*Matthew 8–20: A Commentary*, trans. James E. Crouch, Hermeneia [Minneapolis: Fortress, 2001], 27). In the OT, for instance, God afflicts his people with fever and drought because of their evil deeds (Deut 28:20–22; cf. 2 Chr 21:15, 18–19). Although sins may be the cause of sickness, the story of Job shows that Job's sickness is not concerned with his sins (1:8–12). This indicates that there may be other various factors that cause sickness. See Joel B. Green ("Healing and Healthcare," in *The World of the New Testament: Cultural, Social, and Historical Contexts*, ed. Joel B. Green and Lee Martin McDonald [Grand Rapids: Baker Academic, 2013], 334), who notes a range of etiologies of illness in Second Temple Judaism: "God" (e.g., to discipline or to punish), "divine intermediaries" (e.g., angels or God's Word), "evil spirits" (e.g., demons or fallen angels), "astrological phenomena," "natural factors," and "sin." These lists are drawn

from Larry O. Hogan. *Healing in the Second Tempel* [*sic*] *Period*, NTOA 21 (Göttingen: Vandenhoeck & Ruprecht, 1992), 302–10.

23. Anders Runesson, *Divine Wrath and Salvation in Matthew: The Narrative World of the First Gospel* (Minneapolis: Fortress, 2017), 82.

24. Runesson, *Divine Wrath and Salvation*, 82. Runesson specifically points out that "it is the grave sins of these specific leading figures in Jerusalem that tip the scales (cf. 23:32) and provoke the outpour of divine wrath over Jerusalem" (82). He further writes, "The suffering, which is irreversibly certain to come because of the leaders' adding to the cup of sin of 'their fathers,' will affect all within the people, including the innocent. In the final judgment, however, only the guilty will be held responsible and punished in accordance with their transgressions" (84). As Matthew's narrative bears out, Jesus's critique functions as an attempt to save his people, consistent with his mission as forgiveness of sins (1:21; 26:28). In the end, Jesus judges by becoming judged. Important to note with regard to Jesus's forgiveness of sins is that it entails our accountability, such as repentance (3:3; 4:17).

25. Although the scribes and Pharisees are often depicted in a negative light, we should caution against criticizing them as a whole. In some instances, Matthew presents the Pharisees and the scribes in a positive light (e.g., 13:52; 23:1–2). Since the Pharisees and the scribes sit on Moses's seat, they are to be obeyed (23:1–2). Donald Senior notes that "vigorous challenge to religious authority is an integral part of the biblical story, as the history of the prophets makes clear. It would be absurd to think of Jesus, himself a reverent Jew, as somehow rejecting Judaism or being anti-Jewish because of his opposition to some of the leaders. On the contrary, Jesus challenged the leaders and their viewpoint precisely because of his dedication to Israel" (Donald Senior, *The Passion of Jesus in the Gospel of Matthew*, The Passion Series [Wilmington, DE: Glazier, 1985], 34). W. D. Davies contends that the conflicts between Jesus and the Pharisees in Matthew's narrative in some ways may reflect the conflict between Matthew's community and the Pharisaic reform of Jamnia (*The Setting of the Sermon on the Mount* [Cambridge: Cambridge University Press], 1964). Regarding the Pharisaic reform of Jamnia, see also Shaye J. D. Cohen, "The Significance of Yavneh: Pharisees, Rabbis, and the End of Jewish Sectarianism," *HUCA* 55 (1984): 27–53.

26. Runesson, *Divine Wrath and Salvation*, 83. In a different context, John the Baptist speaks to those who claim to be children of Abraham that mere physical genetics avails nothing (3:7–10). For Matthew, what counts is one's fruit (e.g., 3:10; 7:16–18; 12:33–37).

27. Warren Carter, "Jesus' Healing Stories: Imperial Critique and Eschatological Anticipations in Matthew's Gospel," *CurTM* 37, no. 6 (2010): 492.

28. Ibid., 492–93.

29. Ibid., 494.

30. Givens, "Living into the Kingdom," 13. Givens observes, "God's forgiving us does not occur in a realm separate from our relationships with one another or from the corresponding material conditions of our life" (13).

31. Leprosy would have been quite rare in Jesus's world. The Gospels typically do not refer to leprosy per se, but to various skin diseases. See Green (*Why Salvation?*,

37): "in the Bible 'leprosy' is rarely if ever true leprosy, caused by the bacterium *Mycobacterium leprae* and found in modern medical reference books under the heading 'Hansen's Disease.' Rather, 'leprosy' refers to any of a number of skin conditions that, when diagnosed by a priest, might render a person 'unclean.'" In the CEB, λέπρα is translated as "skin disease" (e.g., Mark 1:42). See Green, "Healing and Healthcare," 333.

32. On the relational dynamic at work between sickness and healing, Green notes the observation of Robert A. Hahn's observation: "*Illness accounts* identify patients as embodied persons in a nest of relationships. The cause and treatment of sicknesses thus require attention to persons in their social environments, with recovery of health measured not only in biomedical but also relational terms" ("Healing and Healthcare," 332–33; emphasis original). See Hahn, *Sickness and Healing: An Anthropological Perspective* (New Haven: Yale University Press, 1995), 28.

33. In John's baptism (3:13–17), Jesus joins the baptism for the forgiveness of sins so that he becomes a vulnerable member of his people, taking his people's sickness and sins as his own.

34. Capernaum is located on the northwest shore of the Sea of Galilee and this city was then known as the border area between Jews and Gentiles. Regarding this city, Davies and Allison note, "In the NT, it occurs only in the gospels, including John. Josephus knew of it" (*Matthew 1–7*, 377). Matthew's narrative shows that there are "a Roman garrison and a customs station" in Capernaum (8:5–13; 9:9–10; 17:24). See Davies and Allison, *Matthew 1–7*, 378. A Roman centurion's servant is healed in this place, and the tax collector Matthew who follows Jesus works here.

35. J. J. M. Roberts, *First Isaiah: A Commentary*, Hermeneia (Minneapolis: Fortress, 2015), 148.

36. For a discussion on slavery in the Roman world, see S. Scott Bartchy, "Slaves and Slavery in the Roman World," in *The World of the New Testament: Cultural, Social, and Historical Contexts*, ed. Joel B. Green and Lee Martin McDonald (Grand Rapids: Baker Academic, 2013), 169–78. Bartchy notes that "ancient and modern slavery are significantly similar in that slavery itself is defined by the 'social death' of the enslaved person, whose owner enjoys total control over the slave's body, including practically unrestricted brutal treatment and sexual exploitation" (172). While slaves in the Roman world were subjected to "beatings, torture, and death (by burning or crucifixion)," they could own property and be educated (171, 173). They also shared cultural values and social codes with their owners and could anticipate being set free (172–74).

37. Elsewhere in Matthew's narrative, Jesus heals paralysis twice (4:24; 8:6, 13). According to Warren Carter, the condition of paralysis may "reflect the trauma and violence of war and occupation" (*Matthew and the Margins: A Sociopolitical and Religious Reading*, The Bible & Liberation Series [Maryknoll, NY: Orbis Books, 2000], 127). The painful, traumatic memory of foreign rule could in part paralyze the condition of the people of Israel.

38. The verb ἀφίημι in 9:2 can be a divine passive. The present passive verb denotes God's action in Jesus's words. The significance of Jesus's statement ("your sins are forgiven," 9:2) is related to Jesus's call. The reader knows that "God has

commissioned Jesus to this role (1:21)," that is, Jesus's mission is focused on delivering his people from their sins. See Carter, *Matthew and the Margins*, 216. Jesus's declaration of "your sins are forgiven" also shows that he takes the initiative in terms of forgiveness rather than waiting for us to forgive others (cf. 6:12, 14–15).

39. Carter, *Matthew and the Margins*, 216. See also Luz (*Matthew 8–20*, 27): "Sin separates the people from God; it also is the cause of sickness." R. T. France nuances the relation between sin and sickness in 9:2: "It is not stated that the paralysis was caused by sin. . . . Sin and disability are linked in this story in that the curing of the latter will be taken as proof of authority to deal with the former, but this does not in itself require us to regard the paralysis as *caused by* sin which Jesus forgives" (*The Gospel of Matthew*, NICNT [Grand Rapids: Eerdmans, 2007], 345; emphasis original).

40. Green, *Why Salvation?*, 37.

41. Thus, while healing is concerned with physical wellness, it should be understood in nonreductionistic ways. It should address the web of one's relations with others. Green observes that "healing does not allow a person or his or her salvation to be reduced to 'parts,' as though inner and outer life could be separated" (*Why Salvation?*, 47).

42. Ibid., 36–37 (emphasis original). Since healing is not reduced to the restoration of individuals, Green rightly points out that "the metaphor of healing serves as an invitation to God's people" to be "a community of compassion and restoration" (48). Cf. Jas 2:13; 5:16, 19.

43. Ibid., 40.

44. In response to Jesus's declaration of forgiveness (9:2), the scribes despise Jesus for what they understand as blaspheming (9:3). They believe that Jesus places himself on the same level with God by proclaiming God's forgiveness. In the eyes of the scribes, Jesus's words threaten the unity of God because forgiveness belongs to Israel's God (e.g., Exod 34:6–7; Isa 43:25; 44:22; Dan 9:9; cf. Mark 2:7). Thus, the scribes do not see "God to be at work in Jesus" (Carter, *Matthew and the Margins*, 216). As the narrative unfolds, the charge of blasphemy against Jesus continues and accelerates so that it culminates in the condemnation and execution of Jesus (e.g., 12:24; 26:65–66). The Pharisees accuse Jesus of healing by exercising the power of Beelzebul (12:24). In its immediate context, their public and verbal maligning of God's forgiving power is to blaspheme the power of the Spirit, which is not forgivable (12:31–32). To blaspheme the power of the Spirit is to speak directly against the very forgiving power of God that touches and heals God's own people. It is to name God's forgiving power of the Spirit itself the satanic power that tears people apart from one another. It is thus not forgivable because of the effect of this public maligning on others as well as those who carry it out with their words.

45. Davies and Allison, *Matthew 8–18*, 92.

46. In Mark's version, it is when Jesus sees the faith of those who lower the paralyzed person through the roof that he says to him that his sins are forgiven (2:4–5). While Matthew does not include the phrase "lower him through the roof," he still retains the comment that Jesus "sees their faith" (9:2). On the term πίστις, Teresa Morgan observes that in Matthew, "*pistis* is what puts human beings, Jewish or gentile, into the right relationship with God" (*Roman Faith and Christian Faith: Pistis*

and Fides in the Early Roman Empire and Early Churches [Oxford: Oxford University Press, 2015], 371–72). For Matthew, therefore, people do not have to be Jewish to trust God. Matthew links *pistis* language with christological titles like *kyrios* (e.g., 8:6, 8, 25; 9:28; 14:28, 30; 15:22, 25; 17:15), a term which can refer to "any human being in a position of power or authority, but in the Septuagint it often refers to God, while in the Greco-Roman world more widely it is given equally to divine and to human rulers" (372). According to Morgan, "[Matthew's] linking of *pistis* with the title *kyrios* affirms that any encounter with Jesus is always, whether or not it is fully recognized as such, an encounter between ruler, human or divine or both, and subject, and reminds readers that encounters with Jesus Christ are always encounters between humanity and God. . . . *pistis* for Matthew characterizes above all the divine-human relationship and community, not intra-human ones" (374). In this sense, *pistis* in Matthew is used to express the distinctive relationship between God and the human.

47. France, *Gospel of Matthew*, 344. Similarly, Carter observes, "Jesus interprets (sees) their action in bringing the man as expressive of their faith" (*Matthew and the Margins*, 215). The pronoun αὐτῶν could include both those who bring the man to Jesus and the paralyzed person. Davies and Allison note that it may or may not be the sick person himself who has faith: "Just as the centurion's faith can gain healing for his servant, so can the faith of the paralytic's friends save the paralytic . . . [but] it is not implied that the lame man was being carried to Jesus against his will. Presumably he was a consenting party and also had faith" (*Matthew 8–18*, 88).

48. In both 9:2 and 9:22, the faith of human being(s) enacts the power of God's healing. In both verses, Matthew uses the term θάρσει ("do not fear") in conjunction with faith (cf. Exod 14:13; Joel 2:21). In the stormy sea, Jesus calms his disciples who are afraid of the storm (8:25–26). In context, fear could paralyze the minds of the disciples rather than build their confidence or faith: "Lord, save [us], we are perishing" (κύριε, σῶσον, ἀπολλύμεθα, 8:25).

49. I am thankful for a discussion with Joseph Chongsu Won, a hematologist and oncologist, who points out the dynamic between faith and healing: Healing of our past and memories is possible when we are with "the light of the world" (5:14; cf. Gen 1:3). That is, "our past wounds can be healed today as Jesus takes us to the past. When we are interwoven or bound with Jesus, time stops as we are in the light moving at 'the speed of light' (C). By faith, we can change the past and future not to mention 'now.' In quantum physics, the observer changes the result of observation" (29 March 2022). In line with quantum physics, faith enables us to transform our pasts and memories in hope rather than in despair. For a brief definition of quantum physics, see the report at https://www.space.com/31933-quantum-entanglement-action-at-a-distance.html (26 May 2022).

50. France observes that Matthew's use of "the Son of Man" is "always used by Jesus himself, not by others about him" (*Gospel of Matthew*, 326–27). Similarly, Davies and Allison observe that "only Jesus employs the phrase [the Son of Man] and that the title is not used confessionally" (*Matthew 8–18*, 51). The "Son of Man," then, is Jesus's self-reference. For further discussion on Matthew's use of the "Son of Man," see Davies and Allison, *Matthew 8–18*, 43–53; Ulrich Luz, *Matthew 8–20:*

A Commentary, trans. James E. Crouch, Hermeneia (Minneapolis: Fortress, 2001), 389–92.

51. D. L. Bock notes that in Matt 26:64, the Son of Man is "pictured as a singular human figure with transcendent qualities, as his riding of the clouds indicates. In the OT it is deity that rides the clouds (Exod 14:20; 34:5; Num 10:34; Ps 104:3; Isa 19:1). So this image is of a human being who also has heavenly qualities" ("Son of Man," in *DJG*, 895). This implies that Jesus as the Son of Man is a human being who has unique and extraordinary power from heaven.

52. The link between the Son of Man in Matthew and Dan 7:13 ("coming with the clouds of heaven") is supported by Matthew's linking of the Son of Man with the phrase "he comes" (ἔρχομαι) in 10:23; 16:28; 24:44; 25:31. See Davies and Allison (*Matthew 8–18*, 51). The interpretation of the Son of Man in Daniel is debated whether this figure is "corporate for Israel," an "angelic figure," or "an eschatological figure." See Bock, "Son of Man," 895.

53. France, *Gospel of Matthew*, 347.

54. *Contra* France (*Gospel of Matthew*, 347), who claims, "The forgiveness of sins as such was not, of course, a part of Daniel's vision of the authority of the Son of Man. Jesus is not expounding Dan 7, but boldly extrapolating from that vision to make a claim for his present status" in Matt 9:6. For a discussion on the relation between the Son of Man and forgiveness of sins, see Joel Marcus ("Authority to Forgive Sins upon the Earth: The Shema in the Gospel of Mark," in *The Gospels and the Scriptures of Israel*, ed. W. Richard Stegner and Craig A. Evans, JSNTSup 104 [Sheffield: Sheffield Academic, 1994], 205): "The statement about the Son of Man forgiving sins may reflect midrashic activity by which other Danielic texts have been linked with Dan 7. In Dan 9:9, for example, we read, 'To the Lord our God belong mercy and forgiveness.' . . . Since the 'one like a son of man' in Daniel 7 is given the authority of the Ancient of Days, it is not hard to imagine that a reader of Daniel would have assumed that this included the authority to forgive sins." Similarly, Bock observes that "what is indisputable" regarding the image of the Son of Man is "an individual with authority to deliver" as found in Second Temple Judaism ("Son of Man," 895).

55. On the lethal quality of human life caused in part by human kingdom(s), see Carter, "Jesus' Healing Stories," 492–94.

56. Carter, *Matthew and the Margins*, 215.

57. Luz, *Matthew 8–20*, 28.

58. On the plural "people" or "human beings" (ἀνθρώποις) in 9:8, see Nolland (*Gospel of Matthew*, 383), who adequately observes, "Almost certainly it anticipates the developing situation in which the Christian community comes to participate in and to continue to benefit from the authority demonstrated here by Jesus" (e.g., 10:1; 18:18–20; 28:18–19).

59. See Herbert Weir Smyth (*Greek Grammar*, rev. Gordon M. Messing [Cambridge: Harvard University Press, 1984], §1469): "The indirect object is commonly introduced in English by *to*"; emphasis original.

60. Jacques Dupont, "La paralytique pardonné (Matthieu 9:1–8)," *NRTh* 82 (1960): 952–53; my translation: "His way of describing the reaction of the Jewish crowd wants to suggest to the Christian community that the crowd must give the

thanksgiving to God for the power which, departed from Jesus in his capacity as Son of Man, remains present in the church through the people to whom Jesus communicated this power."

61. Jesus's discipline of the church in relation to forgiveness will be discussed in detail in chapter 4.

62. That Jesus has all authority in heaven and earth is also hinted at in the beginning of the narrative. The language of γένεσις in 1:1 is resonant with the beginning of heaven and earth in Gen 1:1. This suggests that Jesus himself is the beginning of heaven and earth and its fullness.

63. While the power Jesus as the Son of Man has derives uniquely from him (e.g., 13:41; 24:27, 30, 37, 44; 26:64), what Matthew shows is that the power that Jesus enacts is shared with the disciples. For instance, the power to judge in the parable of the last judgment is uniquely assigned to the Son of Man (25:31–46; cf. 13:36–43; 16:27–28). But as the narrative bears out, the disciples are assigned to minister to the people of Israel (10:5–6), such that Jesus's ruling of Israel is extended to the disciples (19:28). That Jesus's power is extended to and shared with his disciples is what it means for the disciples to be one with Jesus.

64. This is in line with the portrait of the Son of Man in Dan 7:27 LXX, where God's heavenly dominion and kingship is given to his people. Consequently, God's people come to exercise God's heavenly power on earth as they share in God's dominion and the splendor of the kingdoms under the whole heaven.

65. Matthew tells us that Jesus's empowering of the disciples is to care for his people. When Jesus sees his people, he "has compassion" (σπλαγχνίζομαι) on them because they are helpless like sheep without a shepherd (9:36). The language of "sheep without a shepherd" invokes Ezek 34:1–6, where sheep are dispersed because of the irresponsibility and absence of shepherds. To care for, heal, and forgive their sins, Jesus sends his "twelve" disciples to "the house of Israel" (10:2–6).

66. Luz, *Matthew 8–20*, 66.

67. In Matthew's narrative, Jesus is depicted as Israel's shepherd who reigns not only over Israel (2:6; cf. 9:36; Mic 5:2) but all creation as envisioned in Dan 7 (cf. 9:6–8; 28:18–20). Thus, Jesus's forgiveness and healing is for all peoples (e.g., 8:5–13; 12:18–21, 40–42; 15:21–28; 28:19–20). In Matthew's narrative, Jesus calls his followers "the light of the world (κόσμος)" (5:14). The term κόσμος in 5:14 implies that the scope of Jesus's and the disciples' mission is cosmic for all peoples. The narrative unfolds that the "nations" (ἔθνη) will have hope in Jesus's name (12:21; Isa 42:1–4). As the narrative bears out, Jesus also has mercy on a Canaanite mother by healing her daughter who once was the enemy of Israel (15:21–28; cf. Josh 1–24). Further, Jesus commands his disciples to embrace "all the nations" (πάντα τὰ ἔθνη, 28:19). Adela Yarbro Collins observes that the use of πάντα τὰ ἔθνη in 28:19 "differentiates this phrase from the usual reference to the gentiles, τὰ ἔθνη. This conclusion is supported by 1 Clem 29:3" ("Polemic against the Pharisees in Matthew 23," in *The Pharisees*, ed. Joseph Sievers and Amy-Jill Levine [Grand Rapids: Eerdmans, 2021], 154). In a similar manner, Anthony J. Saldarini observes that Matthew affirms an ongoing mission to the Jews in the command to go to "all the nations" (*Matthew's Christian Jewish Community* [Chicago: University of Chicago Press, 1994], 34). In

this sense, πάντα τὰ ἔθνη includes both Jews and gentiles. Regarding the dynamic at work in 28:19, Tommy Givens aptly observes, "The expansion to 'all the nations' does not relativize Israel, but follows Israel's own vocation under the cosmic, eschatological rule of the Son of David. Πάντα τὰ ἔθνη is also where Israel's remaining exiles continue to reside (e.g., Deut 4:27; 28:37, 64; 29:23; 30:1–3; Jer 32:15; 51:8; Ezek 39:23; Amos 9:9; Joel 4:2; Zech 7:14). Thus, what we find in Matt 28:18–20 is not the moving beyond the people of Israel. Nor is it a move from the particular to the universal, or from ethnicity to spirituality. . . . Rather, we find at the close of the First Gospel an extension of Jesus's mission to the furthest reaches of Israel's exile and beyond, whence Israelites are called to be disciples of Jesus and their gentile hosts to be gathered together with them to share in the one covenant people in the flesh under the rule of the Son of David and Son of Man" (*We the People: Israel and the Catholicity of Jesus* [Minneapolis: Fortress, 2014], 329).

68. Marcus, "Authority to Forgive Sins upon the Earth," 205. Regarding the transmission of God's power to his people, see David D. Kupp (*Matthew's Emmanuel*, 149–150), who points out the "continuous experiential chain of divine presence" among his people: God will be with Joshua as he was with Moses (Josh 1:5), "'with' David as he was 'with' Saul, 'with' Solomon as 'with' David, and 'with' Israel as 'with' Israel's forefathers" (1 Sam 20:13; 1 Kgs 1:37; 8:57). This chain of divine presence now applies to Jesus who came to his people as God's Son, God's self, and God's heir. Thus, as Kupp puts it, "Jesus is with his people in the way that YHWH was with Israel" (230). Kupp notes that Matthew depicts "God's personal presence as liberator in the OT as the foundation for describing his same experience of Jesus the Messiah" (230).

69. Givens, "Power of Jesus," 22.

70. W. D. Davies and D. C. Allison Jr., *Matthew 19–28: A Critical and Exegetical Commentary on the Gospel according to Saint Matthew*, ICC (London: T&T Clark, 2004), 169.

71. Craig L. Blomberg, "Jesus, Sinners, and Table Fellowship," *BBR* 19, no. 1 (2009): 46. Citing Frank Stern, Blomberg notes that in the Jewish literature, "Tax collectors were grouped with murderers and robbers. To avoid loss, one could deceive a tax collector. The word of a tax gatherer could not be trusted, nor could his oath believed." See Frank Stern, *A Rabbi Looks at Jesus' Parables* (Lanhan, MD: Rowman & Littlefield, 2006), 141. Stern cites the Mishnaic texts (Ned. 3:4; B. Qam. 10:1–2; Ṭehar. 7:6).

72. To follow Jesus is to unlearn former ways and patterns of feeling, thinking, and behaving, and to learn a new pattern of life revealed and conveyed to us in Jesus. The term ἀκολουθέω thus indicates a commitment to Jesus and calls for another way of life, which costs even one's own life (e.g., 10:18–22, 38–39; 16:24–25).

73. On the relation between discipleship and the acceptance of the kingdom in Matthew, see Ulrich Luz, "The Disciples in the Gospel according to Matthew," in *The Interpretation of Matthew*, ed. Graham N. Stanton (Edinburgh: T&T Clark, 1995), 127. Matthew 13:52 relates "to disciple" (μαθητεύω) to the kingdom of heaven.

74. F. Mendez-Moratalla, "Repentance," in *DJG*, 773. Matthew narrates that the tax collectors and the prostitutes repent and believe the message of John the Baptist

(21:32). The term "repent" (μετανοέω) means "change one's heart" or "a turning." See BDAG 640 s.v. μετανοέω. In the OT, repentance refers to "a turning away from unrighteousness and wicked ways (e.g., Jer 18:11; Zech 1:2–4) and turning to God (e.g., 2 Chr 15:3–4; Isa 55:6–7; Hos 14:1)." See Runesson, *Divine Wrath and Salvation*, 113. On the nature of repentance in Jewish texts generally, Runesson notes that "if repentance is lacking, judgment will follow and may lead to exile or exclusion from the world to come (Sir 48:15; 4 Ezra 9:10–12). God wants repentance, however, and may hold back full punishment for sins committed in order to induce it (Wis 12:10). The basis for this is God's love and mercy" (116).

75. As Joel B. Green observes, repentance/conversion "could never be reduced to an internal realignment of the intellect but rather signified movement from one way of living to another. This was a transformation of *habitus*, a transformed pattern of life" (*Conversion in Luke-Acts: Divine Action, Human Cognition, and the People of God* [Grand Rapids: Baker Academic, 2015], 62). In this sense, repentance is a reorientation or realignment of life that reflects God's purpose.

76. On the relation between forgiveness and repentance, L. Gregory Jones notes, "God's forgiveness should occasion a repentance, a turning, that marks people's new life with and in Christ and results in their showing love to others" (*Embodying Forgiveness: A Theological Analysis* [Grand Rapids: Eerdmans, 1995], 162).

77. Jesus's discipleship as an embodied way of forgiveness is about "seeing and hearing" Jesus. It is about "learning to see one's self and one's life in the context of communion" with God's self. It is through seeing and hearing Jesus that the disciples continue to grow and participate in God's own will. By observing how Jesus acts, the disciples learn what it means to do the will of the Father in heaven (7:21; 12:50). The will of the Father in heaven is manifested in Jesus's words and deeds. Jesus's life can be characterized as a life of forgiveness. Throughout the narrative, Jesus desires mercy and forgiveness (e.g., 5:23–24, 43–47; 9:13; 12:7, 20; 18:27, 33; 20:34; 23:23; 26:28). He sums up the entire law and the prophets through the hermeneutics of love (22:37–40). The will of the Father in heaven, then, is clearly manifest in the practice of mercy and forgiveness. As such, we participate in God's own will by seeing Jesus who embodies forgiveness as a way of life. As the disciples embody forgiveness by virtue of hearing and watching Jesus throughout their lives (e.g., 5:23–24; 9:9–13; 18:21–22; 26:28), forgiveness is not a particular moment of belief. It must be embodied as a way of life throughout our lives. In this process, we are empowered by Jesus's forgiving power to forgive others as "we learn to see ourselves as sinners who have been forgiven" (Jones, *Embodying Forgiveness*, 148). Because we have been forgiven, we are able to see and live as forgiving people, manifesting God's life.

78. Margaret Hannan, *The Nature and Demands of God's Sovereign Rule in the Gospel of Matthew*, LNTS 308 (London: T&T Clark, 2006), 72.

79. Ibid.

80. Stack points out that in Matthew's narrative, the Jewish leaders are constructed as a "composite character," such that "the religious leaders—including the Pharisees, scribes, chief priests, elders, etc.—can be considered a single character since Matthew does not discriminate among them very carefully. They are seen as essentially homogenous in their fundamental opposition to Jesus and in their 'evilness'" (*Metaphor*,

193 n. 12). For further discussion on the character of the Jewish leaders, see Jack Dean Kingsbury, "The Developing Conflict between Jesus and the Jewish Leaders in Matthew's Gospel: A Literary-Critical Study," *CBQ* 49, no. 1 (1987): 57–73; Mark Allan Powell, "The Religious Leaders in Luke: A Literary-Critical Study," *JBL* 109 (1990): 93–110.

81. Yair Furstenberg, "The Shared Image of Pharisaic Law in the Gospels and Rabbinic Tradition," in *The Pharisees*, ed. Joseph Sievers and Amy-Jill Levine (Grand Rapids: Eerdmans, 2021), 217. See also Steve Mason ("Josephus's Pharisees," in *The Pharisees*, ed. Joseph Sievers and Amy-Jill Levine [Grand Rapids: Eerdmans, 2021], 98–100, 109), who similarly discusses Josephus's representation of the Pharisees' "leniency in punishment" and "precise interpretation." Mason notes, "Both Jesus and the Pharisees work among and for the common people and distinguish themselves sharply from the temple-based priestly authorities" (111).

82. Furstenberg, "Pharisaic Law," 217.

83. Ibid., 219.

84. In Matthew's narrative, the righteous are the ones who will "shine like the sun" in the Father's kingdom (e.g., 13:43). Thus, the righteous are not excluded from the kingdom. That Jesus's interest is directed to sinners (9:13) is in line with his care for the least (e.g., 18:5–10; 25:40, 45).

85. If we translate καὶ οὐ simply as "and not," this might signify that "God desires mercy [alone], not sacrifice." However, Matthew envisions Jesus as one who fulfills the law (5:17). Jesus does not deny sacrifice or any cultic law *per se* as Jesus himself defends the law. In this light, the phrase καὶ οὐ should be translated comparatively as "a dialectical negation." Luz notes that this comparative sense is found in a "*Hebraeorum idioma*" (*Matthew 8–20*, 34). This means that God's mercy, which is greater than sacrifice, is a lens through which sacrifice is properly understood.

86. Mbabazi notes that of all the Synoptic writers, Matthew "draws the most winsome picture of God" as merciful, forgiving heavenly Father (*Significance of Interpersonal Forgiveness*, 201). He rightly connects the theme of forgiveness with mercy, love, and reconciliation. In Matthew's narrative, these are all related concepts of forgiveness because forgiveness is an expression of love and mercy (e.g., 5:23–24, 44; 18:27, 33). God's merciful forgiveness as integral to his character is also attested in the OT (e.g., Exod 34:6–7; Num 14:18–19; Pss 25:18; 32:5; 85:2; Isa 55:7).

87. Jesus's table fellowship with the disciples and his way to the cross "for the forgiveness of sins" will be revisited in detail in chapter 5.

Chapter 4

Theosis and Forgiveness

The Oneness of Heaven and Earth

Jesus's teaching in Matt 18:15–35, especially in 18:18–20, epitomizes the transformative dynamics of heaven and earth in Matthew, God and the human revealed in our practice of forgiveness and prayer.[1] On the significance of forgiveness in 18:15–35, Isaac K. Mbabazi observes that "about 60 percent of the material in this chapter is obviously devoted to the issues of brotherly [and sisterly] reconciliation (vv. 15–17) and of interpersonal forgiveness (vv. 21–35)."[2] While the thematic importance of forgiveness has been recognized, what remains to be explored is how the concept of theosis sheds light on the theme of forgiveness in 18:15–35. That is, theosis provides a theological lens that brings into sharper focus the meaning of forgiveness in 18:15–35, especially with respect to the dynamics of heaven and earth and of God and the human in Matthew's Gospel.

This chapter aims to demonstrate how forgiveness fits the transformative dynamics of heaven and earth and of God and the human in Matthew. According to Matthew, our way of exercising forgiveness as an extension of God's way of exercising forgiveness is grounded in embodied practice that enacts God's forgiving nature, presence, and activity (18:33, 35; cf. 5:23–24, 43–48; 7:21; 12:50). To make my argument, I first examine the literary and theological contexts of Jesus's discussion of the discipline of the church (18:15–35) to grasp its significance in Matthew's narrative. In particular, I attend to the opening question of the disciples (18:1) and Jesus's answer (i.e., concerning greatness in the kingdom of heaven, 18:2–14) because they set the stage for all that follows in this discourse, especially with respect to how the kingdom of heaven operates and distributes its power on earth. I then consider Matthew's presentation of the nature of the Father in light of what I have presented on theosis in previous chapters, especially with respect to God's forgiveness (18:6, 10, 12–14, 19, 27) and the nature of our participation in God's forgiveness (18:35).

The final part of the chapter offers an exegesis of 18:15–35 in four steps. Each step has its own distinct emphasis, but together they contribute to an understanding of how a focus on theosis sheds light on forgiveness in Matthew's Gospel. First, I focus on the ethic of forgiveness (18:15–17, 21–22) and challenge the scholarly tendency to interpret this passage as a proof text for excommunication. This passage has often been used to solidify the grip of the church on its sinning members with a view to excommunicating them. While this reading seems plain enough, when this passage is conceived and interpreted in its literary context and with the lens of theosis, it is not well understood as dealing with excommunication, teaching instead the restoration and reconciliation of our relationships with God and with one another.

Second, I examine Matthew's presentation of the oneness of heaven and earth, specifically through embodying forgiveness prayerfully (18:18–20). I challenge the view that heaven and earth are separate or contrasting realities, and suggest that while there is an important distinction between heaven and earth, God's self in Jesus exercises the heavenly rule of God on earth such that there is a relational dynamic between heaven and earth. That is, earth is to be transformed by heaven. Furthermore, I show how the authority to forgive sins is given and extended to the disciples through Jesus (18:18). By sharing Jesus's authority, the disciples exercise God's own authority to bind and loose "on earth," manifesting God's forgiving power from heaven. Accordingly, our action of forgiveness as disciples of Jesus becomes what Jesus himself does.

Third, I consider Jesus's relation to the Spirit to challenge the scholarly tendency to disassociate the presence of Jesus from the presence of the Spirit as if they were not explicitly linked in Matthew's narrative (cf. 18:20). While Jesus and the Spirit should indeed be distinguished from one another, Jesus's presence in the community is empowered by the Spirit, as evident throughout Matthew's Gospel (e.g., 1:20; 3:16; 4:1; 12:28; 28:19–20). Theosis provides a lens that allows us to see the transfer and extension of power at work through the Spirit. That is, the Spirit empowers Jesus and Jesus transfers this power to the disciples. In Matthew's conception, therefore, the nature of Jesus's presence is a matter of the empowering of the Spirit, especially with respect to forgiving power (18:20; cf. 12:24–32).

Finally, I challenge the conditional view of God's forgiveness (18:23–35) and suggest that human forgiving is not a condition of God's forgiveness but the mode in which we participate in God's forgiveness (cf. 6:12, 14–15). I also suggest that repentance is our relational mode of participating in God's gracious forgiveness, such that we embody God's forgiveness in repentance. When discipleship as an embodied practice of repentance is conceived with the lens of theosis, repentance is a way we become reconciled with others and thus reflect and enact God's forgiveness.

THE LITERARY AND THEOLOGICAL CONTEXTS OF MATT 18:15–35

Narratively, Matthew places Jesus's discussion of what might be conceived as the discipline of the church of Christ (18:1–35) at this juncture because Jesus has just established his "church" (ἐκκλησία, 16:18).[3] Thus, 18:15–35 naturally follows Jesus's promise for the founding of his church in Matt 16.[4] In the flow of the narrative, Jesus is now on his way to Jerusalem to die a shameful death that contrasts with what his disciples understand the Messiah to be (16:13–25; 17:22–23).[5] All the pericopae of 16:13–20:34 culminate in exchanges with his disciples, whom Jesus is forming for the future that will open from Jerusalem (21:10)—the way from his death on a Roman cross.[6]

In his discussion of the discipline of the church, Jesus instructs his disciples on how his church embodies heavenly kingdom life on the earth.[7] The discourse begins with the disciples' question, "Who then is greatest in the kingdom of heaven?" (18:1). In response to this question, Jesus sets a nameless child in the midst of the disciples. Jesus exhorts them to become like such a child and to welcome one such child in his name because to receive such a child is to receive Jesus himself (18:3–5). Jesus often identifies himself with the least (e.g., 25:40, 45). Thus, the disciples should learn to be childlike so as to see who Jesus is and how the kingdom of heaven operates, particularly how it is powerful and distributes "greatness." The least are often referred to as "anyone who was not of the ruling orders" in the Greco-Roman world.[8] Children in Jesus's time have little social status and occupy the margins.[9] As the narrative bears out, children are easily despised and neglected (19:13–14). They are thus regarded as one of "the least" (μικρός, 18:6, 10; cf. 11:11).[10] But Jesus proclaims that the kingdom is theirs (19:14), and unless we become like children, we will not enter the kingdom of heaven (18:3). Beryl Rawson observes that in Roman society, "child mortality rates were very high, especially in the years from infancy to about [five]" such that "[p]robably half of all children born had died before the age of 10."[11] In this light, Jesus would have recognized this precarious quality of children's life, thus directing his attention to them and promoting the welcoming of children (e.g., 20:14–15; cf. 9:18–26; 17:14–20).

Further, since their angels in heaven constantly see (ἄγγελοι αὐτῶν ἐν οὐρανοῖς διὰ παντὸς βλέπουσι) the face of the Father, Jesus urges his disciples not to despise the least, like children (18:10). That their angels constantly see the Father in heaven suggests that their lives on earth are closely connected to heaven. As Tommy Givens observes, "That these angels in heaven constantly see the face of Jesus's Father means that the lives of little ones are a primary locus of heavenly power on the earth."[12] Furthermore,

Jesus continues by offering the parable of the lost sheep, saying that it is not the Father's will that any of these little ones be lost (18:14). Margaret Hannan points out that the least can also be connected to "the poor, meek, and persecuted of the beatitudes (5:3–12) to whom it is given to possess the Kingdom of the Heavens."[13] She notes that God's kingdom refers not only to "God's sovereign rule" but also to "the vindicating action of God who acts in the present to reverse the circumstances of the poor, the marginalized, and the oppressed (4.23; 5:3–10)."[14] While the disciples are preoccupied with status and prestige (18:1; cf. 4:8–9),[15] Jesus opposes their expectation by exhorting them to become like children, that is, to humble themselves like the unnamed child placed in their midst (18:3). In this light, Jesus's answer to the disciples implies that in contrast to their expectation, the kingdom of heaven operates through a different distribution of power: "Whoever wants to be great must be a servant, and whoever wants to be first must be a slave" (cf. 20:26–27). Thus, the power of God's heavenly kingdom is invested in one such child (cf. 18:14). The way the childlike are treated, "the extent to which they are welcomed," is how the church embodies and enacts God's heavenly rule on earth.[16] To share in Jesus's rule, then, is to share in childlike humility. This is what our participation in God's life looks like. In this context, Jesus teaches about forgiveness that is to be embodied as childlike humility on the earth (cf. 18:21–22).

THE NATURE OF THE FATHER IN MATT 18:15–35

It is important to consider Matthew's own terms for describing the character of the Father in 18:15–35, especially with respect to the Father's forgiving nature.[17] What is more, Matthew's Gospel offers us an understanding of how we participate in God's forgiving nature. The Father cares for the least (18:3–6; cf. 6:26–32), and their angels "always" (διά παντός) see the face of the Father in heaven (18:10). The Father's loving character is explicitly revealed in the parable of the lost sheep, where Jesus says that it is not the Father's will to lose any of these little ones who go astray (18:12–14).[18] The Father's loving care for us continues in 18:15–35, where the Father in heaven listens to and fulfills our prayer on earth (18:19). In particular, the parable of the unforgiving servant (18:23–35) emphasizes the Father's merciful, forgiving nature.[19] This parable introduces two main characters—a king (βασιλεύς) and his servant(s) (δοῦλος, 18:23). According to Mbabazi, the βασιλεύς or κύριος in this parable is "an *analogy* for God" and the δοῦλος and ἀδελφός are "all analogies for the Church."[20] The servant in the parable has an incalculable debt that is recorded as ten thousand talents (18:24). This amount can be comparable to the whole construction expense of Solomon's temple in the OT (1 Chr 29:4–7). The unthinkable character of the servant's debt leads Jonathan T. Pennington to assert, "This parable depicts clearly how humanity's debt to God is many orders of magnitude greater than the sins others might do against one another" (cf. 18:28).[21] The servant's immeasurable debt leads him to bow down (προσκυνέω) and ask mercy of his lord: "Be patient with me, I will pay everything back to you" (μακροθύμησον ἐπ' ἐμοί, καὶ πάντα ἀποδώσω σοι, 18:26). In response to the servant's plea, his lord "has compassion on" (σπλαγχνίζομαι) him and cancels his incalculable debt (18:27). Thus, this parable reflects the nature of the Father who is merciful and compassionate beyond the human's calculation and understanding (18:33, 35), which is nevertheless to be reflected in the way human beings treat one another. In Matthew, compassion is what Jesus has for his people (e.g., 9:36; 14:14; 15:32; 20:34). Jesus's compassion expresses that of the Father and communicates that compassion to the people such that they are forgiven and healed (cf. 9:13; 12:7).

At the end of this parable, Matthew adds the term "heart" (καρδία, 18:35) to indicate how we are to embody and participate in God's forgiving nature.[22] That is, the way we embody God's forgiveness is to forgive others from the heart (18:35). In line with Jesus's merciful and compassionate heart for his people in Matthew's narrative, we are called to forgive others with a compassionate heart. This suggests that without loving and forgiving others with a merciful and compassionate heart, we cannot fully embody forgiveness in the way Matthew envisions. This is what it means in Matthew to enact a deeper righteousness (5:20).[23] Just as Jesus embodies the Father's compassion, so we are called to embody it so as to be united with God and with others. The nature of our participation in God's forgiveness, then, is not simply following Jesus's action of forgiveness but embodying God's compassion from the heart,[24] thereby conveying on earth the power of heaven (18:35; cf. 6:21).[25]

For Matthew, those who embody God's forgiveness become God's children, God's heirs on earth (5:44–45). Through embodying forgiveness, we thus become brothers (ἀδελφός) and sisters (ἀδελφή) in the household of God (12:50).[26] This is what our participation in God's forgiveness looks like. It looks like being adopted as the children of the Father in heaven in the way we treat one another. Elsewhere in the narrative, Jesus says that the knowledge of the Father is revealed to little children rather than to the wise (11:25). This also confirms that being childlike is a way to access God's heavenly knowledge.[27] To say it another way, being childlike is a way we extend the intimate relationship Jesus shares with the Father in heaven. Thus, being childlike is what enables and empowers us to share in the nature and life of the Father, who is the "Lord of heaven and earth" (κύριε τοῦ οὐρανοῦ καὶ τῆς γῆς, 11:25; cf. 18:5; 19:14–15; 20:26–27).

THEOSIS AND FORGIVENESS: THE ONENESS OF HEAVEN AND EARTH

Theosis and the Ethic of Forgiveness in Matt 18:15–17 and 21–22

Matthew 18:15–17 has often been interpreted to validate and support the church's exercise of excommunication, with the result that the church has used this passage to solidify their grip on the sinning members of the community to excommunicate them (cf. 1 Cor 5:1–5; 2 Cor 2:5–11).[28] W. D. Davies and Dale C. Allison Jr. claim, "To treat someone as a Gentile and toll-collector would involve the breaking off of fellowship and hence mean exclusion from the community. . . . The passage is therefore about excommunication."[29] Anders Runesson contends, "If the offender refuses to acknowledge the need to be forgiven (and thus, refuses to deal with his or her impure status), after a number of steps have been taken, but have failed to make clear to the perpetrator the nature of the offence, the community of Jesus's followers must exclude him or her (Matt 18:15–17; Did 15:3)."[30] Similarly, R. T. France argues that "now their final repudiation of the consensus of the community has made any further accommodation impossible. . . . [T]he disciple is being instructed to suspend normal fellowship with the offender."[31] While the excommunication reading seems plain enough,[32] when this passage is interpreted in its literary context and with the lens of theosis, it is not well understood as merely dealing with excommunication, pointing instead to restoration and reconciliation of our relationship with God and with one another. I thus seek to show how this passage can be better understood in terms of theosis. It is my contention that the framing of this discourse and the rhetorical flow of the larger passage suggest that its purpose is to restore and regain our siblings, as opposed to merely providing a procedure or steps for discipline that may culminate in excommunication. In the language of theosis, we are to be reconciled with the sinning member(s) of the community, thus participating in and enacting God's forgiveness and embodying God's own character and life (cf. 5:23–24).[33]

In light of the framing of this discourse—that is, Jesus's responding to the disciples' ambition for greatness in the kingdom (18:1–5; cf. Mark 9:33–37)—Jesus's concern is forming the disciples of his church to care for the least, like children, that is, forming those who will exercise authority in his kingdom (18:6–14; cf. 19:14; 25:40, 45). As Günther Bornkamm observes, "Of primary importance is the placement of the pertinent question concerning true greatness in the Kingdom of Heaven, which surely sets a standard for all that follows."[34] In this discourse, the least is especially identified as those who are "in danger of straying and perishing" (18:10, 14).[35] Matthew 18:15 begins as follows, "If your brother or sister sins [against you]" (Ἐὰν δὲ ἁμαρτήσῃ [εἰς σὲ] ὁ ἀδελφός σου).[36] Given that Matthew uses the term ἀδελφός to refer to the sinning person (18:15),[37] that sinning person is recognized as the family member of the church, a brother or sister (cf. 12:50). In particular, the sibling idea in Matthew is linked to the theme of forgiveness. For instance, Jesus teaches that one who is angry with a brother or sister must forgive him or her (5:21–26). Reidar Aasgaard observes that this principle is developed further in Matt 18, where "it takes the form of regulations governing the settlement of disputes and forgiveness within the community (18:15–18, 21–22)."[38] Elsewhere in the narrative, Jesus says that we have one Father and thus we are "all brothers and sisters" (πάντες ἀδελφοί, 23:8–9). What Jesus wishes to recount is that God is our Father and we are his children, with the result that we are each other's siblings. Since the sinning person is presented as a brother or sister (ἀδελφός), that person shares the same Father with the community of Jesus's followers (23:9).[39] Accordingly, the whole church carefully discerns and considers the case of their brother or sister to gain him or her (i.e., reconciling forgiveness and repentance).[40] In light of the Father's love for the lost in the preceding segment of the discourse, where Jesus says with the parable of the lost sheep that it is not the Father's will (θέλημα τοῦ πατρὸς) to lose "one of these little ones" (ἓν τῶν μικρῶν τούτων) who go astray (18:12–14), the primary purpose of addressing a sinning brother or sister is to initiate a process oriented to restoring *siblingship*. In conjunction with the opening question of this discourse (18:1), where Jesus reveals that the power of the kingdom of heaven operates through how the least, such as children, are treated (18:2–10), this reconciling process should not be done in a way that maligns and condemns a sinning person. In the reconciling process, repentance is expected of the offender even as mercy is expected of the offended.[41] The offended person could indulge in his or her sense of revenge and in bitterness, thus judging and condemning his or her offender from the heart (5:21–22; 7:1–5; cf. 18:35). Thus, by not judging others self-righteously, the offended person can participate in and enact God's forgiveness. For, as Jesus says in effect, in 18:18–20, in restoring a lost sheep, his disciples are carrying out what has already taken place in heaven (cf. 6:10; 18:14).[42] Likewise, the person who has sinned against the member(s) of the community is called to reflect on the wrong he or she has done. This process could lead the sinning person to repent and humbly ask for forgiveness. Through embodying forgiveness, therefore, they can be reconciled, with the result that they gain access to or rejoin divine communion (cf. 5:23–24; 27:51).

That this reconciling process involves both the offended and the offender suggests that practicing forgiveness is not merely an individual issue.[43] It involves the community as a whole as we are inextricably bound up with others and thus are called to care for one another, especially with respect to "one of these little ones" who is led astray (18:6, 10, 14; cf. 9:7). In line with Jesus's answer to the disciples' question about greatness in the kingdom of heaven (18:1–5), the power of the kingdom of heaven is expressed through how those little ones are treated in the community. According to Matthew's presentation, the reconciling process first takes place in the private conversation between the offender and the offended (18:15; cf. Lev 19:17). From the perspective of the offended, to confront the offender requires courage and love. Thus, to confront the offender is itself an act of repair and an attempt to convince a brother or sister of the wrong he or she has done. Moreover, this private conversation provides "the opportunity for the offender to repent without public scandal."[44] If their brother or sister is convinced, then this reconciling process achieves its goal. If their brother or sister, however, does not admit his or her fault and receive forgiveness, "one or two" (εἷς ἢ δύο) witnesses are brought for this reconciling process in order to continue to search for the straying sheep (18:16; cf. 18:14).[45] If this multivoiced testimony is not sufficient, then the whole church is to intervene to continue this search (18:17).[46] The purpose of this effort is to gain the person, a process that is "conversionary" and ongoing,[47] aiming for a *transformation* of the person and the growth of the community, as opposed to merely providing a procedure or steps for discipline that may culminate in excommunication.[48] As Warren Carter rightly sees, "The three efforts to reconcile the person outlined in 18:15–17 do not finish the process. Though unspecified, restorative efforts continue" to the point of one's transformative participation in God's life (i.e., theosis), through embodying forgiveness.[49]

The ongoing pursuit of forgiveness is expressed in the wandering sheep's becoming like a gentile or a tax collector (18:17).[50] While a gentile or tax collector seems to be portrayed negatively in Matthew (cf. 5:46–47; 9:9–13), they are called to live the life to which the people of God are called (e.g., 9:13; 12:7). As such, exclusion is not the last word for the person who is depicted as a gentile or tax collector. To say that the person is like a gentile and a tax collector is actually a *hint* concerning that person's restoration rather than ostracization (18:17; cf. 1 Cor 5:1–5; 2 Cor 2:5–11).[51] That is, the goal of treating someone as a gentile and a tax collector is "to create a desire to be restored to the community."[52] As L. Gregory Jones observes, "Such exclusion, however, ought to be seen only as temporary and always in the hope that they will return to the fellowship."[53] In this regard, Jesus gives here positive grounds for suspending normal relationship with the unrepentant or the wandering sheep. In the OT, the command to reprove or discipline is connected with the command to love (e.g., Lev 19:15–18).[54] Thus, the church's discernment is to be done in love rather than in condemnation. Further, in the larger literary context of Matthew, Jesus continues to reach out to those regarded as sinners, including gentiles and tax collectors, in order to share

God's fellowship with them (e.g., 9:9–13; 11:19; 21:31–32).[55] Furthermore, in the final scene of Matthew's narrative, Jesus commands the disciples to reach out to all nations, that is, the world of gentiles (28:19–20). Matthew thus consistently narrates Jesus's solidarity with sinners, tax collectors, gentiles, and prostitutes, who are considered "outsiders and people at the bottom of [the] moral scale" in Matthew's narrative world (e.g., 3:13–17; 9:9–13; 11:19; 12:18, 21; 21:31–32; 28:19–20).[56] In this context, the person who has sinned against the member(s) of the community becomes "the object of the community's missionary efforts."[57] Mbabazi similarly observes, "The excommunication reading is problematic because it most likely stands against Matthew's overall teaching and focus in Matt 18, as well as his wider understanding of mission" (e.g., 8:5–13; 15:21–28).[58] Mbabazi adds that Matthew 18 has "a strong emphasis on preservation of the community, expressed in terms of not losing a single member of the community, *one* of the little ones" (e.g., 18:6, 12–14).[59] In line with the immediately preceding parable (18:12–14), the immediately following parable (18:23–35) also points to "*untiring* care for the erring brother [or sister] and readiness to forgive without limit (18:21) on the basis of the divine grace received."[60] Accordingly, both parables encourage our care for those little ones. Elsewhere in the narrative, rather than exclude the unrighteous, God bestows benefaction on both the good and the bad (5:45), and Jesus embodies the mercy and compassion of the Father (9:13; 12:7).

Rather than merely expelling the unrepentant, the ethic of forgiveness is aimed at the restoration of that person.[61] This purpose, restoration of our sinning brothers and sisters, is consistent with Jesus's injunction to love enemies (5:44). Jesus's injunction to love enemies encourages lavish forgiveness. In the rest of the discourse of Matt 18, in response to Peter's question about how much he is to forgive his brothers or sisters (18:21), Jesus answers him to forgive "until seventy-seven times" (ἕως ἑβδομηκοντάκις ἑπτά, 18:22). This answer is not what Peter expects as he thinks seven times are more than enough (18:21). This unexpected, lavish forgiveness implies that forgiveness should be embodied as a way of life rather than a one-time event. As Givens aptly observes, Jesus's point is not that we should be more generous but that "there is no purpose more ultimate than the forgiveness of the little one who has sinned against Peter."[62] Thus, the restoration of the one led astray to the community should be the ultimate purpose no matter what it will take (cf. 18:12–14).[63] Unlimited forgiveness, however, is not to say that one no longer distinguishes good from evil just because everything will be forgiven.[64] Instead, it is only through this limitless pursuit of forgiveness that the church can gain the wayward and have the presence of Christ in its midst (18:20). It is only through this limitless pursuit of forgiveness that the one led astray can see and acknowledge one's own fault(s) and repent.[65] Jesus's emphasis on lavish forgiveness thus encourages us to work tirelessly toward the repair of the broken relationships on the earth—until seventy-seven times (18:22). The recurrent emphasis on forgiveness in Matthew suggests that for Matthew, forgiveness is an important way we embody God's will, thereby participating in God's life. It is through this humble, merciful ruling that we enact the heavenly recovery of the one led astray on the earth (cf. 20:26–28). Granted, forgiveness is not an easy task. It is "costly" and perhaps a "lifelong struggle" because it involves "acknowledging and experiencing the painful truth of human sin."[66] As Jones puts it, "Christian forgiveness involves a high cost, both for God and for those who embody it. It requires the discipline of dying and rising with Christ."[67] Thus, there is no shortcut to embodying forgiveness. Nevertheless, Jesus, God-with-us, will guide *us* to the point of reconciliation, sharing God's life with us as theosis, "until the completion of the age" (ἕως τῆς συντελείας τοῦ αἰῶνος, 28:20; cf. 1:23; 18:20). In this way, our hearts are transformed in a way that produces the fruit of love and forgiveness, manifesting God's heart, God's will, and God's character (5:8; 7:21; 12:50; cf. 7:17–18; 12:33–35; 15:11).[68]

The Oneness of Heaven and Earth in Matt 18:18–20

We have seen in this study that the transformative, dynamic relation between God and human beings at work in Matthew is especially concerned with the heaven-earth relation.[69] Pennington observes that heaven and earth are frequently interwoven throughout Matthew's narrative: "heaven and earth is a key theological and literary theme in the First Gospel."[70] According to Pennington, heaven and earth are connected "over twenty times in some form in Matthew," whereas "Mark has only two instances of the heaven and earth pair and Luke five."[71] This statistic shows that heaven-and-earth is something of a Matthean particularity. Distinctly in Matthew's narrative, the heaven-earth relation manifests the God-human relation. Arguably, Matthew uses the phrases "kingdom of God" and "kingdom of heaven" synonymously to refer to the same reality (e.g., 4:17; 12:28; 19:23), but is able to accentuate the nuance of the dynamic relation between heaven and earth with his preferred phrase, "kingdom of heaven." Matthew also frequently refers to God as the "Father in heaven" or "the heavenly Father" (e.g., 6:1, 9, 14, 32; 7:21). Thus, Matthew's enrichment of the God-human relation with the heaven-earth relation offers an inviting locus for considering Matthew's Gospel through the lens of theosis.

Matthew 18:18 has an explicit formulation of the transformative dynamics of heaven and earth: "Whatever you bind on earth will have been bound in heaven, whatever you loose on earth will have been loosed in heaven" (ὅσα ἐὰν δήσητε ἐπὶ τῆς γῆς ἔσται δεδεμένα ἐν οὐρανῷ, καὶ ὅσα ἐὰν λύσητε ἐπὶ τῆς γῆς ἔσται λελυμένα ἐν οὐρανῳ). The periphrastic participles ἔσται δεδεμένα ("he/she/it will have been bound") and ἔσται λελυμένα ("he/she/it will have been loosed") are in the future and perfect tenses rather than simply the future. This suggests that heaven is already filled with God's perfect will and that earth comes to participate in heavenly life, as opposed to imagining contrastive or conflicting realities.[72] This is also confirmed by the Lord's Prayer that God's will be done on earth "as it is in heaven" (6:10). In this light, that binding and loosing has already taken place in heaven indicates that earth becomes a place where heaven unfolds.[73] In God's self in Jesus, heaven and earth, God and the human, are interrelated, such that earth participates in heavenly life and the heavenly life becomes the reality of human life on the earth.[74]

Matthew 18:18 is given in the context of reconciling forgiveness between the offended and the offender (18:15–17; cf. 18:21–35).[75] The discerning process of the church is described as "binding and loosing" (18:18).[76] According to Jones, "In relation to forgiveness, to 'bind' is to withhold fellowship, to 'loose' is to forgive."[77] Similarly, Mark Allan Powell observes, "Matthew considers binding and loosing to be a constitutive aspect of the church's mission on earth," that is, "the church's authority to forgive or retain sins."[78] Thus, the process of binding and loosing is a communal practice of discernment and forgiveness. Here, the process of binding and loosing is to be done prayerfully by "two" (δύο) of the church members (18:19). It is in that way that the Father in heaven works in the church. Jesus says that where "two or three" (δύο ἢ τρεῖς) are gathered prayerfully in his name, he is "in their midst" (ἐν μέσῳ αὐτῶν, 18:20; cf. Aboth 3:2).[79] The church thus comes to exercise the power of binding and loosing through the practice of prayer. On the nature of the church's authority and power, Powell observes that "the church possesses such authority not because Christians have shown themselves to be wiser or more faithful than Pharisees but because Christ dwells in their midst (18:20; cf. 28:20)."[80] Through our communal prayer, Jesus, God's presence with us, is in our midst and grants his heavenly power to the church (cf. 1:23; 28:18).[81] According to Allen Verhey, "Prayer is not a technology, not magic. Prayer is simple attention to God."[82] Verhey goes on to say that "in our prayers of confession, we learn humility, and we are freed from the compulsive need to defend our own little righteousness."[83] In our prayers, moreover, "we are called and formed to be forgiving others."[84] The practice of prayer, then, is a way to forgiveness. The prayerful support of brothers and sisters in Christ may lead the unrepentant to acknowledge his or her sins, with the result that the church can embody forgiveness. In our prayers, therefore, we may experience the renewing work of the presence of Jesus in the church (18:20). The presence of Jesus will guide "our discernment and our developments of doctrines and rules, our binding as well as our loosing."[85]

In this way, embodying forgiveness prayerfully leads the church to "possess the authority and sanction of heaven."[86] Consequently, "whatever you bind on earth will have been bound in heaven, whatever you loose on earth will have been loosed in heaven" (18:18). We thus unfold God's forgiving power from heaven, as well as God's ongoing repair of what remains unforgiven, through the embodied practices of prayer and forgiveness. This fits the picture of the Lord's prayer, where God's forgiveness of our sins and our forgiving others are tied together (6:14–15). By embodying forgiveness prayerfully on earth, we participate in the will of the Father in heaven manifested in the Lord's prayer (6:12). Embodying forgiveness prayerfully, then, is a way of theosis, the union of God and the human and thus the oneness of heaven and earth. That is to say, heaven and earth are not merely contrastive or conflicting realities, but they converge through our embodied practices of forgiveness and prayer on earth. Through this embodied practice, we participate in God's life by binding our anger and bitterness and loosing the love and forgiveness of God over our life and broken relationships (cf. 5:23–24, 44–48). In this way, we participate on earth in the heavenly life revealed in Jesus who wields his power (ἐξουσία) from heaven to forgive sins (cf. 9:2, 6).

Jesus and the Spirit: Jesus's Presence and Forgiving Power in Matt 18:20

To understand the nature of Jesus's presence and forgiving power in Matthew, it is important to consider Matthew's connection of Jesus with the Spirit. Scholars like David D. Kupp contend that Matthew is "particularly careful with his Spirit language, apparently avoiding the suggestion that the Holy Spirit is the Spirit of Jesus."[87] Kupp insists further that while "Matthew clearly supports straightforward references to πνεῦμα as the Spirit of God in OT terms, a divine agent of blessing, approval and inspiration working on behalf of his people," Matthew "actively reject[s] a 'pneumatology' or Spirit terminology which he may not even have had access to."[88] In a similar vein, Luz contends that Matthew "speaks of the presence of Jesus, rather than the presence of the Spirit."[89] While Matthew seems to speak of the continuing presence of Jesus as distinct from that of the Spirit in the community (e.g., 18:20), the presence of Jesus involves the presence of the Spirit, especially with respect to God's forgiving presence and power.[90] I contend that the nature of Jesus's relation to the Spirit is better understood with the framework of theosis, especially with respect to the power at work between the Spirit, Jesus, and his disciples. That is, the Spirit empowers Jesus and Jesus transfers this power to the disciples.

In the beginning of the narrative, Jesus is conceived by the creative power of the Spirit (1:20). The Spirit then descends on Jesus in John's baptism for the forgiveness of sins (3:16).[91] The Jordan River, where Jesus's baptism takes place, is a place of revelation as heaven is opened and the Spirit of God descends on Jesus (3:16).[92] Jesus thus receives God's revelatory knowledge ("my beloved Son," 3:17) by the empowering of the Spirit and it is no coincidence that Jesus is led by the Spirit into the wilderness in the subsequent narrative (4:1). Jesus thus operates in the sphere of the Spirit, even though the presence of the Spirit is not explicitly mentioned elsewhere in the narrative. Put another way, the Spirit with whom Jesus is anointed at his baptism becomes an ongoing presence in him. The Spirit, then, empowers Jesus for carrying out the work of the Father in heaven throughout the narrative. This is also evidenced by the scene where Jesus casts out demons by the Spirit of God (12:28). We should bear in mind that this is not to say that Jesus and the Spirit are identical without any distinction, as though Matthew sees the Spirit as Jesus or vice versa. As Runesson observes, "The person of Jesus is presented more as a tool, a channel through which the powers of the Spirit can work unhindered."[93] In this way, Jesus's ministry is empowered by the Spirit, with the result that the power of the Spirit is channeled through Jesus.

For Matthew, the power of the Spirit is especially depicted as the forgiving power of God (12:24–32), since to blaspheme the power of the Spirit is to speak directly against the forgiving power of God that touches and heals God's own people. It is to name God's forgiving power of the Spirit itself as satanic power that tears people apart from one another. No forgiveness will be given to those who blaspheme the Spirit (12:32; cf. 12:29).[94] Matthew tells us that just as the nature of the power of the Spirit is forgiving power in Matthew, so the nature of Jesus's power is presented as power (ἐξουσία) to forgive sins (9:6). Further, just as the Spirit empowers Jesus to enact God's forgiving power from heaven, so Jesus empowers the disciples with the power he has received (9:8; 10:1, 5; 18:18), power that is associated with his conception (1:20), his anointing with the Spirit in baptism for the forgiveness of sins (3:16), and throughout his ministry (4:1; 9:6; 12:24–32; 27:50).

In this light, when Jesus says he is in the midst (ἐν μέσῳ) of his disciples (18:20; cf. 1:23), Jesus's presence implies the presence of the Spirit, the forgiving power of God, which is transferred to his community. That Jesus's presence is especially a matter of God's forgiving power in 18:20 is evident per the literary context, where the process of reconciling forgiveness between the community members is discussed. In this reconciling process, the community of Jesus, empowered by the presence of Jesus, exercises an authority to bind and loose, unfolding God's forgiving power from heaven (18:18–20). Furthermore, the "name" (ὄνομα) of Jesus in 18:20 supports the implication of the presence of the Spirit. The particular phrase εἰς τὸ ὄνομα in 18:20 appears in 28:19, where the name is that of the God we may identify as triune—Father, Son, and the Spirit (28:19–20). The name of the triune God in 28:19 is not a sudden invention at this juncture of the narrative. That the proto-, narrative trinitarian God appears in Jesus's baptism in 3:16–17 also suggests that God is implicitly active as triune from the beginning of the narrative. The name of the triune God in 28:19 thus indicates that Jesus's name in 18:20 involves the reality of the triune God. Although the Spirit is not explicitly named in 18:20, the larger literary context of the passage signals the reality and presence of the Spirit. Accordingly, the presence of Jesus in the community does not exclude the presence of the Spirit, who accompanies Jesus from his conception throughout his ministry, and is conveyed to his followers (9:8; 10:1, 5; 18:18, 20; 27:50; 28:19–20).

Forgiveness and Repentance as Relational Mode in Matt 18:23–35

As we have explored in the Lord's Prayer (6:12, 14–15), this study endeavors to read forgiveness as mode rather than as a condition we meet in order to earn God's forgiveness (see chapter 2, above). The parable of the unforgiving servant is often read as an example of conditional forgiveness. For instance, Mbabazi notes that in the parable of the unforgiving servant, while the lord mercifully forgives his servant's debt, "the lord goes on to take back the forgiveness he generously granted" (18:33).[95] He contends that this parable is an example of "the use of the concept of conditionality": "It is quite clear that the lord's own behaviour is based on the behaviour of the slave toward his fellow slave; the lord treats him as he himself has treated his fellow slave. In so doing, Matthew restates explicitly the *conditioned* forgiveness and *conditioned* mercy."[96] He adds, "This [reciprocal] principle comes to fuller expression in 6:12, 14–15 and 18:32b–35."[97]

While there may be some conditionality at work in the parable of the unforgiving servant, through the lens of theosis, forgiveness can be better understood as relational mode rather than a question of meeting divinely imposed conditions. That is, our forgiveness is the mode in which we participate in and enact God's own forgiveness. In the parable, the servant's enormous debt is forgiven (18:27), but he does not treat his colleague the way he was treated by his lord. In response to the small, unpaid debt of his fellow servant (σύνδουλος), he grabs and chokes him (18:28). His fellow servant begs as he himself has begged his lord, with the words, "be patient with me, I will pay it back to you" (18:29), the same words of his own begging (18:26). But he has his fellow servant thrown into prison until he pays back the relatively small debt (18:30). His lord thus speaks to the unforgiving servant that "it is necessary" (ἔδει) for him "to have mercy" (ἐλεῆσαι) on his debtor just as the lord has had compassion on him (18:33; cf. 5:7; 9:13, 36; 12:7). Given that forgiveness can be understood as an embodied way of life in our relationship with God and with others (i.e., the way we treat others), the servant does not embody God's forgiveness in his relations with others and, as such, the servant does not come to enjoy the fullness of his lord's forgiveness. That is to say, to embody forgiveness is to abide in the realm of God's mercy, thus enjoying God's forgiveness. In the Sermon on the Mount, for instance, Jesus teaches that if we are angry with or insult our brother or sister, we will be liable to judgment and the hell of fire (5:22). This could mean that if we hang on to anger and bitterness, we come to torment ourselves (cf. 18:34). If we hang on to anger and bitterness, we cannot enter or enjoy the fullness of what God has for us. Jesus thus invites us to reconcile with one another so as to enter the divine communion (5:23–24). Rather than indulging in bitterness and rage, we are called to bind our anger and loose God's love and forgiveness over our life (cf. 18:18). In this way, we come to reflect and enjoy God's forgiveness. Forgiveness is thus not simply a precondition for our worship. It is the mode in which we give proper worship to God rather than a condition we have met for the reward of worship. Forgiveness, then, is a way of theosis, which takes place with God's initiative and the work of our response, not as a consequence of conditions that we meet before God acts.

The implication of the parable of the unforgiving servant is that just as the Father mercifully forgives our debts (18:27, 33, 35), so we are called to embody that forgiveness. It is more than a question of imitating God or reciprocity through a condition to be met. This is evidenced by the preceding question of Peter and Jesus's answer (18:21–22), where Jesus teaches that forgiveness has no limits, and, as such, it is not conditional as though God would depend on or wait for human forgiveness (cf. 18:27). Thus, it is not a matter of entirely distinct agencies that are reciprocal or sequential, human and then divine (cf. 6:12, 14–15). If we understand human forgiveness as a matter of participating in God's forgiveness, our forgiveness mirrors and extends God's own forgiveness, such that if we are not forgiving others, we are not enjoying God's forgiveness ourselves. God's forgiveness is being received by those who are embodying and extending God's forgiveness in the way they treat and forgive others from the heart (18:33, 35). Such a heart is merciful and childlike in nature (18:33; cf. 18:2–5).

The parable of the unforgiving servant also tells us that God has already extended forgiveness to us (18:27, 33), and, as such, we receive and embody that forgiven-ness in repentance as an embodied way of life.[98] Here, we should bear in mind that God's forgiving action always underlies and shapes our action, such that the priority of God's forgiveness should not be viewed merely as temporal priority. While God's merciful forgiveness is already given, this does not imply that God's forgiving grace is based on our action but that our forgiveness becomes God's way of extending forgiveness. That is, God forgives through the way we treat and forgive one another. Our forgiveness thus expresses our participation in what God does rather than merely pointing to our sequential action following God's action. Rather than a condition we meet in order to earn forgiveness, we receive and embody God's forgiveness in repentance, since repentance is our relational mode of participating in God's gracious forgiveness.[99] This suggests that God's forgiveness does not neglect our responsibility to repent and forgive others.[100] God's merciful forgiveness invites and empowers us to repent and show mercy to others (4:17; 5:7; 9:13; 12:7; 23:23; cf. 2 Cor 5:14).[101] By not forgiving his colleague, the servant does not embody forgiveness in repentance—that is, "a transformed pattern of life" (i.e., from one way of living to another).[102] Accordingly, our repentance is a key to embodying and enjoying God's forgiveness. When the practice of repentance is conceived with the lens of theosis, repentance as an embodied way of life is a way we become reconciled with others, enabling us to participate more fully in God's forgiveness.

SUMMARY

This chapter endeavored to demonstrate how forgiveness is a hermeneutical key to understanding the transformative dynamics of heaven and earth, God and the human in 18:15–35. For this purpose, I explored the literary and theological contexts of the passage to grasp its significance in Matthew's narrative. In particular, I attended to the opening question of the disciples (18:1) and Jesus's answer (i.e., concerning greatness in the kingdom of heaven, 18:2–14) because they set the course for all that follows in this discourse, especially with respect to how the heavenly kingdom operates and distributes its power on earth. I contended that to share in Jesus's heavenly rule on earth is to share in childlike humility. I then examined the forgiving nature of the Father in heaven by attending to the Father's loving care for the least and compassion for his debtor (18:6, 10, 14, 19, 27, 35). Just as the Father mercifully cares for us and forgives us, so we are called to extend care and forgiveness to others. We thus participate in God's forgiveness with a merciful and compassionate heart (18:27, 33, 35). Our participation in God's life is empowered by the childlike humility of Jesus (e.g., 11:25; 16:25; 18:1–10; 19:14; 20:26–28).

In my exegesis, I examined the ethic of forgiveness (18:15–17, 21–22) and challenged the tendency to interpret Jesus's teaching as culminating merely in excommunication. In light of the larger literary context and rhetorical flow of the discourse, I demonstrated how this passage points to restoration and reconciliation of our relationship with God and with one another rather than authorizing excommunication. While the excommunication reading seems plain enough, I suggested that the ultimate purpose of 18:15–17 is to restore the one led astray, consistent with the Father's will for the lost (18:14). I then examined Matthew's presentation of the oneness of heaven and earth, specifically through embodying forgiveness prayerfully (18:18–20). Along the way, I challenged the view that heaven and earth are merely separate or contrasting realities, and demonstrated how earth is a place where heaven unfolds, specifically through the practice of prayer and forgiveness. Next, I discussed the nature of Jesus's presence and forgiving power in relation to the Spirit (18:20). While Jesus and the Spirit are mutually distinguishable, Jesus is conceived by the Spirit and then carries out his mission empowered by the Spirit (e.g., 1:20; 3:16; 4:1; 12:28; 18:20; 28:19) through which he empowers the disciples (9:8; 10:1, 5; 18:18). Thus, the way Jesus shares his power with his disciples, power that is the Spirit he has received from the Father, is clarified as a matter of theosis of disciples' participating in the life of God through the Spirit Jesus shares with them. Finally, I challenged the conditional view of God's forgiveness in reading the parable of the unforgiving servant and demonstrated how forgiveness is the very mode in which we embody with one another God's own forgiveness (18:23–35; cf. 6:12, 14–15). I also suggested that repentance is our relational mode of participating in God's gracious forgiveness, such that we embody God's forgiveness in repentance. Through the embodied practice of forgiveness and repentance, we participate in God's forgiveness in our relationship with others (cf. 18:33).

NOTES

1. Matthew 18:15–35 is an appropriate unit of study because this pericope is unified by the theme of forgiveness and the nature of the Father in heaven (18:19, 35). Also, the term ἀφίημι appears four times in this unit (18:19–20, 27, 35). Matthew 18 is often framed as the community discourse. See Dale C. Allison Jr., *Studies in Matthew: Interpretation Past and Present* (Grand Rapids: Baker Academic, 2005), 137. This discourse is specifically given to/for the church (ἐκκλησία), the community of Jesus (18:15–20; cf. 16:18).

2. Isaac K. Mbabazi, *The Significance of Interpersonal Forgiveness in the Gospel of Matthew* (Eugene, OR: Pickwick, 2013), 188.

3. We should bear in mind that Matthew envisions continuity between the church and Israel (cf. 5:17; 13:52). On this issue, see Richard B. Hays (*The Moral Vision of the New Testament: Community, Cross, New Creation: A Contemporary Introduction to New Testament Ethics* [San Francisco: HarperSanFrancisco, 1996], 199, 308), who notes that "the meaning of the New Testament's vision of community is decisively conditioned by the covenant community of Israel." See also Jonathan T. Pennington (*Heaven and Earth in the Gospel of Matthew* [Grand Rapids: Baker Academic, 2007], 89): "Matthew's use of ἐκκλησία, like many of his other terms, alludes to the

Septuagint—specifically, the assembly or people of God in the Old Covenant (around 75x including Deut 4:10; 1 Kgs 8:14; Ezra 2:64)."

4. In Matt 16, Peter confesses Jesus as "the Messiah and the Son of the living God" (16:16). Joel B. Green observes that Jesus's founding of his church (16:18) is in line with Peter's confession: "Jesus' point is focused on the foundational apostolic testimony to Jesus' identity as 'Messiah, Son of the living God,' a revelation originating with the heavenly Father" ("Kingdom of God/Heaven," in *DJG*, 475). In context, since Jesus addresses God as "my Father in heaven" (16:17), the possessive personal pronoun (μου) implies that Jesus is of heavenly origin like the Father.

5. The point of departure of this entire section of the narrative (16:13–20:34) is a question from Jesus: "Who do people say the Son of Man is?" (16:13). Donald Senior notes that 16:13–15 "channel[s] the flow of the narrative toward the culmination of Jesus' mission in Jerusalem" (*The Passion of Jesus in the Gospel of Matthew*, The Passion Series [Wilmington, DE: Glazier, 1985], 31). He further writes, "Jesus's death on the cross is presented as the ultimate outcome or consequence of the entire mission of the Son of God" (30). In 16:21–25, Peter plays Satan, rebuking Jesus's coming suffering and death. Thus, while Peter confesses that Jesus is "the Messiah, the Son of the living God" (16:16), he does not seem to understand what the Messiah is to be (16:21).

6. The geographical locus of 16:13 is the district of Caesarea Philippi. W. D. Davies and D. C. Allison Jr. note that the city was named "in honour of the god Pan, who there had a cave shrine. Augustus gave it to Herod the Great" (*Matthew 8–18: A Critical and Exegetical Commentary on the Gospel according to Saint Matthew*, ICC [London: T&T Clark, 2004], 616). Thus, this city has a connection with Roman imperial power. In this geopolitical context, Matthew presents Jesus's identity as "the Messiah, the Son of the living God" in contrast to the Roman power. Jesus's identity as the Messiah reveals that his way to rule is done through suffering and death, specifically through embodying forgiveness rather than through domination (16:21). Likewise, the term ἐκκλησία (16:18; 18:17) is set in contrast to the groups under Roman imperial power. Richard A. Horsley observes that Jesus's community exists as "an alternative society to Roman imperial order . . . rooted in the history of Israel, in opposition to *pax Romana* . . . in God's guidance of human affairs, history, which had been running through Israel and not through Rome" ("Building an Alternative Society: Introduction," *Paul and Empire: Religion and Power in Roman Imperial Society*, ed. Richard A. Horsley [Harrisburg, PA: Trinity Press International, 1997], 209).

7. On the relation of the church to the kingdom, Jeannine K. Brown and Kyle Roberts note that "church and kingdom clearly overlap to some degree, and yet cannot be equated without remainder. The Gospel of Matthew resounds with the centrality of the kingdom of God. The church is comprised of local, covenantal communities of believers witnessing to the kingdom's arrival" (*Matthew*, THNTC [Grand Rapids: Eerdmans, 2018], 284). In this sense, the church is a key witness to the presence and nature of the kingdom of heaven on the earth.

8. C. R. Whittaker, "The Poor in the City of Rome," in *Land, City and Trade in the Roman Empire* (Aldershot: Variorum Ashgate, 1993), 8; there is no sequential pagination throughout this volume.

9. Matthew's social world was characterized by rank, status, and power. For discussions on social and economic stratifications in the Greco-Roman world, see Gerhard Lenski, *Power and Privilege: A Theory of Social Stratification*, 2nd ed. (Chapel Hill: University of North Carolina Press, 1984), 284; Bruce W. Longenecker, *Remember the Poor: Paul, Poverty, and the Greco-Roman Word* (Grand Rapids: Eerdmans, 2010), 45, 53. See Lynn H. Cohick ("Women, Children, and Families in the Greco-Roman World," in *The World of the New Testament: Cultural, Social, and Historical Contexts*, ed. Joel B. Green and Lee Martin McDonald [Grand Rapids: Baker Academic, 2013], 184): "With no middle class, the majority of children grew up in poverty or at a subsistence level." See also see Paul J. Achtemeier, Joel B. Green, and Marianne Meye Thompson (*Introducing the New Testament: Its Literature and Theology* [Grand Rapids: Eerdmans, 2001], 48): "In a father-oriented society like this one, children, like slaves, were among the weakest, most vulnerable among the population. They had little implicit value as human beings, a reality that is perhaps related to the high likelihood that they would not survive into adulthood. Even if women procured their place in the household by bearing children, especially sons, the children themselves were of low status." Cf. On children's rearing and health-care in Roman society, see Beryl Rawson, *Children and Childhood in Roman Italy* (Oxford: Oxford University Press, 2003), 126–33; 213–19; 223. Rawson observes, "Family members usually took responsibility for the sick and dying. That specialized health-care developed only for childbirth and early childhood indicates something of the priorities of Roman society. . . . Poorer persons used whatever help was available and could be afforded" (132). Despite the support and help provided by parents and surrogate parents, Rawson notes, "The young child did not qualify for full recognition of its existence and individuality until the age of 10" (104).

10. There is little debate among scholars on the meaning of μικρός in Matthew (e.g., 10:42; 11:11; 18:6, 10). It clearly refers to Jesus's followers. See Davies and Allison, *Matthew 8–18*, 763; Ulrich Luz, "The Disciples in the Gospel according to Matthew," in *The Interpretation of Matthew*, ed. Graham N. Stanton (Edinburgh: T&T Clark, 1995), 128. Matthew presents John the Baptist as one who is "less than the least" in the kingdom of heaven (11:11). This also confirms that the kingdom of heaven distributes power through the least.

11. Rawson, *Children and Childhood in Roman Italy*, 82, 126. In a similar vein, Cohick notes that "life expectancy [of a child] was short, and losing a parent or sibling was sadly familiar. Terms such as 'stability' and 'safety' cannot be used to describe a child's life in the Hellenistic and early imperial periods" ("Slaves and Slavery in the Roman World," 184). See also Beryl Rawson ("Children in the Roman *Familia*," in *The Family in Ancient Rome: New Perspectives*, ed. Beryl Rawson [Ithaca, NY: Cornell University Press, 1986], 196): "Many must have been orphans in some sense, either through parents' death or through separation due to slave sales and transfers or through exposure of the children. Of 431 *alumni*, only 16 record a natural parent's name; of 564 *vernae*, 70 do so."

12. Givens, "Jesus and His Church," 32.

13. Margaret Hannan, *The Nature and Demands of God's Sovereign Rule in the Gospel of Matthew*, LNTS 308 (London: T&T Clark, 2006), 158.

14. Ibid., 61.

15. When tempted by Satan, Jesus refuses to take worldly power and greatness (4:8–9). Jesus himself thus shows what it means to humble oneself (cf. 16:24–25; 20:20–28; 26:39, 42).

16. Givens, "Jesus and His Church," 27. See also Sharyn E. Dowd ("Is Matthew 18:15–17 about 'Church Discipline'?," in *Scripture and Traditions: Essays on Early Judaism and Christianity in Honor of Carl R. Holladay*, ed. Patrick Gray and Gail R. O'Day [Leiden: Brill, 2008], 148), who observes that how we as the community of Jesus "behave toward the 'little ones' has consequences that [we] must not take lightly."

17. For further discussion on the Father's nature in Matthew, see chapter 2.

18. Some manuscripts (D K L^{mg} N W Γ Δ Θ^{c} 078^{vid}) add 18:11: "for the Son of Man came to save the lost" (ηλθεν γαρ ο υιος του ανθρωπου σωσαι το απολωλος).

19. Regarding the relation between 18:21–22 and 18:23–35, Mbabazi observes that the discourse marker διὰ τοῦτο "seems to indicate a *connection*" and, as such, 18:23–35 follows "an example or proof of the *logion* in 18:21–22" (*Significance of Interpersonal Forgiveness*, 161; emphasis original). Davies and Allison note that both 18:21–22 and 18:23–35 "have to do with forgiving" (e.g., 18:21, 35), but they have different emphases: 18:21–22 is "a memorable call for repeated forgiveness," and 18:23–35 is a "vivid reminder that the failure to forgive is failure to act as the heavenly father acts" (*Matthew 8–18*, 794).

20. Mbabazi, *Significance of Interpersonal Forgiveness*, 161; emphasis original. The king's merciful character (18:27, 33) is clearly aligned with that of the Father in heaven (18:35; cf. 5:7; 9:13; 12:7). See also Bernard Brandon Scott ("The King's Accounting: Matthew 18:23–34," *JBL* 104, no. 3 [1985]: 430): "The king is no longer a king, but God. The last line (v. 35), with its identification of the king as God, determines the narrative as an allegory."

21. Jonathan T. Pennington, *The Sermon on the Mount and Human Flourishing* (Grand Rapids: Baker Academic, 2017), 229.

22. The term καρδία signifies "seat of physical, spiritual and mental life" as "source of the whole inner life, with its thinking, feeling, and volition." See BDAG 508 s.v. καρδία. Judith V. Stack observes that in Matthew, the heart is a metaphor for the "inner person" or "one's inner self" rather than merely a single organ of the body. For further discussion, see Stack, *Metaphor and the Portrayal of the Cause(s) of Sin and Evil in the Gospel of Matthew*, BibInt 182 (Leiden: Brill, 2020), 168–70.

23. For Matthew, righteousness (δικαιοσύνη) is the quality of those who seek the kingdom life from heaven. The theme of righteousness is developed in 3:14–15; 5:6, 10, 20; 6:33; 21:28–32; 25:31–46.

24. Jesus declares that where one's treasure is, there one's heart is (6:21). In context, this means that one's heart is to be in heaven. W. D. Davies and Dale C. Allison Jr. note, "A heart or mind directed towards heaven, and therefore acting in accordance with heaven's will" (*Matthew 1–7: A Critical and Exegetical Commentary on the Gospel according to Saint Matthew*, ICC [London: T&T Clark, 2004], 632). That Matthew's Jesus values the heart is because one's inner self empowers one's action

or fruit (e.g., 7:16–20; 12:33–35; 13:8, 23). As Hays observes, "Speech and action are the outward manifestation of what is in the heart" (*Moral Vision*, 99).

25. On the relation between the Father's compassionate and merciful character and 18:34–35, the point is not that our ability to forgive calculable debts is the condition of God's forgiving our incalculable debt. Instead, the parable accentuates the relation between God's abundant forgiveness and the relatively small demands of our forgiving one another, that is, that Peter and the disciples, including us, cannot expect to enjoy God's abundant forgiveness if we are stingy with much less demanding forgiveness, because less demanding forgiveness is partly how God's forgiveness happens, how our forgiveness participates in God's. One might think of this as the physics of how God operates among and in us, as opposed to the description of a conditional system. Thus, it is like saying that if one drops a rock from the cliff, gravity pulls it to the ground. The point is not to say that one has to drop a rock from the cliff in order for gravity to act, as if dropping it were a condition of gravity. The point is to say, this is how rocks fall, how gravity works, how falling rocks participate in gravity in a particular way (gravity is of course already acting on them before they are dropped and fall). Similarly, this is how God forgives—we forgive one another. And since God's forgiveness precedes and exceeds our forgiveness—as gravity does the falling of rocks—the way we forgive one another is just one tiny way in which God forgives.

26. Elsewhere in the NT, the NRSV sometimes translates the term ἀδελφός as "members of God's family" (Gal 1:2) and "members of God's church" (1 Tim 6:2). For further discussion, see Andrew D. Clarke, "Equality or Mutuality? Paul's Use of 'Brother' Language," in *The New Testament in Its First Century Setting: Essays on Context and Background in Honour of B. W. Winter on His 65th Birthday*, ed. P. J. Williams, Andrew D. Clarke, Peter M. Head, and David Instone-Brewer (Grand Rapids: Eerdmans, 2004), 154–55. Clarke observes that ἀδελφός language in Pauline letters conveys "a sense of affection, mutual responsibility, and solidarity," but need not include the notion of equality (158). Clarke's quotation is from David G. Horrell, "From ἀδελφοί to οίκος θεοῦ: Social Transformation in Pauline Christianity," *JBL* 120, no. 2 (2001): 299. See also Reidar Aasgaard ("Brothers and Sisters in the Faith: Christian Siblingship as an Ecclesiological Mirror in the First Two Centuries," in *The Formation of the Early Church*, ed. Jostein Ådna, WUNT 183 [Tübingen: Mohr Siebeck, 2005], 288): Siblingship in classical antiquity was "associated with love," and "harmony among siblings was regarded as ideal."

27. One of children's features is simplemindedness. Thus, to be childlike is to be simple rather than being confused. See Ulrich Luz, *Matthew 8–20: A Commentary*, trans. James E. Crouch, Hermeneia (Minneapolis: Fortress, 2001), 162–63.

28. For a discussion on the church's exercise of expulsion in the history of interpretation, see Luz, *Matthew 8–20*, 453–54.

29. Davies and Allison, *Matthew 8–18*, 785.

30. Anders Runesson, *Divine Wrath and Salvation in Matthew: The Narrative World of the First Gospel* (Minneapolis: Fortress, 2017), 124.

31. R. T. France, *The Gospel of Matthew*, NICNT (Grand Rapids: Eerdmans, 2007), 694.

32. On the excommunication reading, see also Göran Forkman, *The Limits of the Religious Community: Expulsion from the Religious Community within the Qumran sect, within Rabbinic Judaism, and within Primitive Christianity*, ConBNT 5 (Lund: Gleerup, 1972); Donald A. Hagner, *Matthew 14–28*, WBC 33B (Dallas: Word, 1995), 532; Graham N. Stanton, "The Communities of Matthew," *Int* 46, no. 4 (1992): 384; Luz, *Matthew 8–20*, 452.

33. Matthew 5:24 reads: "First be reconciled to your brother or sister, and then come and offer your gift [to God]." The theme of forgiveness in Matthew is closely related to the themes of "mercy, reconciliation, love, and non-retaliation." See Mbabazi, *Significance of Interpersonal Forgiveness*, 27. These are all related concepts of forgiveness because forgiveness is an expression of love, mercy, and reconciliation (e.g., 5:7, 21–26, 38–42, 43–48; 6:12, 14–15; 7:1–2, 12; 9:2–6; 18:15–17, 21–35).

34. Günther Bornkamm, "The Authority to 'Bind' and 'Loose' in the Church in Matthew's Gospel," in *The Interpretation of Matthew*, ed. Graham N. Stanton (Edinburgh: T&T Clark, 1995), 105; Scott, "The King's Accounting," 429.

35. Bornkamm, "'Bind' and 'Loose,'" 106.

36. Some manuscripts (א B 0281 *f*[1] 579 sa bo[pt]) omit the phrase εἰς σέ. But the use of "between you and him [or her] alone" (μεταξὺ σοῦ καὶ αὐτοῦ μόνου, 18:15) in the next clause suggests that a brother or sister sins against another brother or sister. France contends that the shorter reading of א B is to be preferred because "to introduce it [personal concern] here, where it is the brother's [and sister's] welfare, not 'your' interest, which is in focus, is premature" (*Gospel of Matthew*, 689). But the sin that a brother or sister commits against another brother or sister is not necessarily confined to a personal concern but is applied to the entire church as each member of the church is bound up with one another. As Luz adequately notices, "It is a biblical, Jewish, and early Christian conviction that every sin affects the entire church" (*Matthew 8–20*, 451). Thus, it seems appropriate to include the phrase εἰς σέ in reading 18:15.

37. The term ἀδελφός in Matthew is used to refer to Jesus's followers (e.g., 5:21–26; 7:1–5; 12:50; 18:15–17; 23:8–9; 25:40). On Matthew's use of ἀδελφός, see Aasgaard, "Brothers and Sisters," 298–99.

38. Aasgaard, "Brothers and Sisters," 298–99. That Matthew connects siblingship with the theme of forgiveness is resonant with the siblingship in classical antiquity. See Aasgaard, "Brothers and Sisters," 288. Aasgaard observes that the author of Matthew appeals to "traits which were characteristic of notions of siblingship in antiquity, such as the emphasis on love, emotional closeness, harmony, tolerance, forgiveness" (313).

39. Reidar Aasgaard notes the observation of Plutarch that we do not choose our brothers and sisters, "but are born into community with them, and thus under obligation to love them" ("Brotherhood in Plutarch and Paul: Its Role and Character," in *Constructing Early Christian Families: Family as Social Reality and Metaphor*, ed. Halvor Moxnes [London: Routledge, 1997], 169). Aasgaard goes on to say that for Plutarch, "leniency" and "mutual forgiveness" are important features that govern brotherly and sisterly love: "A brother [or sister] is given, not chosen, thus his [or her] weaknesses should be tolerated" (173).

40. Stack rightly sees that "the instructions [in 18:15–17] are particularly focused on proceeding in such a way that there can be forgiveness and reconciliation" (*Metaphor*, 121). While the repentance of those led astray appears to be lacking in 18:15–17, the underlying purpose of addressing their condition is to gain them back through their repentance. Similarly, Mbabazi points out that "one may assume the idea of repentance to be incorporated in that of reconciliation" in 18:15–17 (*Significance of Interpersonal Forgiveness*, 153).

41. In this reconciling process, Mbabazi contends that the stress is on "the responsibility of the offended person in forgiving" (*Significance of Interpersonal Forgiveness*, 153). He goes on to say, "In both 18:15–17 and 18:21–22, the response of the one sinned against is what is in view. The emphasis on both texts is likely on the injured person's responsibility toward their injurer" (159). Yet, this should not exclude the offender's responsibility toward the injured person as God's forgiveness is expressed in the way both the offender and the offended treat one another.

42. The dynamic relation between heaven and earth in 18:18–20 will be discussed below.

43. Portions of this paragraph are adapted from my published article, Kangil Kim, "A Theology of Forgiveness: Theosis in Matthew 18:15–35," *JTI* 16, no. 1 (2022): 48–49, doi:10.5325/jtheointe.16.1.0040. Used with permission from Penn State University Press.

44. Hays, *Moral Vision*, 102.

45. On the nature of the "one or two" conversation, Givens points out, "Here it is also to keep the circle of possible shame for the one who has sinned as small as possible, even as that may add to the shame felt by the offended disciple, who is kept from shifting it to the weakened shoulders of the one who has sinned against him" ("Jesus and His Church," 34). This multivoiced testimony is reminiscent of Deut 19:15, "Only on the evidence of two or three witnesses shall a charge be sustained" (NRSV). The intertextual connection indicates that this pattern of practice receives "divine authorization" (Brown and Roberts, *Matthew*, 171).

46. This enduring process may involve tolerance envisioned in Paul and Plutarch. As Aasgaard observes, "Brothers [and sisters], since they *are* brothers [and sisters], ought to be lenient towards one another, and indulge each other's weaknesses and mistakes. . . . Such tolerance also implies that one should be willing to forgive a sinning brother [or sister]. And also to ask for his [or her] forgiveness" ("Brotherhood in Plutarch and Paul," 179; emphasis original). Cf. See France (*Gospel of Matthew*, 693), who contends, "Anyone who is not willing to accept such united testimony may then properly be regarded as no longer a fit member of the community."

47. The term "conversionary" is drawn from Joel B. Green, *Conversion in Luke-Acts: Divine Action, Human Cognition, and the People of God* (Grand Rapids: Baker Academic, 2015), 124, 132. Like forgiveness, repentance is an embodied way of life rather than a particular event. As Green observes, repentance/conversion should be understood "in terms of 'process' rather than 'event,' with ongoing transformation occurring as the individual learns his or her role as a convert" (134). On the embodied nature of forgiveness and repentance, see further L. Gregory Jones, *Embodying Forgiveness: A Theological Analysis* (Grand Rapids: Eerdmans, 1995), xii, xvi, 15.

48. Since the reconciling process in 18:15–17 is conversionary in nature (i.e., reconciling forgiveness and repentance), the process outlined in 18:15–17 cultivates conversionary life through repentance rather than promoting excommunication. Through cultivating this habit of repentance, we as the church learn to see ourselves as sinners rather than condemning and judging others self-righteously (cf. 7:1–5). Jones rightly sees that habits and practices are "central means for forming people in the virtues necessary for friendship with God" and with others (*Embodying Forgiveness*, xiii).

49. Warren Carter, *Matthew and the Margins: A Sociopolitical and Religious Reading*, The Bible & Liberation Series (Maryknoll, NY: Orbis Books, 2000), 368.

50. Portions of this paragraph are adapted from Kim, "A Theology of Forgiveness," 52–53.

51. Luz contends that while Paul envisages the possibility of readmission or salvation (e.g., 1 Cor 5:1–5; 2 Cor 2:5–11), in Matthew there is "no mention of the possibility that the sinner at a later date will be readmitted to the church" (*Matthew 8–20*, 452). But this reading does not fit the flow of the narrative. Jesus blesses gentiles with healing in their household (8:5–13) and even acclaims a Roman centurion's faith (8:10). Further, he continues to share table fellowship with tax collectors (e.g., 9:9–10; 11:19). Thus, although there is no specific mention of the readmission of the sinner in 18:15–17, Jesus's recurrent encounters with them and being their friend (11:19) points to their recovery and restoration.

52. Brown and Roberts, *Matthew*, 170.

53. Jones, *Embodying Forgiveness*, 194. Jones goes on to say that "Jesus's injunction to treat such people as 'Gentiles and tax collectors' suggests both their self-exclusion from the community *and* the requirement to reach out continually to draw them back in—precisely for the sake of their salvation" (255; emphasis original). In a similar vein, Hays writes, "The goal of the community's disciplinary action must always be the restoration of the sinner to fellowship" (*Moral Vision*, 102).

54. For instance, Lev 19:17–18 runs as follows: "you shall reprove your neighbor . . . but you shall love your neighbor as yourself" (NRSV).

55. Assuming that Matthew is identical with the figure of the tax collector (9:9–10), he himself is evidence of Jesus's unreserved forgiveness. Matthew depicts Jesus as "a friend" (φίλος) of tax collectors and sinners (11:19). Gentiles will hope in Jesus's name (12:18, 21; cf. 4:15–16). Moreover, Matthew's narrative unveils that tax collectors believe John the Baptist who proclaimed the way of righteousness (21:31–32).

56. Mbabazi, *Significance of Interpersonal Forgiveness*, 158.

57. Hays, *Moral Vision*, 102. In a similar vein, Carter writes, "Gentiles and tax collectors are objects of mission, people to be won over to the community of disciples" (*Matthew and the Margins*, 368).

58. Mbabazi, *Significance of Interpersonal Forgiveness*, 155. Mbabazi suggests, "'Dissociation' may be suggested as a more appropriate term than 'excommunication' because the former tends to fairly describe how the injurer is to behave toward the straying fellow" (158).

59. Ibid., 156 (emphasis original).

60. Bornkamm, "'Bind' and 'Loose,'" 106 (emphasis mine).

61. Portions of this paragraph are adapted from Kim, "A Theology of Forgiveness," 53–54.

62. Givens, "Jesus and His Church," 36.

63. We should bear in mind that in 18:12–14, the heavenly kingdom is more focused on one sheep led astray than on ninety-nine sheep. Similarly, see Dowd ("'Church Discipline'?," 138): "The lost brother [or sister] must not be allowed to stray; extreme measures must be taken to restore broken relationships."

64. Luz, *Matthew 8–20*, 467.

65. In Matthew, God's forgiveness empowers our repentance (18:15–17, 27, 33; cf. 3:3; 4:17). God's merciful forgiveness is what enables us to unlearn our former patterns of feeling, thinking, and behaving, and to learn the new pattern of life as forgiven and forgiving community. In a similar vein, Jones observes that God's forgiveness occasions "a repentance, a turning, that marks people's new life with and in Christ," such that God's forgiveness provides "the paradigm for how we are to understand our own vocation to be forgiven and forgiving people" (*Embodying Forgiveness*, 162, 153). In repentance, therefore, we learn that because we have been forgiven (18:27, 33), we are able to see and live as forgiving people. Consequently, we gradually learn to see the way Jesus sees, becoming Christ-like people who reflect and enact God's forgiving love in our life.

66. Jones, *Embodying Forgiveness*, 163, 197.

67. Ibid., 5.

68. Jesus states that one's fruit comes from one's heart (12:33–35). Jesus's emphasis on the heart is well illustrated in the parable of the sower (13:1–23), where only a good soil/heart bears abundant fruit (13:23).

69. The transformative dynamics of heaven and earth are evident throughout Matthew's narrative. As explored above, in the Lord's Prayer, heaven becomes a present reality on the earth in and through Jesus, who delivers God's heavenly forgiveness on earth. Through praying and embodying Jesus's prayer, the full reality in the heavenly realm is to become fully present on the earth: "on earth as it is in heaven" (6:10). Thus, 6:10 indicates that our prayer enacts the dynamics of heaven and earth. In Jesus's healing of the paralyzed person, moreover, Jesus exercises the authority to forgive sins, as a human person who embodies God's heavenly forgiving power on earth (9:2, 6). The narrative shows that Jesus's authority to forgive and heal is extended to the disciples (10:1). Thus, the disciples, now sharing in Jesus's authority, extend the forgiveness of sins by enacting God's heavenly forgiving power. This chain of authority shows the sequence of power whereby we come to have the full authority of God in and through Jesus.

70. Pennington, *Heaven and Earth*, 238.

71. Jonathan T. Pennington, "The Kingdom of Heaven in the Gospel of Matthew," *Southern Baptist Journal of Theology* 12, no. 1 (2008): 46.

72. Pennington contends that Matthew repeatedly sets up "a *contrast* between two realms—the heavenly and the earthly—which stand for God on the one hand, and humanity on the other" ("Kingdom of Heaven," 47; emphasis original). According to Pennington, Matthew urges us to sense that there is "a great disjunction between heaven and earth, between God's way of doing things and ours" (47). Pennington

suggests, Jesus's identity is "very much defined through his connection with heaven" (e.g., 3:17; 4:17; 11:27), which "stands in contrast to the earth, which repeatedly is identified with the human (6:19–21; 18:18–20; 21:25–26; 23:9)" (*Heaven and Earth*, 83). For Pennington, therefore, Jesus's association with the divine indicates his contrast to the earth, which is identified with the human. This contrastive view is also found among other Matthean scholars, like Kari Syreeni, who contends, "The emphasis [of heaven and earth in Matthew] is . . . on the dichotomy, the innate separateness of the heavenly and mundane spheres" ("Between Heaven and Earth: On the Structure of Matthew's Symbolic Universe," *JSNT* 40 [1990]: 3). While Pennington rightly emphasizes the thematic importance of heaven and earth in Matthew, a theosis framework suggests a more nuanced understanding of the relation between heaven and earth, specifically, the oneness of heaven and earth, God and the human. While there is indeed a crucial distinction between heaven and earth (e.g., God's heavenly rule and kingdom and earthly kingdoms or rulers; see Pennington, *Heaven and Earth*, 322), that Jesus takes on human flesh and exercises the heavenly rule of God on earth as a human being points to a formative, relational dynamic between heaven and earth rather than merely a contrast (e.g., 6:10; 18:18; 28:18), even if this relational dynamic involves confrontation.

73. The dynamic relation between heaven and earth is also seen in the OT, where Jacob wrestles with God or his representative in Peniel (the Jabbok) (Gen 32:22–32). Before Jacob encounters his brother Esau, who wanted to kill him (Gen 27:41), he first wrestles with God or his representative, with the result that his hip is wrenched and he receives the heaven-given name, "Israel." After this heavenly wrestling, Jacob could meet his brother Esau and be reconciled. This narrative implicitly shows that the heavenly struggle and result in Peniel affect the outcome of life on the earth, that is, earth becomes a place where heaven unfolds (i.e., reconciliation of Jacob and Esau). The identity of the counterpart with whom Jacob wrestles is not within the purview of this study.

74. I am thankful for a discussion with Joseph Chongsu Won, who points out the dynamic at work in the God-human relationship in conjunction with quantum physics/entanglement: "We—you and me and Jesus—are entangled. Beyond time and space, when one's spin changes, the other changes instantaneously. Even past events change others into future completed action. When two electrons are created in orbit, their spin must be the opposite due to Pauli's exclusion principle. When they are sent apart far away, even many light years away to the end of the universe, as one electron changes the spin, the other changes beyond time and space. Jesus offers the free gift of an extra dimension; we accept those by the miraculous response of faith. Faith entangles us to God beyond where we are and what time it is" (30 April, 2022). In this light, in the context of Matt 18:18, where the process of reconciling forgiveness between the community members is discussed, forgiveness entangles us with God beyond time and space, thus making a fruitful, dynamic relation between heaven and earth. Forgiveness is thus a way God and the human, heaven and earth, are entangled and thus tied together.

75. Portions of this paragraph are adapted from Kim, "A Theology of Forgiveness," 49–50. The cross-reference in the margin of 18:18 in NA[28] points to John 20:23, which deals with forgiveness.

76. The language of binding and loosing is connected to Jesus's promise made to Peter in 16:19. Through this intratextual connection, Matthew indicates that Jesus's promise made to Peter extends to the whole church. Similarly, Mark Allan Powell points out, "It is no longer to be exercised by one gifted leader (e.g., Peter) but is now to be exercised by the community as a whole" ("Binding and Loosing: A Paradigm for Ethical Discernment from the Gospel of Matthew," *CurTM* 30 [2003]: 443).

77. Jones, *Embodying Forgiveness*, 192.

78. Powell, "Binding and Loosing," 438.

79. The phrase ἐν μέσῳ αὐτῶν forms an *inclusio* with 18:2, where Jesus sets a child "in their midst" (ἐν μέσῳ αὐτῶν). This is predicated on Jesus's identification of himself as children or the least (e.g., 18:5; 25:40, 45). Since the church gathers in Jesus's name, Jesus is the *center* of God's people.

80. Powell, "Binding and Loosing," 443.

81. In 28:18, Jesus says that all power in heaven and on earth is given to him. By sharing in Jesus's power, Jesus's followers can exercise the same power Jesus has. On the connection between Jesus's divine presence and his power in Matthew, see David D. Kupp, *Matthew's Emmanuel: Divine Presence and God's People in the First Gospel*, SNTSMS 90 (Cambridge: Cambridge University Press, 1996), 199.

82. Allen Verhey, *Remembering Jesus: Christian Community, Scripture, and the Moral Life* (Grand Rapids: Eerdmans, 2002), 428. Verhey places the practices of Christian community at the center of NT ethics. For Verhey, since the Christian community is a community of moral discourse (i.e., what we should do), the Christian community must take on certain practices, such as prayer, reading of Scripture, care for the suffering, the least, and the poor. These practices characterize a community that remembers Jesus.

83. Ibid., 428. For Verhey, the Christian community must take on a certain character, that is, humility.

84. Ibid., 429.

85. Jones, *Embodying Forgiveness*, 203.

86. Hannan, *God's Sovereign Rule*, 161.

87. Kupp, *Matthew's Emmanuel*, 229.

88. Ibid.

89. Luz, "Disciples," 131; Kupp, *Matthew's Emmanuel*, 230.

90. On the role of the Spirit in Matthew's narrative, see Blain Charette, *Restoring Presence: The Spirit in Matthew's Gospel*, *Journal of Pentecostal Theology* 18 (Sheffield: Sheffield Academic, 2000).

91. In John's baptism for the forgiveness of sins, Jesus is anointed with the Spirit (3:16). While the way John baptizes people (i.e., water, 3:11) is different from the way Jesus will baptize people (i.e., the Spirit, 3:11), the nature of their work is similar because they both work for the forgiveness of sins (3:6; 9:6; 20:28; 26:28). Since Jesus himself is anointed with the Spirit, the way God indwells and empowers Jesus

is the power of the Spirit (3:16). As bearer of the Spirit, Jesus saves his people by unleashing God's forgiving power in Matthew.

92. On the revelatory character of rivers in Scripture, see, e.g., Ezek 1:1; Dan 8:2–8; 10:4–7.

93. Runesson, *Divine Wrath and Salvation*, 159.

94. Blasphemy against the Spirit is "the renunciation of the power of God," a denial of God's forgiveness and salvation as "the Spirit is inextricably linked to God's salvific work," such as "binding the strong man" (12:29) in Matthew. See Runesson, *Divine Wrath and Salvation*, 132.

95. Mbabazi, *Significance of Interpersonal Forgiveness*, 184.

96. Ibid. (emphasis original).

97. Ibid. Mbabazi insists that "in 6:12 the conditional element occurs for the first time; in 6:14–15, it is elaborated and stressed" (164). He goes on to say that in the parable of the unforgiving servant, "the idea of *conditional* forgiveness and that of *conditional* mercy are juxtaposed" (188; emphasis original). In a similar vein, France contends that the principle of reciprocity or conditionality in Matthew is embodied in 5:7 ("mercy for mercy") and "is expressed more generally in the 'measure for measure' epigram of 7:2" and the "golden rule of 7:12 establishes the same principle at the heart of Jesus's ethic" (*Gospel of Matthew*, 168). But the mercy-for-mercy and measure-for-measure epigrams are not necessarily to be understood as conditionality. A theosis framework enables us to see them as mode. That is, our merciful act is the mode in which we participate in and enact God's mercy in our relationships with others.

98. See Miroslav Volf (*Free of Charge: Giving and Forgiving in a Culture Stripped of Grace* [Grand Rapids: Zondervan, 2005], 182), who nuances the relation between "given and "received": "God's forgiveness was given, it was sent," but "we need to receive it. We receive the gift by trusting that God has indeed forgiven us."

99. Runesson views repentance as a condition we meet in order to earn forgiveness: "Forgiveness cannot be given without repentance" (*Divine Wrath and Salvation*, 119, 124). Elsewhere he contends, "God's forgiveness is made conditional upon individual human forgiveness" (121). What theosis allows us to see, however, is that repentance is not merely a condition we meet in order to earn God's forgiveness but rather is our relational mode and proper response to God's gracious forgiveness.

100. In the OT, God's forgiveness is often associated with proper human response, namely, repentance (e.g., 2 Chr 7:14; Isa 1:16–18, cf. 1 John 1:9).

101. In a similar vein, Brown and Roberts note the dynamic of the God-human relation: "God's merciful forgiveness of the enormous debt incurred by humanity provides the *basis* as well as the compulsory *rationale* for forgiven sinners to practice lavish forgiveness for others" (*Matthew*, 71; emphasis mine).

102. See Green (*Conversion in Luke-Acts*, 62), who observes that repentance could "never be reduced to an internal realignment of the intellect but rather signified movement from one way of living to another," that is, "a transformation of *habitus*, a transformed pattern of life." In this sense, repentance is a reorientation or realignment of life that produces fruits that reflect God's character and will.

Chapter 5

Theosis and the Death of Jesus

"Blood for Many for the Forgiveness of Sins"

Jesus's declaration at the Last Supper, "for the forgiveness of sins," is significant for this study because it epitomizes the nature of Jesus's death as presented by Matthew (26:28), signaling the transformative, relational dynamics of heaven and earth revealed in and through Jesus's death (27:51–54).[1] While the Last Supper has regularly been read in Matthean scholarship as a forgiveness text, what remains to be explored is how the concept of theosis sheds light on the meaning of the death of Jesus, especially with respect to the dynamics of God and the human and of heaven and earth.[2] Narratively, Jesus repeatedly teaches and embodies forgiveness (e.g., 5:22–24; 6:12, 14–15; 9:1–13; 12:7; 18:15–35; 22:37–40), but the phrase, "for the forgiveness of sins" (26:28) appears climactically at the end of the narrative, forming an *inclusio* with "he will deliver his people from their sins" (1:21), indicating the culmination of God's forgiving power in the progression of Matthew's narrative. The phrase "for the forgiveness of sins" appears among the Synoptic Gospels only in Matthew's version of the sayings at the Last Supper (cf. Mark 14:24; Luke 22:20). Matthew thus clearly associates the forgiveness of sins with the death of Jesus. As God's Son, God's heir (3:17; 7:21; 11:27; 12:50; 16:16; 26:39; 28:18), Jesus offers his own body for many for the forgiveness of sins. As Matthew portrays Jesus, the way he wields his heavenly power on earth is climactically revealed in the way he gives up his life for many (20:26–28; 26:28, cf. 27:51–53). Further, just as Jesus embodies forgiveness even to the point of his own death, so he empowers his followers to embody his cruciform life as a way of discipleship (26:37–42).

To make my argument, I first examine how 26:28 expresses the culmination of the motif of God's forgiveness in Matthew's narrative. The meaning of Jesus's forgiveness of sins depends on the progression of the narrative.

From the beginning of the narrative, Jesus's role is defined as delivering his people from their sins (1:21). Accordingly, Jesus's mission is oriented to delivering his people, not least through forgiveness (e.g., 9:2, 6).[3] At his final Passover meal, Jesus shares table fellowship with his disciples, declaring explicitly the forgiveness of sins (26:28). To understand this narrative presentation, an examination of 26:28 in virtue of its location in Matthew's narrative is required. Next, I consider the nature of Jesus's table fellowship at the Last Supper because it implies that the forgiveness of sins has been frequently expressed in his table fellowship (e.g., 9:9–13; 11:19; 26:20–29; cf. 21:31–32). Jesus's table fellowship reflects and enacts God's gracious forgiveness, thereby inviting and enabling people to embody the life of the heavenly kingdom on the earth.

I then offer an exegesis of 26:28 in three steps. Each step has its own distinct emphasis, but together they contribute to an understanding of how theosis sheds light on the death of Jesus in Matthew's narrative. First, I consider the nature of Jesus's death in conjunction with the blood of the covenant enacted in Exodus (24:8) and a new covenant envisioned in Jeremiah (31:31–34). By alluding to Exod 24:8, Matthew shows that Jesus's blood heals and repairs a familial bond between God and human beings. Jesus's blood thus enables us to become children of God, the heirs and sharers of the nature and life of God. Also, Jesus's sharing the blood of the covenant, as envisioned in Jeremiah, transforms the relationship between God and his people as God's laws are inscribed on our heart (Jer 31:33). Consequently, we come to know God's own ways, thereby reflecting God's life in the way we live.

Second, I examine discipleship in Matthew according to the significance of theosis and the death of Jesus—that is, discipleship as participation in Jesus's cruciform life. Discipleship in Matthew is about bearing one's cross through embodying forgiveness as Jesus embodies it, even to the point of death (e.g., 10:37–39; 16:24–25). I examine how, in his Gethsemane prayer, Jesus invites the disciples to participate in his suffering and death through prayer (26:37–42). I show that Jesus's teaching of discipleship empowers his followers to share in Jesus's death, thereby reflecting and enacting God's life.

Finally, I examine Jesus's death in relation to the transformative, relational dynamics of heaven and earth in 27:51–54. By examining the significance of the torn veil, I show that Jesus's shedding of blood for the forgiveness of sins enables and empowers our access to the fullness of God's knowledge and presence, as a matter of theosis. Also, I highlight that Jesus's death for the forgiveness of sins occasions cosmic events that display the dynamics of heaven and earth (27:51–53), which reveal who he is—God's Son (27:54). That Jesus is revealed as God's Son as the result of God's action points to the significance of the Father-Son relationship for understanding the forgiving power of Jesus's death (cf. 11:27; 12:50). Just as the Father-Son relation is what enables the Father to manifest his heavenly power at the death of his Son, so the way we participate in God's power depends on the way we share in the Father-Son relationship as embodied in Jesus's death. Thus, the Father-Son relationship as developed by Jesus's death is the paradigm for our transformative participation in divine life, namely, theosis. In this way, this study endeavors to demonstrate how Jesus's death can be better understood with the framework of theosis, especially with respect to the transformative, relational dynamic between God and humanity and thus between heaven and earth (28:18).

MATTHEW 26:28 AS THE *CULMINATION* OF GOD'S FORGIVENESS IN MATTHEW'S NARRATIVE

From the beginning of the narrative, Jesus is presented as one who delivers his people from their sins (1:21). Jesus's name as "God is savior" (*yēšūa'*) and his mission as deliverer indicate that his life will be oriented to delivering his people from their sins. It is "Jesus" who sheds his blood for the forgiveness of sins (26:28). As Paul Kunjanayil observes, "The fullness of the being and mission of Jesus may be seen in his name" (cf. Gen 3:20; 4:1; 5:29).[4] Matthew indicates that, as the meaning of Jesus's name as savior, Jesus's saving his people from their sins will be a matter of God's saving Israel from their sins according to the patterns of that salvation in Israel's biblical history (cf. Jer 31). As we have seen in the Lord's Prayer (6:12, 14–15) and the forgiveness and healing of the paralyzed person (9:2–8), forgiveness of sins is a matter of repairing the damage of inherited debts. That is, forgiveness is more than a one-off transaction but a process of transformation of Israel's condition and broken relationships in the land. In Israel's biblical history, Jeremiah presents a new covenant for Israel and Judah as a matter of forgiveness of the people's iniquity (31:31), which is explicitly repairing the damage to their life on the earth—that is, their living the curse of slavery to gentile powers in exile.[5]

The narrative then teaches that Jesus fulfills God's saving purpose particularly through his suffering and death, effecting the salvation of the people through the forgiveness of their sins (1:21). That is to say, it is climactically through suffering and death that Jesus saves his people (26:28). Daniel M. Gurtner observes, "That σώζω in Matthew's gospel can refer to deliverance from physical danger (8:25), disease (9:21–22), or death (24:22) suggests that Jesus offers forms of 'salvation' through various aspects of his ministry as well as through his death."[6] Thus, the saving power of Jesus's death should be understood in light of the other ways the narrative presents him as savior. In particular, Dale C. Allison Jr. identifies six key scenes that are closely connected to Jesus's suffering—the persecution of the infant Jesus (2:1–18), turning the other cheek (5:38–42), the disciples' mission (10:17–23), the martyrdom of John the Baptist (14:1–12), Jesus's transfiguration (17:1–8), and true service (20:20–28).[7] Each scene carries Matthew's readers forward to its conclusion—that is, Jesus's suffering and death. As anticipated in his infant narrative (e.g., 2:13–18) and his prediction of suffering and death (e.g., 16:21; 17:22–23; 20:17–19; 26:2; cf. 12:40), the narrative implies that Jesus's public ministry will culminate in his passion and death.[8] The disciples' suffering also anticipates Jesus's own suffering later in the narrative as the disciples are called to embody what their teacher Jesus does (5:38–42; 10:17–23, 25). Further, the martyrdom of John the Baptist anticipates Jesus's passion and death (14:1–12). Just as John the Baptist is executed unjustly, so Jesus will be executed unjustly.[9] And both in Jesus's transfiguration and his crucifixion, Jesus is declared God's Son (17:5; 27:54), and people are greatly terrified (17:6; 27:54).[10] As the narrative bears out, entrance into the kingdom must be accompanied by the cup of suffering (20:20–28). While the disciples request positions of honor—that is, sitting at Jesus's right and left hand (20:20–21; cf. 18:1)—Jesus asks them in reply whether they can drink the cup of suffering he drinks (20:22; cf. 26:39, 42). What Jesus shows them later is that those ruling with him to his right and his left are the two insurgents hanging on Jesus's right and left sides (27:38).

We should bear in mind that for Matthew, Jesus's suffering and death is the particular way his forgiving power is revealed, since it is through his suffering and death that Jesus sheds his blood for the forgiveness of sins (26:28; 27:28–31, 34–35, 50). In his Sermon on the Mount, Jesus exhorts his followers to turn the other cheek, obeying the restraining principle of an eye for an eye more rigorously than current authorities are teaching (5:38–42).[11] The idea in 5:38–42 is not to abandon that part of the law but to fulfill it (cf. 5:17). That is, while many authorities of Jesus's and Matthew's day are interpreting it as justification for measures of retaliation, Jesus presents it as commanding restraint when people are tempted to retaliate, restraint whose fullness is loving the enemy rather than responding to the enemy's injustice retributively (cf. 5:44–46). We can see how Jesus embodies this teaching in the way that he suffers and dies, bringing transformative justice to his people by forgiving and loving his enemies to the point of his own death instead of resorting to something retaliatory. In his trial, Jesus is struck and does not strike back (26:67; cf. 5:39); his clothes are taken and he does not claim his rights (27:31, 35; cf. 5:40; Isa 50:4–11). Matthew thus shows that Jesus embodies forgiveness through his suffering and death.

For Matthew, the nature of Jesus's suffering and death is ordained and purposed by God (26:3–5, 39, 42), the Father who is the source of Jesus's power as Son (11:27; 28:18).[12] In 16:21, Matthew's use of δεῖ indicates the necessity of Jesus's suffering ordained by God (cf. 26:54).[13] In context, the necessity of Jesus's suffering and death is related to his identity as Christ (16:17), who must suffer and die, rather than conquer by violence, if he is indeed to deliver his people from their sins once and for all (16:21; 26:28). In particular, in Jesus's passion prediction, Matthew uses the term παραδίδωμι, which resonates with the motif of Yahweh's Suffering Servant in Isaiah, who is handed over for many (17:22; 20:18–19; cf. Isa 52:13–53:12).[14] Like the Suffering Servant, Jesus is afflicted and crushed for his people's sins (27:4, 19; cf. Isa 53:2, 5–6, 9). Like the Suffering Servant, Jesus remains silent and is handed over (παραδίδωμι) for many (26:24, 28, 63; cf. Isa 53:7, 12; Ps 38:13–14). In this way, Matthew alludes to the Suffering Servant of Yahweh in Isaiah, who comes to give his life for many for the forgiveness of sins (20:26–28; 26:28).[15] Further, this shows that Jesus saves his people through suffering by a pattern that others share with him (e.g., 10:17–21), which is itself a pattern whereby Jesus is revealed as the Servant of Yahweh. This goes to the dynamics of theosis—that is, we are saved not only by Jesus's doing something for us but also by Jesus's enabling us to participate, as his disciples, in his own self-giving, which is itself the self-giving of God as God hands over God's own heir for the salvation of God's people.[16]

Jesus's servanthood is linked to his forgiving ministry throughout the narrative. As he begins his ministry, the first thing Jesus does is to identify himself with his people by joining them in the baptism for the forgiveness of sins (3:6, 11, 13–17). As Isaiah knows Israel's sins as his own (Isa 6:5), Jesus takes his people's sins as his own by being baptized with them (cf. Isa 53:6, 8, 11). During his ministry, Jesus continually embraces sinners and embodies merciful forgiveness (9:13; 11:19; 12:7; 21:31–32). As a way to embody merciful forgiveness, Jesus touches and heals the weak, the blind, and the needy (e.g., 8:1–9:38). In this process, Jesus proclaims God's justice to the gentiles by the power of the Spirit and does not break a bruised reed (12:17–21; cf. Isa 42:1, 3). In the context of Isa 42, Yahweh's Servant delivers his people from the prison of those who sit in darkness (Isa 42:7). Like Yahweh's Servant, Jesus is presented as one who delivers his people sitting in darkness (e.g., 4:16; cf. Isa 9:1–2).[17] By sharing in their darkness—the vulnerable condition of Israel envisioned in Isa 42:3—Yahweh's Servant brings light to the people of Israel. In this light, Jesus's delivering his people from their sins involves his sharing in their darkness and his being a suffering member of his people (8:17; cf. Isa 53:4),[18] which will come to final expression in his death for his people.[19] Rowan Williams observes that Jesus's suffering and death reveals the truth about God and how God is recognized in Jesus. Even though "the prophets imagine God bringing the charges," in trial, it is God, "who is left silenced" and, as such, "God, paradoxically, is the vulnerable one" (27:12, 14; cf. Isa 53:2).[20] That is, God becomes recognizable as God only on this lowly ground (cf. 18:2–5), the place of suffering and humiliation (e.g., 16:25;

20:26–28). The Jerusalem authorities mock Jesus, saying that he saves others but cannot save himself (27:42); God can save him now if Jesus is the Son of God (27:43). Despite this mockery, Jesus remains silent, and it is in Jesus's becoming vulnerable unto death for our sake that God decisively reveals who Jesus is through the lips of the centurion and those with him—Son of God (27:54). That is to say, it is through suffering and weakness that God is decisively active and present in Jesus (1:23).[21] This is how Jesus, who is God's presence with God's people in human flesh (1:23), reveals who he is and thus who God is.

As the narrative develops further, Jesus "set his face to go to Jerusalem rather than somewhere else apparently more promising, even when that road of solidarity [for many] led to the cross"; that is, shameful death in Jerusalem is Jesus's way to deliver his people (16:21).[22] The development of the narrative nears its climax as Jesus shares the Last Supper with the disciples, declaring his death for the forgiveness of sins as that death is embodied by the meal (26:28). The Last Supper is a meal between Jesus and the disciples, the *culmination* of their fellowship throughout their journey with Jesus.[23] It is climactic in the sense that the Last Supper is the farewell meal as Jesus is about to depart from the disciples and is looking to his death. While Jesus predicts his suffering and death earlier in the narrative (16:21; 17:22–23; 20:17–19, 28), the nature of his death is explicitly highlighted at the Last Supper: "for many for the forgiveness of sins" (26:28). Matthew's genealogy at the beginning of the narrative also reminds us that Jesus's birth is located in the context of Israel's history,[24] "culminating in exile and still awaiting" its restoration (1:12), which is revealed on the earth apocalyptically, and thus paradoxically, in his life as completed by his death.[25] Thus, the peculiar way he sheds his blood in death enables the long-promised healing of his people on the earth (cf. 27:51–54).

The death of Jesus can also be conceived as the culmination of the growing conflict between Jesus and other teaching authorities throughout the narrative (cf. 7:28–29). The opposition to Jesus accumulates as the narrative develops, which culminates in his trial and death (27:25). The religious authorities see Jesus as one who is in league with Satan (9:34; 12:24). They recurrently test him (12:38; 15:2; 16:1; 19:3). They are angry at the crowd's praise of Jesus (21:15), challenging his authority (21:23). They attempt to arrest him (21:46). They also plan to entrap Jesus in what he says (22:15). In particular, Jesus is charged with blasphemy because of his mercifully forgiving a paralyzed person (9:2–6, 13). This prepares the reader for the passion account, where Jesus is condemned for blasphemy by the Jerusalem authorities (26:65). In response to stiff opposition, Jesus refuses to violently resist (26:51–54), shedding his blood for the forgiveness of sins, which culminates in the Last Supper and the cross. In Jesus's trial, "all the people" (πᾶς ὁ λαός) are in opposition to Jesus, willing him to die (27:25).[26] In response to the opposition of all the people, Jesus sheds his blood "for many" (περὶ πολλῶν), spreading God's forgiveness to all.[27]

THE NATURE OF JESUS'S TABLE FELLOWSHIP, THE LAST SUPPER, AND FORGIVENESS

The Nature of Jesus's Table Fellowship in Matthew's Gospel

Jesus's forgiveness is often expressed in table fellowship in Matthew's narrative. After Jesus has set his course for the cross (16:21), he shares the Last Supper with the disciples (26:20–29). Earlier in the narrative, Jesus shares table fellowship, especially with those who are deemed sinners (e.g., 9:9–13; 11:19; 15:21–28). For this reason, Jesus is characterized as a "friend" (φίλος) of tax collectors and sinners (11:19).[28] In the Jewish background, eating together symbolizes "the ratification of a covenant" (e.g., Gen 26:26–31).[29] I. Howard Marshall observes that "a meal was often a social occasion to be enjoyed in the company of other people and it could serve as an expression of hospitality, friendliness, and unity" (e.g., Lev 7:11–21).[30] The reconciliation between Jacob and Laban is sealed by a meal (Gen 31:54–55). Also, since the people of Israel offer certain parts of an animal in sacrifice to Yahweh (Lev 3:3–16), and they eat before Yahweh (Deut 12:7), the meal can be regarded as "an occasion of communion between Yahweh and his people."[31] In a similar vein, Joachim Jeremias notes that "every table fellowship is a guarantee of peace [and] of trust" (e.g., Gen 43:25–34; Josh 9:1–15).[32] Thus, when Jesus shares a meal with sinners and outcasts, it expresses the acceptance of those who are deemed sinful and thus "the assurance of forgiveness."[33] In this light, Jesus's sharing a meal with sinners and "the tax collectors and the prostitutes" (οἱ τελῶναι καὶ αἱ πόρναι, cf. 21:31–32) is "deemed scandalous because it appears to imply acceptance and/or approval of the sinners."[34]

Once we reach the Last Supper, Jesus presents bread as his body and the cup as his blood of the covenant (διαθήκη),[35] which is poured out for many for the forgiveness of sins (26:27–28). While Matthew does not explicitly narrate that Jesus forgives sinners in table fellowship elsewhere in the narrative, the Last Supper reveals the nature of Jesus's table fellowship—that is, its power to forgive sins. This later development of the nature of Jesus's table fellowship enriches what Jesus does earlier in the narrative (e.g., 9:9–13; 11:19; 14:14–21; 15:32–38). Earlier passages in the narrative like Jesus's sharing a meal with tax collectors and sinners (9:9–13) are "implicitly understood to provide the ground for" what Matthew wants to develop later in the narrative.[36] This suggests that forgiveness is already implicit especially in Jesus's other table meals with those who are deemed sinners, whose culmination is the Last Supper. This does not mean that all occasions of table fellowship are events in which people are forgiven in Matthew, since Jesus does not eat only with those whom the narrative might refer to as sinners (e.g., 26:7–13).[37]

As in the Last Supper, Jesus's meals in Matthew often convey the hope that sinners are being forgiven and thus inheriting the coming kingdom as they come to foretaste the heavenly banquet (e.g., 26:29; cf. 9:13; 21:31). In this sense, Jesus's table fellowship reflects God's gracious forgiveness, thereby inviting people to repent and receive God's forgiveness, which is to embody together the life of the heavenly kingdom on the earth (21:31–32; cf. 4:17).[38] In this process, Jesus does not simply give sinners a status of being forgiven but acts, by virtue of sharing their table, to affect the conditions of their life, moving them from a place of being despised to one of being welcomed and thus healed. Jesus's sharing their table thus conveys the welcome, reintegration, and healing of those who are despised and neglected (e.g., 9:9–13; 11:19; 15:28). Jesus's sharing of meal in this sense entails incorporation of sinners into the community of Jesus. Meals shared by Jesus are thus key sites where the healing and repair of broken relationships take place on the earth. That is, Jesus's meal serves as an important medium by which forgiveness and healing are conveyed.

Theosis and the Last Supper

The Last Supper can be conceived with the framework of theosis, with respect to Jesus's forgiving power that transforms the conditions of Israel's life on the earth. To begin, it is worth observing the connection between the Last Supper and Jesus's act of feeding multitudes earlier in the narrative, though they may not be related in the sense of something "eucharistic."[39] Earlier in the narrative, Jesus feeds the people in Jewish territory (14:13–21) and then feeds them again with gentiles among them (15:32–39). Both of these meals take place in Jewish Galilee, but the meal for the four thousand men and their families does appear to include gentiles who have joined the crowds following Jesus as he moved in the border regions to the north in the preceding segment of the narrative (e.g., 8:5–13; 15:21).[40] The significance of these two feeding stories lies partly in their connection to the Last Supper at the end of Matthew's narrative, with respect to Jesus's provision and forgiveness for his people. That Jesus's two feeding stories take place in the desert (14:13; 15:33) evokes God's feeding of Israelites in the desert (e.g., Exod 16). As Markus Barth observes, "Für das Passa oder/und das Fest der Ungesäuerten Brote war der Exodus maßgebend, der von den Propheten als Macht- und Liebes-Erweis des Schöpfers von Himmel und Erde und als Prototyp für die Rückführung Israels aus dem Exil verstanden wurde."[41] Through this feeding, God not only satisfies his people's hunger but also repairs the conditions of Israel's life, thus showing his love and forgiveness that is operative in famine conditions, so much so that the abundance of Israel's desert banquet spills over as bread for even their gentile enemies (e.g., 15:22–28). Jesus's encounter with a gentile woman in 15:22 is not a random encounter with gentiles, but with a Canaanite, a person representing Israel's enemy in biblical history (e.g., Josh 1–11).[42] Jesus's healing of the sickness of the Canaanite woman's daughter would signify the repair of the broken relationships with gentile enemies, namely, a transformation of the intergenerational fabric of the life of Israel (cf. 27:54). In context, Jesus's healing of the Canaanite woman's daughter is expressed as Jesus's sharing a table meal (15:27–28). Thus, Jesus's meal brings forgiving power to bring peace with gentile peoples. This means that Jesus's healing and forgiveness involve peace with gentile peoples. This is also confirmed by the following segment of the narrative, where Jesus has mercy on (σπλαγχνίζομαι) the crowds that appear to include gentiles and feeds them all (15:32–34).[43]

Jesus's feeding in the desert also foreshadows the heavenly banquet envisioned in Isa 25:6–8, where the meal—the abundance of well-matured wine and rich meat—is portrayed as an eschatological vision for our fellowship with God (Isa 25:6–8; cf. Matt 8:11; Rev 19:7–9).[44] Through this heavenly meal, God will swallow up death forever, wiping away the tears of all faces and removing the disgrace of his people (Isa 25:8). Through Jesus's feeding that foreshadows the heavenly banquet, then, his people are being nourished, healed, and restored. Thus, the significance of Jesus's feeding lies not only in remembering God's provision and saving action in the past but also in the future hope among God's people for the healing of the conditions of their life on the earth. At the Last Supper, Jesus himself also looks forward to drinking the fruit of the vine in the Father's kingdom (ἐν τῇ βασιλείᾳ τοῦ πατρός, 26:29)—that is, the heavenly banquet.[45] Thus, just as Jesus's act of feeding multitudes brings the healing of the conditions of his people on the earth, so the Last Supper connects the spirit of hope and salvation to the death of Jesus, signaling a transformation of the conditions of Israel's life on the earth by the change that Jesus's death will effect.

Next, we should bear in mind that the Last Supper in Matthew is a Passover meal, since Jesus sends the disciples to prepare for the Passover (πάσχα) meal on the first day of Unleavened Bread—the day of the Passover (26:17, 19; cf. Mark 14:12; Luke 22:7).[46] In Israel's history, the Passover is known as a feast that commemorates God's liberation of the people of Israel from slavery.[47] That Matthew presents Jesus as God-with-us (1:23) indicates that God's liberation for his people works in and through Jesus (1:21; cf. Exod

11:5; 12:29).[48] This implies that just as the God of Israel liberates his people from slavery in the Passover, so Jesus will be delivered up for his people in the Passover to liberating effect (26:2, 18; cf. 1:21). Thus, for Matthew, the Passover meal is not only an occasion for remembering what God has done for them but also an occasion for anticipating the coming deliverance of God through Jesus. In this way, Jesus's Passover meal expresses the culmination of his forgiving power as it is embodied by his death.

At the Passover meal, Jesus begins as follows: "one of you will betray me" (26:21). Jesus knows what is about to happen. He predicts Judas's betrayal and Peter's denial (26:25, 34), consistent with his earlier passion predictions (16:21; 17:22–23; 20:17–19, 28).[49] In response to Jesus's words, Matthew narrates that the disciples "grieve greatly" (λυπούμενοι σφόδρα) and speak to one another, "Surely I am not [the one]" (26:22). Peter, who claims that even though all will desert Jesus, he will "never" (οὐδέποτε) desert Jesus (26:33) and even "die with" (σὺν ἀποθανεῖν) him (26:35), ends up denying Jesus three times and weeping bitterly (26:69–75).[50] The narrative reports that "all the disciples" (οἱ μαθηταὶ πάντες) desert Jesus and flee (26:56).[51] Craig L. Blomberg observes that in Scripture, "more than just expressions of hospitality, meals increasingly establish networks of human allegiance, so that treachery against those with whom one has eaten proves all the more heinous (1 Kgs 13; 18:19)."[52] Jesus's Last Supper thus goes so far as to embrace and forgive those who deny, desert, and betray him.

Given that the meal with the disciples takes place during the Passover according to Matthew, when the people of Israel are protected and delivered from death (Exod 12:21–36), God's protection and deliverance are expressed by the power of Jesus's death to forgive the failure of the disciples. In fact, Jesus's mercy on them signals how his death is merciful for the many. In this redemptive meal, by sharing his body and blood (i.e., breaking bread and sharing a cup), Jesus mercifully gives himself to the disciples and dies for them (cf. 9:13; 12:7; 20:28), such that he becomes one with them, forgiving their faults and failure (26:26–28; cf. 6:11).[53] Their faults and failure are not strong enough to stop the spread of Jesus's forgiving power; in fact, Jesus's power is such that their faults and failure become the soil of his power for them and for others. By receiving the bread and the cup, the disciples come to receive the forgiving power of his death.[54] Accordingly, the Last Supper is a vivid expression of Jesus's forgiveness and friendship.[55]

Earlier in the narrative, Jesus teaches the community of his followers to serve and love one another, embracing even their enemies (e.g., 5:43–46; 20:26–27; 22:38). Jesus also teaches that it is not the Father's will to lose "one of these little ones" who go astray (18:12–14; cf. 10:6; 15:24). Further, Jesus teaches that the sum of the entire law and the prophets is the practice of love (22:37–40). Jesus himself embodies and fulfills his teaching by embracing the disciples at the Last Supper in the midst of their failure. Jesus takes the failure of his disciples as his own finally by shedding his blood for them on a cross. That Jesus conveys forgiveness to the disciples at the Last Supper is expressed by the way that the community of Jesus who remembers him does not give up on sinners but works at the repair of relationships broken by failure and betrayal (cf. 18:15–18). The welcome Jesus conveys to sinners earlier in the narrative (e.g., 9:9–13; 11:19) is the welcome he conveys to his disciples who deny, desert, and betray him, and thus the welcome the community of Jesus receives and conveys to sinners (cf. 18:15–18). Since Jesus already knows their failure at the Last Supper (26:21, 34), Matthew has it that Jesus forgives his disciples not simply as those who would deny, desert, and betray him but as those who had already denied, deserted, and betrayed him. Through the community of Jesus's people who shares meals that express mutual love and forgiveness, sinners are welcomed (cf. 9:9–13).[56]

As the fruit of Jesus's forgiving power, the disciples are restored to communion with Jesus and commissioned to embody and teach Jesus's words (28:19–20). In this light, Jesus's forgiveness must be understood as a transformation of life that comes by means of his death for the forgiveness of sins (26:28) and in accord with the Father's merciful character throughout the narrative (e.g., 5:45; 9:13; 12:7; 18:33). The Last Supper, then, transforms the conditions of life on the earth for the sinners who share their table with Jesus. Through this meal, Jesus heals the conditions of life for sinners and welcomes them into his community as brothers and sisters—that is, fruitful kinship with God.

THEOSIS AND THE DEATH OF JESUS

Theosis and Jesus's Blood of the Covenant in Matt 26:28

A theosis framework clarifies the concept of covenant in relation to Jesus's death. Yahweh steps intimately into history to form a covenant relationship with the people of Israel.[57] Scot McKnight defines covenant as "the promissory relationship that Yahweh would be Israel's God and Israel would be Yahweh's people."[58] In the OT, that Yahweh would be Israel's God points to the reality that Israel becomes God's child (e.g., Exod 4:22–23; Deut 8:5; Hos 11:1). That is, covenant in Scripture refers to the familial bond between Yahweh and his people, one that is manifest in the manifold earthly conditions of Israel's life. Key figures with whom Yahweh makes a covenant relationship are Abraham, Moses, and David (e.g., Gen 12:1–3; 15:6; 17:1–14; Exod 24:1–8; 1 Sam 7:8–16). In particular, Yahweh promises that he will not only be Israel's God but also live among them (Exod 29:45–46; Lev 26:12;

cf. Matt 1:23). Although the people of Israel break the Mosaic covenant (Jer 31:32), God remains faithful to his covenant and promises a "new" covenant for his people (Jer 31:31–34) that includes forgiveness and restoration (Jer 31:27–34; Ezek 34:25, 27). Rolf Rendtorff observes the nature of the new covenant in Jer 31 as follows: "the renewed and re-enacted covenant here being expressly termed 'new' for the first (and only) time. But in substance the parallelism with the renewed establishment and endorsement of the covenant in Exod 34:10 is quite clear. An essential point in this connection is that in both texts the new establishment of the covenant is indissolubly linked with the forgiveness of Israel's sins (e.g., Exod 34:9; Jer 31:34)."[59] In response to Moses's plea, God forgives Israel's sins and establishes the covenant (Exod 34:9–10). In Jeremiah, God promises that he will be Israel's God and forgives their sins (31:33–34). The nature of both covenants points to "the restoration of the covenant relationship" as envisioned in Lev 26:42–45.[60] Thus, both covenants confirm God's promise of forgiving Israel's sins.

Matthew 26:28 alludes to Exod 24, where Moses takes the blood of a slaughtered ox and dashes it on the people, which establishes "the blood of the covenant" (τὸ αἷμα τῆς διαθήκης) with God (24:8).[61] The effect of shedding blood from a sacrifice includes the forgiveness of sins through which God and his people are reconciled (cf. Lev 4:1–5:13).[62] By drawing on Exod 24:8, Matthew shows that the blood of the covenant is embodied in Jesus himself. Given Matthew's interest in the fulfillment of the OT (cf. 5:17), it seems appropriate to reason that Matt 26:28 presents Jesus's blood of the covenant as the fulfillment of the covenant envisioned in Exodus. Jesus thus enacts the covenant by blood as envisioned in Exodus, blood that restores us to become God's covenantal family, though not in the sense of sharing of biological blood.[63] In this way, those who receive the blood of Jesus become God's covenant people. Since blood signifies the source of life in Scripture (cf. Lev 17:11), Jesus's blood of the covenant establishes the life-giving bond between God and his people.[64] That is, Jesus's pouring of blood signifies his life-giving act, such that Jesus's death is the vivid expression of the Father's life-giving act in Jesus, which unites the people to God as his covenant people and thus his family. In a similar vein, John Paul Heil observes, Jesus "relates the blood to be shed by his death to the sacrificial 'blood of the covenant' that Moses threw against the altar," which was the "ceremony establishing the covenant [and] concluded with a meal that united the people of Israel in the covenantal relationship with God (Exod 24:9–11)," a familial relationship.[65]

We have seen in our study that family language is an important element of theosis (see chapter 2). Jesus enjoys the Father's knowledge and power because he relates to the Father as "the Son" (e.g., 3:17; 7:21; 11:27; 12:50; 16:16; 26:39). Sharing in Jesus's life is thus key to participating in the life of divine family. Further, Jesus shares his blood with his twelve disciples who signify the twelve tribes of Israel (cf. 10:2–6; 19:28). Through them, Israel is to be restored in its covenantal, familial relationship with God in the conditions of their life on the earth.[66] In this way, Jesus enacts reconciliation through his blood sacrifice, the offering of his life as a gift, which is key to the transformation of the conditions of Israel's life on the earth. That is, Jesus's forgiveness addresses the "death" of drought, famine, brokenness within Israel, and enmity with gentile peoples.[67] This indicates that reconciliation through the forgiveness of sins involves the healing of these conditions on the earth. Jesus's reconciliation through forgiveness, then, conveys blessings of a shared family life that repair and heal the broken relationship with God. Accordingly, the way Jesus shed his blood restores our relationship with God, empowering us to become the heirs and sharers of God's life. Forgiveness of sins through the shedding of Jesus's blood is not a matter of only imitating Jesus. It is a matter of being made a sharer, by relationship, in God's own familial life on the earth. In this regard, the theosis of forgiveness through Jesus is already anticipated in Israel's covenant history, and that history is fulfilled in Jesus, who sheds the blood of the covenant for many for the forgiveness of sins.

Matthew's allusion to Jer 31:31–34, where Israel's God promises to make a new covenant with the people of Israel (31:31), shows a further aspect of theosis.[68] Jeremiah envisions the forgiveness of sins as part of this new covenant (31:34). Joel B. Green observes that the prophet Jeremiah "anticipates the time when God would renew the covenant with his people, forgiving their iniquity and remembering their sin no more" ("I will forgive their iniquity and remember their sin no more," Jer 31:34).[69] The advent of this era has arrived, Jesus declares in his final Passover meal, as Jesus enacts the covenant that conveys the forgiveness of sins (26:28). In the context of Jeremiah, the prophet shows the renewal of God's covenant with his people in terms of Israel's return to the land and the end of enmity with gentiles (31:8–10, 16–17, 23; cf. 24:6).[70] In this process, Jeremiah envisions that God's forgiveness brings the transformation and healing of Israel's bodily life on the earth (31:13–14; cf. 31:3; 2 Chr 7:14). The themes of Israel's return and healing involve Israel's repentance (31:18–19) and a renewed relationship with God (31:31–34). This healing is not merely a one-off transaction but a process of transformation of the fabric of Israel's life, with respect to peace with gentile peoples. In the process of the transformation of Israel's life, God's mercy is operative for his people (31:3, 20), and, as a result, Israel is depicted as God's child—that is, its life is an expression of the Father-children relationship (31:9, 20). Similar to the covenant envisioned in Exodus, God's renewing of the covenant with his people in Jeremiah is also associated with restoring the familial relationship with Israel. By drawing on Jeremiah, Matthew describes Jesus's death as effecting the promised covenant in which Israel's bodily life is repaired and healed.[71] By forgiving his people's sins envisioned in Jeremiah, Jesus repairs the relationship between God and his people, thereby restoring their fellowship and thus the mutual flow of life such as the relationship of mutual care, forgiveness, and healing (31:34). Furthermore, Jeremiah sees that Israel is healed as God's covenant people by the way they embody God's way as God's laws are inscribed on their hearts (31:33).[72] That God's laws are inscribed on their hearts implies a renewal of the mind—that is, the rending of their wicked hearts (31:34; cf. Ezek 36:26; Matt 27:54).[73] As a result, their hearts are transformed in a way that mirrors and displays God's ways. In line with Jeremiah's vision, Jesus's shedding the blood of the covenant enables and empowers his people to participate in and enact God's merciful ways, knowledge, and character as sharers in God's own life.

Discipleship as Participation in Jesus's Cruciform Life in Matt 26:37–42

Earlier in this study (see chapter 3), we observed the extension of God's own forgiving power working itself out through Jesus in the community of Jesus (9:8; 10:1). Participation in the life of Jesus, which is the life of God as Jesus is the presence of God-with-us (1:23), is a matter of the transformation of the reality of the human, namely, discipleship. As Michael J. Gorman observes, "[D]iscipleship is not about imitation or even obedience to an external call or norm. It is about transformation, theosis."[74] Thus, discipleship is not merely following Jesus or imitating what Jesus does. As the narrative unfolds, Matthew shows a further aspect of theosis, with respect to discipleship as participation in Jesus's cruciform life, the very light of God reflected in them through Jesus. For Matthew, taking up the cross is presented as a metaphor for discipleship (e.g., 10:38–39; 16:24–25). Discipleship as theosis is divinely empowered human life, such that God exercises God's own power in us. We thus reflect Jesus's cruciform life as the result of God's forgiving power working itself out in our lives (cf. 18:27, 33).

After the Last Supper with the disciples, Jesus prays in Gethsemane in the face of his death. Jesus's Gethsemane prayer is about forgiveness as he discerns the Father's will during the prayer and willingly accepts bearing a cross and thus shedding blood for the forgiveness of sins: "your will be done" (γενηθήτω τὸ θέλημά σου, 26:42; cf. 6:10, 12; 18:18–20).[75] For Matthew, to forgive is to renounce any requirement of retribution because to wield forgiving power from heaven is not to destroy one's enemies or to avoid death but to love one's enemies and submit one's will to God's unto death (5:44; 16:24–25; 26:42). Thus, the life of the cross—suffering and death—is connected to Jesus's life specifically in terms of forgiveness. The cross by nature is not for the sake of himself but "for many for the forgiveness of sins" (26:28), such that Jesus gives up his right to defend himself (27:12–14) and thus submits his right to the Father (26:42). As Matthew portrays the matter, to embody that forgiveness is not easy but involves a painful process. In Gethsemane, Jesus himself is deeply grieved as he has to take the cup of suffering—that is, the cross he has to bear (26:37–39).[76] Jesus struggles by throwing himself on the ground and praying to the Father that the cup of suffering may pass from him, "if it is possible" (26:39). At the end of this painful process of struggling, Jesus submits to the will of the Father in heaven—death for the forgiveness of sins—thereby manifesting the Father's will on earth (26:28, 42; cf. 16:21; 17:22–23; 20:28). Thus, the nature of Jesus's death is portrayed as an act of obedience to the Father in heaven (26:42). It is through Jesus's obedient death, then, as the culmination of Jesus's life, that Jesus saves his people from their sins (cf. 1:21).

A theosis framework suggests a more nuanced understanding of Jesus's prayerful forgiveness. In his Gethsemane prayer, Jesus invites the disciples to pray together: "stay awake with me" (γρηγορεῖτε μετ' ἐμοῦ, 26:38).[77] Jesus emphasizes the practice of prayer twice more before his arrest (26:40–41; cf. 24:42–43; 25:13). The phrase "with me" (μετ' ἐμοῦ) indicates "the bond between Jesus and his disciples" (cf. 1:23; 26:18, 20, 29).[78] Also, the phrase resonates with 1:23, where Matthew narrates that God is "with us" (μεθ' ἡμῶν) in Jesus. This suggests that the disciples can share in divine fellowship in and through Jesus, who is God's presence with us. Since Jesus embodies God's presence (1:23), those who share in Jesus's life also participate in God's life. Accordingly, Jesus's sharing his own life with others itself is God's life with us. We thus participate in God's life that is in Jesus. Since Jesus addresses God as Father in this prayer (26:39; cf. 6:9), his injunction to pray together with him invites the disciples to participate in the life of God. Being watchful prayerfully with Jesus, then, is to share in divine fellowship. Further, to participate in Jesus's prayer signals our share in his suffering (26:38, 40). Thus, Jesus's injunction to his disciples to pray with him includes imparting the communion of Father and Son to the disciples through their sharing his suffering and death for the forgiveness of sins. They do this partly by the remembrance of their failure to keep watch and their caving to temptation when they forsook Jesus, who nevertheless did not forsake them. The underlying implication of Jesus's injunction to pray together is that just as Jesus embodies forgiveness as a way of life that leads to the cross, so his followers are called to share in the life of the cross. We as disciples of Jesus thus embody forgiveness as an extension of Jesus's cruciform life (e.g., 5:44–45; 6:12, 14–15; 10:38–39; 11:29–30; 16:24–25; 18:5, 20; 28:20).

The extension of Jesus's cruciform life to his followers is not a sudden invention at this juncture of the narrative (i.e., Matt 26). In his mission discourse, for instance, Jesus teaches that "it is adequate (ἀρκετός) for the disciple to be like (ὡς) the teacher" (10:25).[79] In context, to be like the teacher, Jesus, is itself to embody his life, even his death (10:38–39). For Matthew, anyone who does not take up his or her cross and loses his or her life for the sake of Jesus is not worthy of Jesus (10:37–39; 16:24–25).[80] Jesus also teaches that before they enter into glory with Jesus, the disciples are called to share in his suffering and death (20:22–23; 26:28). To share in the life and glory of Jesus, then, is to share in his cup of suffering (20:22). Just as Jesus suffers and dies, so his followers are called to embody the loss of his life in the way they give of their own. This implies that Jesus's suffering and death do not exempt others from such burdens but empowers them to carry the very burdens that put Jesus on the cross (cf. 11:29–30).[81] What theosis allows us to see is that Jesus's life of the cross is not only the model but also the enabling basis of the disciples' life of the cross. That is, Jesus's teaching of discipleship empowers his followers to share in Jesus's own forgiveness, even his death. The life of Jesus and the life of the disciples, then, are tied together through sharing in the life of the cross.[82] It is through sharing in the life of the cross that we become like (ὡς) Jesus, thereby participating in God's own life.

Jesus's Death and the Heaven-Earth Relation in Matt 27:51–54

The pericope under consideration offers a telling witness to the death of Jesus, with respect to the dynamic relation between heaven and earth and thus between God and the human, which can be seen more clearly through the lens of theosis. Through his sacrificial death for the forgiveness of sins,[83] Jesus enacts with a kind of finality the transformative, relational dynamics of heaven and earth. Matthew reports the tearing of the temple veil as the direct effect of Jesus's death, thus signaling the dynamics of the heaven-earth relation (27:50–51). To begin, it is worth observing the significance of the veil that is torn at the death of Jesus. In the OT, the sanctuary—the spaces of the Holy Place and the Holy of Holies—signifies God's presence among the people (e.g., Exod 25:8; 1 Kgs 8:6–11).[84] At the heart of God's presence is the Holy of Holies (Lev 16:2).[85] Since Matthew uses the singular noun "veil" (καταπέτασμα), the torn veil in 27:51 could be either the outer veil that covers the entrance to the sanctuary or the inner veil that divides the Holy Place from the Holy of Holies and conceals the ark of the covenant (e.g., Exod 26:31–37).[86] Matthew does not specify which of the two curtains of the temple is torn (27:51).[87] In Exodus LXX, the term καταπέτασμα, translated from the Hebrew term פרכת, is used to refer to the inner veil that separates the Holy place from the Holy of Holies (26:33).[88] Gurtner observes that "the 'inner veil' appears as פרכת 26 times in the MT, and פרכת never refers to anything but the 'inner veil.' Of its 26 occurrences in the MT, 25 [occurrences] refer to the inner veil of the tabernacle and 1 (2 Chr 3:14) to the inner veil of Solomon's temple."[89] On the day of atonement for the forgiveness of sins, Aaron and his sons alone could enter behind the inner veil (פרכת, καταπέτασμα) and make sin offerings (Lev 16:2, 12, 15; cf. Num 18:7). In the NT, the term καταπέτασμα appears outside the Gospels only in Hebrews. In Hebrews, καταπέτασμα refers to the inner veil in conjunction with the role of the chief priest (6:19–20; 9:3, 7; cf. Exod 26:31–35; Lev 16:1–5).[90] Given that the פרכת veil functions to regulate our access to God's very presence in the Holy of Holies, through the priesthood, the rending of the inner veil signifies the extension of Yahweh's presence among his people as promised in Jesus, who is God-with-us (1:23). Since this inner veil can be penetrated only on the day of atonement when the blood of a sacrifice is sprinkled on the front of the mercy seat (Lev 16:14, 19), Jesus's shedding of blood for the forgiveness of sins serves to enable and empower our access to the very presence of God, not only to the Holy Place (cf. Exod 24:8; Lev 16:2; Heb 9:7).[91] Thus, in Matthew, the torn veil is most likely the inner veil, the veil before the Holy of Holies.[92] As Paul Lamarche rightly puts it, "Par la mort du Christ le voile se déchire, le Saint des Saints nous est révélé, et il nous est donné, par la foi du Christ, d'entrer gratuitement dans la demeure et l'intimité du vrai Dieu."[93]

The significance of the rending lies in our access to the fullness of God's presence, which takes place at the death of Jesus. Given that the veil limits human access, the rending can be understood as a removal of the veil that separates (בדל) us from God, thus enabling our access to the presence of the Father in heaven (cf. 11:25–27),[94] which was only permissible to the chief priests (e.g., Lev 16:1–5; Num 4:20; 18:1–7; cf. 2 Cor 3:16–18; Eph 2:11–19; Heb 6:20; 10:19). This is not to say that the veil was an impediment to God's forgiveness. The veil limited our access to protect us from God's lethal glory.[95] The veil thus reveals God's merciful protection for his people rather than a mere separation. More importantly, given that the veil also functioned as mediation between God and Israel, through the priesthood, and thereby mediation between God and other peoples, who were in various relationship with Israel as priest (e.g., 8:5–13; 27:54), the rending of the veil brings the fullness of God's presence that is in Jesus (cf. 1:23). That is to say, the rending brings the full mediation of God's presence to his people through Jesus's forgiveness and death. Jesus, then, is the mediation of heaven and earth that ministers God's forgiveness. This is in some ways resonant with the extension of God's knowledge, which was uniquely shared between Father and Son (e.g., 11:25–27), to his people through Jesus (e.g., 1:23; 6:9; 9:8; 10:1; 18:18–20; cf. 28:19–20). The intimate, privileged access to the Father Jesus has is extended to his followers through his atoning death, much as God's presence is accessed by means of the blood of sacrifices (e.g., Lev 16:14,

19).[96] Jesus's death is thus the means by which Jesus shares God's presence with us, being God-with-us (1:23).

The rending of the veil at the death of Jesus further invites us to see the transformative, relational dynamics of heaven and earth (e.g., 5:34–35; 6:9–10; 9:2, 6; 18:18–20; 28:18). The rending of the veil is parallel to the rending of heaven in Jesus's baptism (3:16).[97] The passive verb ἠνεῴχθησαν in 3:16 is a divine passive,[98] with the result that the opening of heaven is the result of God's action from heaven. Likewise, the passive verb ἐσχίσθη in 27:51 indicates God's action from heaven. This is evidenced by Matthew's portrayal that the veil of the sanctuary is torn "from top to bottom" (ἀπ' ἄνωθεν ἕως κάτω, 27:51).[99] The direction of this rending is downward, from heaven to earth. Both the opening of heaven in 3:16 and the rending from heaven in 27:51, then, are God's action from heaven (cf. Isa 64:1). That the veil is torn from top to bottom, from heaven to earth, suggests that God acts from heaven through Jesus's death to tear the veil. That is, God's heavenly power is decisively revealed at the death of Jesus. This suggests that Jesus's death is a way of theosis as God decisively acts in human flesh that is in Jesus.

Jesus's death ushers in cosmic events in history that display the dynamics of heaven and earth—the rending of the veil, earthquake, opening of the tombs, and raising of the dead and their entrance to Jerusalem (27:51–52). The tearing of the veil is first and is followed by the earthquake, the rending of the rocks, the opening of the tombs, and the raising of the dead.[100] The logical order of these cosmic events is significant. Again, the passive verbs—ἐσείσθη (27:51), ἐσχίσθησαν (27:51), ἀνεῴχθησαν (27:52), and ἠγέρθησαν (27:52)—indicate that these events are the result of God's action (cf. 1 Kgs 19:11; Isa 48:21; Nahum 1:5–6). The raising of the dead as a consequence of the earthquake is the culminating act of God in Jesus's death (cf. Isa 52:1–2; Ezek 37:11–14; Dan 12:2; Zech 14:5; 1 En. 93:6). The cosmic events happening at the death of Jesus are particularly associated with the eschatological vision of Ezekiel, where dry bones rise and return to their homeland from exile (Ezek 37:11–14).[101] By alluding to Ezekiel's vision, Matthew shows that God enacts restoration in and through the death of Jesus (cf. Ezek 37:6, 13–14).[102] That is, God's action in Jesus brings the transformation and healing of Israel's bodily life on the earth as the people of Israel return to their homeland from exile (27:52–53; cf. 9:7). This eschatological transformation is linked to the confession of the centurion and the soldiers with him—"Son of God" (θεοῦ υἱός, 27:54; cf. 2:15; 3:17; 17:5; 26:39).[103] That is, a key expression of this transformative hope in Matthew's scene of Jesus's death is the gentile enemy's echoing the words of Israel's God about Jesus as Son (27:54). The forgiveness of Israel's sins is a matter of peace with its gentile enemies on the earth, the seed of which is presented in the confessing centurion—Son of God—at the cross as Jesus dies. Given that the centurion and the Roman soldiers with him are gentile enemies who are involved in Jesus's torture and death, that they are moved by Jesus's death points to a seed for peace with gentile peoples.[104] Consequently, Jesus's death transforms Israel's condition of life on the earth, with respect to peace with its gentile enemies (cf. 8:11; 15:27–28; 28:19).

That Jesus is revealed as God's Son at his death reveals the transformative fatherhood of God, thus pointing to the significance of the Father-Son relationship (cf. 11:27; 12:50). That is to say, the Father-Son relation is manifest in and through the Father's heavenly power at the death of his Son. This gives us the insight that we participate in God's power in Jesus's death by sharing in the Father-Son relationship. The Father-Son relation, then, is the context of our transformative participation in the divine life, namely, theosis. As we have seen in this study (see chapter 2), Jesus's unique filial relation to his Father is shared with Jesus's followers, as his Father is the same Father we know as such (e.g., 6:9). We thus become God's children, the heirs and sharers of God's power, in and through Jesus. In becoming God's children and heirs through Jesus, we receive God's life, thereby participating in God's presence, knowledge, and power (cf. 6:9–10; 10:1; 11:25–27; 18:18–20; 28:18–20). It is through this familial relationship, then, that we come to enact God's power from heaven like Jesus (cf. 9:6, 8; 10:1).

At the end of the narrative, Jesus declares that "all power in heaven and on earth" (πᾶσα ἐξουσία ἐν οὐρανῷ καὶ ἐπὶ [τῆς] γῆς, 28:18) has been given to him—that is, power over the entire cosmos (28:18; cf. Phil 2:9–11; Col 1:18–20; Eph 1:20–22).[105] That Jesus has "all power" in heaven and on earth confirms Matthew's earlier presentation of Jesus as the Son who receives "all things" (πάντα) from the Father in heaven (11:27).[106] This is also confirmed by Jesus's healing of a paralyzed person in Capernaum, where he, as the Son of Man, extends God's forgiving power from heaven to human life (9:6). Likewise, his death produces an extension of heavenly reality on earth, rending the veil from top to bottom (27:51). Moreover, Jesus commands his disciples to teach, to spread "all things" (πάντα) he has commanded them (28:20), with particular focus on his discourses of teaching that structure the narrative. The adjective πάντα refers to his life in its totality including his forgiveness, suffering, and death. Thus, the disciples are called to reflect the life Jesus teaches. Since Jesus has fully inherited God's power in heaven and on earth as Son and heir (11:27; 28:18; cf. 1:23; 3:17), he shows the path his followers will take. That is, by sharing in Jesus's life of forgiveness, we come to fully inherit what Jesus is, thereby becoming God's children and God's heirs, sharing in Jesus's own power, his power as himself God-with-us (cf. 12:50).

Matthew's narrative concludes with Jesus's promise of his ongoing presence with his people (28:20; cf. 1:23). Jesus's presence in the community of discipleship means we have continued access to his living memory, whereby we learn and reflect his own life and participate in his presence. Thus, Jesus is God's ongoing presence with us, transforming our life into God's life, which does not become a life that is less ours but the fullest expression of ourselves. We as disciples of Jesus carry on his forgiving work in his name (18:20), God-with-us, "the name of the Father and of the Son and of the Holy Spirit" (28:19). We thus provide a faithful witness to the kingdom from heaven, embodying forgiveness wrought by Jesus in the Spirit.

SUMMARY

This chapter endeavored to demonstrate the nature of Jesus's death in terms of theosis, especially with respect to the transformative, relational dynamic between God and the human and thus between heaven and earth. For this purpose, I examined Matthew's presentation of forgiveness throughout the narrative and how 26:28 expresses the culmination of God's forgiveness narratively. From the beginning of the narrative, Jesus's death is anticipated as he is declared as one who delivers his people from their sins (1:21). Accordingly, Jesus's mission is oriented to delivering his people from their sins, specifically through embodying merciful forgiveness and healing (e.g., 9:2–8, 13; 12:7; 21:31–32), which culminates in the Last Supper, where Jesus is about to depart from the disciples, and he looks forward to his death for the forgiveness of sins (26:28). I then considered the nature of Jesus's table fellowship because in Matthew, Jesus's table fellowship often expresses his forgiveness (e.g., 9:9–13; 11:19; 26:20–29; cf. 15:27). Although not all occasions of table fellowship are occasions in which people are forgiven in Matthew, Jesus's meals in Matthew often convey the hope that sinners are being forgiven and welcome. Regardless of the disciples' failure, in fact through their failure, Jesus's table fellowship with them in the Last Supper is an expression of forgiveness and friendship. Next, I examined how the nature of Jesus's death can be conceived in the framework of theosis, with respect to Jesus's shedding the blood of the covenant for the forgiveness of sins envisioned in the OT, discipleship, and the heaven-earth relation in Matthew. Jesus's death enacts the promised covenant as envisioned in Exodus and Jeremiah and effects the transformative, relational dynamics of heaven and earth, that is, the oneness of God and his people and thus the oneness of heaven and earth (27:51–53; 28:18; cf. 11:25–27). Consequently, Jesus's life of forgiveness and death effects our transformative relationship with God—our life as God's children and heirs (1:23; 5:44–45; 6:9; 11:19; 12:50; 28:19–20).

NOTES

1. The Lord's Supper is identified in various ways, such as "the Holy Communion," "the Last Supper," "the Breaking of Bread," and "the Eucharist." On this issue, see I. Howard Marshall, *Last Supper and Lord's Supper* (Exeter: Paternoster, 1980), 14–15. In this study, I use the term "the Last Supper" to indicate Jesus's last table meal with the disciples before his death.

2. On the thematic importance of forgiveness in the Last Supper, see, e.g., Paul Kunjanayil, "The Interconnection between the Emmanuel Theme and the Forgiveness of Sins Theme in the Gospel of Matthew," *Studia Biblica Slovaca* 13, no. 1 (2021): 20–48, esp. 34–42; Paul M. Hoskins, "A Neglected Allusion to Leviticus 4–5 in Jesus's Words Concerning His Blood in Matthew 26:28," *BBR* 30, no. 2 (2020): 231–42; John Paul Heil, "The Blood of Jesus in Matthew: A Narrative-Critical Perspective," *PRSt* 18, no. 2 (1991): 117–24. But scholars have not provided adequate attention to the death of Jesus according to the significance of theosis.

3. On the overlapping meanings of salvation and forgiveness, see chapter 1, n. 4, above.

4. Kunjanayil, "Emmanuel Theme," 22.

5. The patterns of God's saving Israel from their sins envisioned in Jer 31 will be discussed further below.

6. Daniel M. Gurtner, *The Torn Veil: Matthew's Exposition of the Death of Jesus*, SNTSMS 139 (Cambridge: Cambridge University Press, 2007), 128.

7. Dale C. Allison Jr. calls the six key scenes that anticipate Jesus's passion "intratextual allusions" (*Studies in Matthew: Interpretation Past and Present* [Grand Rapids: Baker Academic, 2005], 233–34; see further, pp. 218–32).

8. Jonah's sign in 12:40 (i.e., the Son of Man's three days and three nights like Jonah) alludes to Jesus's death. On the connection between Jonah's sign and Jesus's death, see Ulrich Luz, *Matthew 8–20: A Commentary*, trans. James E. Crouch, Hermeneia (Minneapolis: Fortress, 2001), 217.

9. On further connection between John the Baptist and Jesus, see n. 38, below.

10. Allison observes that in both scenes, the number six appears: "after six days" (17:1) and "from the sixth hour" (27:45) (*Studies in Matthew*, 228).

11. The theme of suffering discipleship we find in 5:38–42 continues in 10:17–23. Like Jesus, the innocently suffering righteous one (27:4, 19), the disciples will be handed over (10:17–21). Like Jesus, so the disciples will be brought before governors and kings and whipped (10:17–18; 26:59; cf. 27:1–2, 11–26). Like Jesus, they will have the Spirit come upon them to bear testimony (10:20; cf. 3:16; 4:1; 12:28). Like Jesus, they will be betrayed by their loved ones (10:21; cf. 26:14–16, 21, 34, 56).

12. Richard Beaton, *Isaiah's Christ in Matthew's Gospel*, SNTSMS 123 (Cambridge: Cambridge University Press, 2002), 18.

13. By necessity, I mean Jesus's suffering must take place according to God's will (26:39, 42).

14. On the connection between Jesus's suffering and Yahweh's Suffering Servant in Isaiah, see Joel B. Green, *The Death of Jesus: Tradition and Interpretation in the*

Passion Narrative, WUNT 2/33 (Tübingen: Mohr Siebeck, 1988; Eugene, OR: Wipf & Stock, 2011), 239–40. Citations refer to the Wipf & Stock edition.

15. Matthew 20:28 narrates, "The Son of Man did not come to be served but to serve and to give his life [as] a ransom (λύτρον) for many" (cf. Isa 53). Ransom means "deliverance by payment," indicating "the manumission of slaves and release of prisoners of war." Since the payment is made with Jesus's life, "the life for life principle is here operative" (e.g., Exod 21:28–32; Lev 25:51–52; Num 18:15). See W. D. Davies and D. C. Allison Jr., *Matthew 19–28: A Critical and Exegetical Commentary on the Gospel according to Saint Matthew*, ICC (London: T&T Clark, 2004), 95. Scholars have debated the connection between 20:28 and 26:28. R. T. France, for example, argues that the expression "for many" in 26:28 is familiar to us from 20:28, with respect to "the purpose of Jesus's death" (*The Gospel of Matthew*, NICNT [Grand Rapids: Eerdmans, 2007], 994). J. Christopher Edwards, however, contends that "there is no evidence from the reception history that the ransom logion is ever associated with the Eucharist, or Last Supper traditions from the synoptics or Paul" (*The Ransom Logion in Mark and Matthew: Its Reception and Its Significance for the Study of the Gospels*, WUNT 327 [Tübingen: Mohr Siebeck, 2012], 116; see pp. 118–21). While the explicit verbal connection between 20:28 and 26:28 may be lacking, the motif of giving up one's life operates both in the ransom logion and in the Last Supper. The cross-reference in the margin of Matt 20:28 in NA[28] also points to Matt 26:28 and Isa 53:10–12 LXX. See also Luz (*Matthew 8–20*, 546), who notes that Matt 20:28 is "an organic train of thought that begins (v. 18) and ends (v. 28) with the suffering of the Son of Man."

16. The disciples' participation in Jesus's own suffering and self-giving will be discussed further below.

17. For further discussion on Jesus's delivering power for his people sitting in darkness, see chapter 3.

18. Isaiah 53:4 reads: "He took our weaknesses and bore [our] diseases." Leroy A. Huizenga argues that Matthew's quotation of Isa 53:4 in 8:17 is concerned with healing and Gentile inclusion rather than Jesus's suffering (*The New Isaac Tradition and Intertextuality in the Gospel of Matthew*, NovTSup 131 [Leiden: Brill, 2009], 198–201). But Jesus's healing is related to his suffering, since his healing and forgiving ministry climactically issues in his suffering and death.

19. Donald Senior adequately notices the meaning of Jesus's death in relation to the suffering people of God: "The fact that crucifixion was a punishment reserved primarily for slaves, lower classes, and foreigners without rights—what the majority might view as the dregs of society—brings a startling depth of meaning to the association of Jesus with the poor and the outcasts" (*Why the Cross?*, Reforming New Testament Theology [Nashville: Abingdon, 2014], 7).

20. Rowan Williams, *Christ on Trial: How the Gospel Unsettles Our Judgement* (Grand Rapids: Eerdmans, 2000), xi. Williams goes on to say that the image of God revealed in Jesus is not a version of "whatever makes us feel secure and appears more attractive than other familiar kinds of security" (15). It is "precisely at the moment when no worldly condition secures or makes sense of this" that Jesus shares in who God is (22).

21. This resonates with Paul's teaching: "For whenever I am weak, then I am strong" (2 Cor 12:10). For Paul, the way God's power dwells in him is revealed in his weakness (12:9). On the relation between God's power and the weakness of Jesus, see also Dietrich Bonhoeffer, *Christ the Center*, trans. Edwin H. Robertson (New York: Harper & Row, 1978), 46–47, 54.

22. Tommy Givens, "The Election of Israel and the Politics of Jesus: Revisiting John Howard Yoder's *The Jewish Christian Schism Revisited*," *Journal of the Society of Christian Ethics* 31, no. 2 (2011): 88.

23. In Matthew's narrative, Jesus shares the meal table with tax collectors and sinners (e.g., 9:9–13; 11:19), and a Canaanite woman, a person representing Israel's historic enemy (15:21–28), thereby embracing Israel's enemies (cf. 5:44–55; 12:18–21; 28:19–20). Jesus continues to touch the lives of gentiles (8:5–13), drawing them to Israel to grow into "one people of covenant peace" (cf. 12:18–21; 28:19–20). See Givens, "Election of Israel," 89.

24. In Matthew's conception, one of the significant elements in this genealogy lies in a figure named David (1:6). Like Abraham, David's name forms an *inclusio* within the genealogy (1:1, 17). According to a Jewish numerological system (i.e., gematria), each letter of David's name in Hebrew (דוד) is numbered as four (ד), six (ו), and four (ד), which is fourteen in sum. Matthew sees David as a key to understanding who Jesus is—that is, Israel's king. In line with the significance of the number fourteen, Matthew divides Jesus's genealogy into three sets of fourteen generations—from Abraham to David, from David to the deportation to Babylon, and from the deportation to Babylon to Jesus the Messiah (1:17). Matthew has conceived this scheme because David is also in the fourteenth position from Abraham in 1 Chronicles. Matthew tells us that Jesus comes as the Son of David (1:1, 6, 17; 21:9), such that he has a legal right to sit on the throne of David. In line with his birth, Jesus dies as Israel's king (27:37). Jesus as Son of David exercises his kingly rule not by dominating others but by humbly serving others (18:5; 20:26–27), specifically through embodying forgiveness. Since Jesus is also presented as the Son of God (e.g., 16:16; 27:43, 54), he is not only the legal king of Israel but also the legal heir of the Father in heaven. As Steven M. Bryan observes, "If the portrayal of Jesus's kingship as specifically Davidic is important for Matthew, so too are other themes introduced within the genealogy. Thus, the genealogy designates Jesus not only as the son of David but also as the son of Abraham and as the Christ" ("Onomastics and Numerical Composition in the Genealogy of Matthew," *BBR* 30.4 [2020]: 519; see further, pp. 522–39).

25. Catherine Sider Hamilton, *The Death of Jesus in Matthew: Innocent Blood and the End of Exile*, SNTSMS 167 (New York: Cambridge University Press, 2017), 196. See also Richard B. Hays ("The Gospel of Matthew: Reconfigured Torah," *HTS* 61 [2005]: 187), who notes that Israel's Scripture in Matthew's narrative is "a story that outlines a broad arc of God's dealing with Israel. It is a story whose plot may be summed up in the following narrative sequence: election, kingship, sin, exile, and messianic salvation. This is precisely the plot sketched in the *opening genealogy*" (emphasis mine).

26. Donald Senior notes that λαός is used in a "collective sense" in Matthew's Gospel, referring to the people of Israel "as a whole" (*The Passion Narrative according to*

Matthew: A Redactional Study, BETL 39 [Leuven: Leuven University Press, 1975], 259). Similarly, Hamilton notes that the phrase πᾶς ὁ λαός refers to "the people of Israel in its entirety (e.g., Deut 27:15–26; Josh 1:2; 3:17; 4:1; 6:5; 10:15; Judg 20:8; 2 Sam 8:15; 2 Chr 7:4–5; 36:23)" (*Death of Jesus*, 185–86). She adds that, "in Deuteronomy, the term πᾶς ὁ λαός is connected not only to the constitution of the people as the covenant people, but to their future in the land" (186). As such, Hamilton notes, "By his use of the term πᾶς ὁ λαός" (27:25) reflected in Jeremiah, Matthew suggests that in his narrative, "what is at issue in the blood of the innocent poured out upon the land is exile, Jerusalem's defeat and the loss of the land (23:36–9; 24:2ff)" (187). The prophet Jeremiah says to the rulers and all the people (πᾶς ὁ λαός) that if they put him to death, they will bring innocent blood (αἷμα ἀθῷον) on themselves and on this city and its inhabitants (33:12–15 LXX). First Enoch 6–11 and Jub. 6–7 similarly narrate that blood brings flood and disasters to the land. But this is not to say that Matthew's terms are anti-Jewish. The opposition to Jesus is due in part to their misconstrual of God's will who mercifully embodies forgiveness. Donald Senior notes, "Matthew's words cannot be understood as anti-Jewish or anti-semitic. . . . God's graciously offered message of love and forgiveness is paradoxically rejected. Such rejection leads to judgment but also to repeated offers of forgiveness when Israel comes to its senses and accepts God's mercy" (*The Passion of Jesus in the Gospel of Matthew*, The Passion Series [Wilmington, DE: Glazier, 1985], 120). In a similar vein, Hamilton notes, "The holy ones who are raised are Jewish" saints (27:52–53) and "the women who announce the resurrection with joy are Jewish" (28:8) (*Death of Jesus*, 225).

27. The sense of the term "many" in 26:28 is not "some, as opposed to others who are denied the redemptive benefits of the death of Jesus, but all." See John T. Carroll and Joel B. Green, "'His Blood on Us and on Our Children': The Death of Jesus in the Gospel according to Matthew," in *The Death of Jesus in Early Christianity* (Peabody, MA: Hendrickson, 1995), 44. Matthew could possibly relate "the many" for whom Jesus's blood is shed with Abraham's fatherhood in Gen 17:5 LXX. Just as many nations come to inherit the blessings promised to Abraham, so many will be forgiven and blessed by Jesus's forgiveness of sins, who comes to fulfill Abrahamic blessing (1:1; cf. 8:11; 28:19). See Tommy Givens, *We the People: Israel and the Catholicity of Jesus* (Minneapolis: Fortress, 2014), 327. Cf. Exod 1:9; 12:35–39; Hos 1:10–11; Isa 25:6–7; 52:14; 53:12; 56:7. Regarding the language of "many," Matthew could possibly draw on Isa 53:12 LXX, where the prophet Isaiah also declares that "his soul was handed over to death, and he was accounted among the lawless ones, and he bore [the] sins of many (ἁμαρτίας πολλῶν) and was handed over because of their sins." See Joachim Jeremias, *The Eucharistic Words of Jesus*, trans. Norman Perrin, The New Testament Library (London: SCM, 1966), 227–29.

28. E. P. Sanders observes that the significance of Jesus's eating with sinners is not primarily concerned with purity: "from the point of view of Judaism, everyone, except the priests, often live in a state of ritual impurity," such that the Pharisees did not think that the failure to eat food in ritual purity was a sin (*Jesus and Judaism* [Philadelphia: Fortress, 1985], 210). In this sense, sinners in Jesus's time were not simply those who did not keep the purity laws of the Pharisees. For further discussion on purity issues, see Yair Furstenberg, "The Shared Image of Pharisaic Law in the

Gospels and Rabbinic Tradition," in *The Pharisees*, ed. Joseph Sievers and Amy-Jill Levine (Grand Rapids: Eerdmans, 2021), 199–219.

29. Mark Allan Powell, "Table Fellowship," in *DJG*, 925. In Gen 26:26–31, Isaac makes a covenant with Abimelech, holding a feast. In the Passover meal, Jesus also makes a covenant (διαθήκη) with his disciples (26:28).

30. Marshall, *Last Supper*, 18.

31. Ibid., 19.

32. Jeremias, *Eucharistic Words of Jesus*, 204. In Gen 43:25–34, for example, Joseph invites his brothers to his table as an expression of reconciliation and forgiveness (cf. 45:5–9; 50:20).

33. Ibid. Cf. Josephus narrates that King Agrippa invites Silas to his table as his guest to signify that he forgives him (*Ant.* 19.321).

34. Powell, "Table Fellowship," 925. That Matthew links tax collectors with prostitutes and sinners (11:19; 21:32) shows that tax collectors would have been regarded as sinners in Matthew's narrative world (cf. 9:9–13).

35. The "breaking" of the bread could primarily mean "distribution" rather than "killing" as Jesus distributes it to the disciples. See Marshall, *Last Supper*, 86. But since the bread signifies Jesus's body (26:26), it could also mean his death as his body is broken and dead on a cross (27:26, 50). The cup clearly refers to Jesus's death in Matthew's narrative (e.g., 20:22; 26:39), containing the blood of the covenant. The blood especially speaks of "violent" death. By violent, I mean actions that enact physical harm or death. The bread and the cup become one of the important elements of Christian worship (e.g., 1 Cor 10:14–22; 11:17–34).

36. Joel B. Green, "Narrative Criticism," in *Methods for Luke*, ed. Joel B. Green, Methods in Biblical Interpretation (Cambridge: Cambridge University Press, 2010), 95.

37. When Jesus sits at the table ("while he was eating," NLT), a woman comes in with an alabaster jar of ointment and pours it on Jesus's head (26:7). The woman's act is viewed variously as part of celebration, the anointing of Jesus who is Israel's king, priest, and Messiah, and honoring of Jesus. Cf. Exod 29:7; Lev 21:10; Pss 23:5; 45:7–8; 133:2; Prov 27:9 LXX; Isa 61:3; Wis 2:7–9. See the lengthier discussion by John Nolland, *The Gospel of Matthew*, NIGTC (Grand Rapids: Eerdmans, 2005), 1052–55; France, *Gospel of Matthew*, 974; Davies and Allison, *Matthew 19–28*, 445–48.

38. *Contra* Sanders (*Jesus and Judaism*, 200–211), who contends that "Jesus did not call sinners to repent as normally understood, which involved restitution and/or sacrifice, but rather to accept his message, which promised them the kingdom. This would have been offensive to normal piety" (210). Sanders insists that the message of John the Baptist was focused on repentance, but Jesus did not emphasize repentance (though he did assume it), requiring only obedience to his message (206, 322). From the beginning of the narrative, however, Jesus calls sinners to repentance in light of the coming kingdom from heaven (4:17). Jesus's ministry thus encompasses what John the Baptist proclaims in his preaching. This suggests that to enter the kingdom in Matthew involves an ethic of repentance—a turning from one way of life to another that aligns with the kingdom (e.g., 5:1–7:27). As the narrative unfolds, Jesus critiques the unrepentant cities (11:20, 23). Matthew 21:31–32 also narrates that the tax

collectors and the prostitutes "repent" (μεταμέλομαι) and believe the message of John the Baptist, thereby entering the kingdom of God. This also suggests the continuity between John the Baptist and Jesus, with respect to repentance. On further parallelism between Jesus and John the Baptist, see Allison, *Studies in Matthew*, 225–26; Janice Capel Anderson, *Matthew's Narrative Web: Over, and Over, and Over Again*, JSNTSup 91 (Sheffield: JSOT Press, 1994), 172–74.

39. The fish in the feeding miracle cannot be equated with the cup of wine in any sense. But the feeding in the desert commonly points to Jesus's provision for his people. Marshall points out that there is no clear connection between the feeding miracles and the Last Supper. But he admits that "we can see the Last Supper as an example of the table fellowship through which Jesus bound his disciples closely to him and as a foretaste of the heavenly banquet; the feeding miracle stories fall within this general framework," though there is no justification for seeing "the feeding miracle stories as 'eucharistic' in the proper sense of the term" (*Last Supper*, 97). See also Ulrich Luz (*Matthew 8–20: A Commentary*, trans. James E. Crouch, Hermeneia [Minneapolis: Fortress, 2001], 345): "It is true that the feeding is not a Lord's Supper but a regular meal with bread and fish. . . . It did, however, remind the church *also* of the Lord's Supper and helped it understand that something of what is reported here also happened in its own realm of experience" (emphasis original).

40. W. D. Davies and D. C. Allison Jr., *Matthew 8–18: A Critical and Exegetical Commentary on the Gospel according to Saint Matthew*, ICC (London: T&T Clark, 2004), 546.

41. Markus Barth, *Das Mahl des Herrn: Gemeinschaft mit Israel, mit Christus und unter den Gästen* (Neukirchen-Vluyn: Neukirchener Verlag, 1987), 22; "For the Passover or/and the Feast of the Unleavened Bread, the Exodus [motif] was decisive, which was understood by the prophets as a vindication of power and love of the creator of heaven and earth and as a prototype for the reparation of Israel from exile."

42. Luz notes that Canaanite is also "the self-designation of the Phoenicians at the time of Matthew" (*Matthew 8–20*, 338). While Jesus's second desert banquet may not primarily be a feeding of gentiles as it takes place in Jewish Galilee (15:29), Jesus's journey into gentile territory (15:21) could draw gentiles who come to join the crowds, thereby participating in the desert meal. *Contra* Luz (*Matthew 8–20*, 338), who claims that a feeding of gentiles is "certainly not the case in Matthew."

43. In Matthew, compassion is what Jesus has for his people and is what enables him to heal and forgive (e.g., 9:13, 36; 12:7; 14:14; 15:32; 18:27; 20:34).

44. On the connection between Jesus's table fellowship and heavenly banquet envisioned in Isa 25:6–8, see János Bolyki (*Jesu Tischgemeinschaften*, WUNT 2/96 [Tübingen: Mohr Siebeck, 1998], 193), who observes, "Diese wunderbare Metapher von der Universalität des Heils beschreibt das Heil selbst, das den Reichtum der Tischgemeinschaft, Gottes Anwesenheit und das gemeinsame Sich-zu-Tisch-Setzen der Völker in sich fasst. Damit werden die Heilsverheißungen im Rahmen der Tischgemeinschaften Jesu verständlich" (This wonderful metaphor of the universality of salvation [in Isa 25:6–8] describes salvation itself, which encompasses the richness of table fellowship, God's presence and the joint dining of the peoples at the table. In this way, the promises of salvation within the framework of Jesus's table fellowship

become comprehensible). In line with Isaiah's vision, Matt 8:11 also narrates that many will come from east and west to dine with Abraham, Isaac, and Jacob in heaven. This picture is of the heavenly banquet.

45. In 26:29, Matthew uses the phrase "with us" (μεθ' ὑμῶν) to indicate that the heavenly banquet will be shared with the disciples. The phrase "with us" forms an *inclusio* with the *Emmanuel* motif (God-with-us, μεθ' ἡμῶν ὁ θεός, 1:23). Similarly, Ulrich Luz observes that the *Emmanuel* motif "forms a bracket or inclusion around the entire Gospel of Matthew . . . explicitly in passages such as 17:17, 18:20, and 26:29, implicitly in the story of the miracles, which symbolically tell of the presence of Jesus in his community" (*The Theology of the Gospel of Matthew*, trans. J. Bradford Robinson, New Testament Theology [Cambridge: Cambridge University Press], 31). This suggests that Jesus shares God's presence with us by sharing the heavenly meal envisioned in the Last Supper with us.

46. In John's Gospel, the Jews had not yet commemorated the Passover at the time when Jesus stands before Pilate (18:28). John also presents the day of the crucifixion as the day of preparation of the Passover (19:14). For a detailed discussion of chronological harmonization on the difference between the Synoptic Gospels and John's Gospel, see Marshall, *Last Supper*, 71–75. After the review of various theories, Marshall adopts a view that "the synoptic Gospels and John reflect the use of different calendars," that is, "Jesus followed the Pharisaic calendar and practice, and the synoptic Gospels report the Last Supper from this point of view, while the priests followed the Sadducean calendar, and John reports events from their point of view" (72, 74). As Matthew portrays the Last Supper as a meal that takes place in the Passover, the Last Supper can be a Passover meal. For an extensive discussion on the connection between the Last Supper and a Passover meal, see Jeremias, *Eucharistic Words of Jesus*, 41–62. See also Huizenga, *New Isaac Tradition*, 240–41.

47. Marshall, *Last Supper*, 77; Senior, *Passion of Jesus*, 66.

48. On the relation between Jesus as God-with-us and God's liberating power, see chapter 3.

49. Green, *Death of Jesus*, 315.

50. Peter's failure recurs elsewhere in Matthew's narrative, where he plays Satan, silencing Jesus and denying Jesus's suffering and death (16:22–23). Nevertheless, failure is not the last word for the disciples. Matthew presents the disciples as those who will carry on Jesus's mission (28:18–20).

51. The disciples' failure is due in part to their misunderstanding of Jesus as "the Messiah, the Son of living God" (16:16). As Matthew portrays, Jesus as the Messiah must suffer and die (16:21; 17:22–23; 20:28). But the disciples respond to Jesus's predictions of passion with denial (16:22) and great distress (17:23).

52. Craig L. Blomberg, "Jesus, Sinners, and Table Fellowship," *BBR* 19, no. 1 (2009): 39.

53. The bread of the Last Supper in 26:26 also resonates with the petition for "daily bread" in the Lord's Prayer (6:11). The phrase "daily bread" evokes Israel's manna in the desert provided by the God of Israel (Exod 16:4, 31–32; Num 21:5; cf. Pss 78:23–25; 104:14–15; 132:15; Prov 30:8). The underlying assumption of God's provision is that just as the Father provides our daily provision, so God's children are

called to do for others. Likewise, just as Jesus breaks bread and shares a cup as a way to enact forgiveness, so his followers are called to embody it.

54. Jeremias, *Eucharistic Words of Jesus*, 233, 236–37. In a similar vein, Marshall observes, "It is important that the bread and wine are actually received by the disciples. The action indicates not merely the offering of a gift but the reception of a gift. By accepting what Jesus gave to them the disciples accepted the symbolical significance of the gift and thus gave their assent to his offer. Thus in due course the Lord's Supper became a sign not simply of the offer of salvation but also of the reception of salvation" (*Last Supper*, 84–85).

55. Despite the betrayal of Judas, Jesus still addresses Judas as friend (26:50). Yet, this is not to say that one's responsibility with regard to one's action and decision is exempt (cf. 26:24). On friendship in the Greco-Roman world, see Andrew D. Clarke ("Equality or Mutuality? Paul's Use of 'Brother' Language," in *The New Testament in Its First Century Setting: Essays on Context and Background in Honour of B. W. Winter on His 65th Birthday* [Grand Rapids: Eerdmans, 2004], 157): There was "the widespread social custom of a Graeco-Roman patron publicly addressing his client as 'friend' (*amicus*), when the relationship is self-evidently one of hierarchy." Clarke observes that in the NT, the language of friend expresses a level of affection (26:50; cf. Rom 7:4; 1 Cor 14:26; 2 Cor 11:9; Gal 4:12; 5:11; 6:1; Phil 4:21). See further Paul J. Achtemeier, Joel B. Green, and Marianne Meye Thompson, *Introducing the New Testament: Its Literature and Theology* (Grand Rapids: Eerdmans, 2001), 48; John T. Carroll and Joel B. Green, "Why Crucifixion? The Historical Meaning of the Cross," in *The Death of Jesus in Early Christianity* (Peabody, MA: Hendrickson, 1995), 177; Marshall, *Last Supper*, 95.

56. In a similar vein, Givens notes, "The discipline enjoined upon us is not that of pretending to shape the people of God by pronouncing the good guys in the people of God and the bad guys out—and of course always identifying ourselves with the good guys" ("Election of Israel," 88).

57. Key figures with whom Yahweh makes a covenant relationship are Abraham, Moses, and David (e.g., Gen 12:1–3; 15:6; 17:1–14; Exod 24:1–8; 1 Sam 7:8–16).

58. Scot McKnight, "Covenant," in *Dictionary for Theological Interpretation of the Bible*, 141.

59. Rolf Rendtorff, *The Covenant Formula: An Exegetical and Theological Investigation*, trans. Margaret Kohl, OTS (Edinburgh: T&T Clark, 1998), 86.

60. Ibid., 85–86.

61. The cross-reference in the margin of Matt 26:28 in NA[28] points to Exod 24:8 LXX. See also Edwards, *Ransom Logion*, 118–19. In the OT, blood signifies the life in the flesh, that is, the source of life (e.g., Lev 17:11). Regarding the significance of blood in the OT, John Paul Heil notes that "the blood of sacrificed animals was 'poured out' by priests on the altar as a sin offering to atone for the sins of the people (Lev 4:7, 18, 25, 30, 34), so the blood that will be 'shed' or 'poured out' by the death of Jesus represents a sacrifice for the atonement of sins 'for,' that is, 'on behalf of' 'many' people" (*The Death and Resurrection of Jesus: A Narrative-Critical Reading of Matthew 26–28* [Minneapolis: Fortress, 1991], 37). The nature of blood in Matthew

is presented as "innocent blood" (e.g., 2:16–18; 23:35; 27:3–10, 24–25). See Hamilton, *Death of Jesus*, 33–43.

62. Hoskins argues that Matt 26:28 alludes to Lev 4:1–5:13: "Matt 26:28's combination of blood, poured out, for (περί) the sinner, and the forgiveness of sins is found in only one passage in the OT, namely, Lev 4:1–5:13" ("Neglected Allusion," 234; see further, pp. 235–40). The expression "pouring out blood" (ἐκχέω + αἷμα) is found in both Matt 26:28 and Lev 4:7, 18, 25, 30, and 34. The nature of the pouring out of the blood of a sacrifice in Leviticus is the sin offering. That is, the blood of a sacrifice is poured out only in the sin offering. In this light, the idea that Jesus's blood is poured out presents Jesus's blood and death as the blood of a sacrifice. Also, just as the blood of the sin offering is for (περί) the people of Israel—priests, leaders, and the assembly—for the forgiveness of sins (e.g., Lev 4:20, 26, 31, 35; 5:13; cf. Isa 53:11–12), so Jesus's blood is for (περί) many for the forgiveness of sins (26:28). It is through this sacrificial death that Jesus delivers his people from their sins (1:21). See also Stanislas Lyonnet and Leopold Sabourin, *Sin, Redemption, and Sacrifice: A Biblical and Patristic Study*, AnBib 48 (Rome: Pontifical Biblical Institute, 1970), 181.

63. On fictive kinship in the Greco-Roman world, see Achtemeier, Green, and Thompson, *Introducing the New Testament*, 47–48.

64. In Matthew's narrative, the bond between Jesus and God's people is also affirmed through Jesus's name as God-with-us (1:23; cf. 18:20; 28:20). Similarly, Senior observes that Moses's sprinkling of the blood signifies "the bond of life now binding God and the people," such that Jesus becomes the "living blood bond between God and God's people" (*Passion of Jesus*, 67).

65. Heil, *Death and Resurrection*, 36.

66. On the connection between the twelve disciples and the twelve tribes of Israel, see Luz, *Matthew 8–20*, 66. The specific number *twelve* thus indicates that Jesus's forgiveness and healing is directed to the whole people of Israel, especially those that are gathered in the promised land in his generation.

67. For instance, Jesus's feeding multitudes implies famine and drought in the land (e.g., 14:15; 15:32–33). Enmity with gentile peoples is implied in the narrative, where people come to ask Jesus why he dines with tax collectors who work for Rome (e.g., 9:11; 11:19; cf. 8:10; 15:22–28). For further discussion on the brokenness and healing of the conditions of Israel's life, see chapter 3.

68. The cross-reference in the margin of Matt 26:28 in NA[28] points to Jer 31:31. But Matthew does not use the term "new" (καινός): "blood of the covenant." Cf. Luke 22:20. On Matthew's allusion to Jer 31:31–34, see Dale C. Allison Jr., *The New Moses: A Matthean Typology* (Eugene: OR: Wipf & Stock, 1993), 189.

69. Joel B. Green, *Why Salvation?*, Reframing New Testament Theology (Nashville: Abingdon, 2013), 51.

70. Leslie C. Allen, *Jeremiah: A Commentary*, OTL (Louisville: Westminster John Knox, 2008), 347.

71. Frank J. Matera, *Passion Narratives and Gospel Theologies: Interpreting the Synoptics through their Passion Stories*, Theological Inquiries: Studies in Contemporary Biblical and Theological Problems (New York: Paulist, 1986), 93. See also Edwards, *Ransom Logion*, 119.

72. Since God's laws are written on the human heart, Heil observes that the nature of the covenant envisioned in Jeremiah is "profoundly internal to the people, 'written upon their hearts,' and characterized by a universal knowledge of God and the forgiveness of sins (31:31–34; 32:37–41)" (*Death and Resurrection*, 36–37). It is "universal" in the sense that "the atoning blood of Jesus will be poured out on behalf of 'many,' a common Semitic expression for 'all people,'" which "indicates the universal nature of the covenant, which brings forgiveness and salvation to 'all'" (37). Thus, Jesus's death has a salvific effect not only for the people of Israel but for all people.

73. On the connection between Jer 31:34 and Ezek 36:26, see Allen, *Jeremiah*, 356. The rending of the heart is in some ways resonant with the centurion's renewed recognition ("Jesus is God's Son") after witnessing to Jesus's death (27:54). The centurion comes to perceive what he did not perceive previously. This could indicate the centurion's transformed mind and conception—that is, conversion. Joel B. Green observes that a transformation of one's conception of God is associated with conversion: "conversion signals . . . a transformed imaginative framework within which what was previously inconceivable is now matter-of-fact" (*Body, Soul, and Human Life: The Nature of Humanity in the Bible*, STI [Grand Rapids: Baker Academic, 2008], 128).

74. Michael J. Gorman, *Inhabiting the Cruciform God: Kenosis, Justification, and Theosis in Paul's Narrative Soteriology* (Grand Rapids: Eerdmans, 2009), 170.

75. In Matthew's narrative, the will of the Father is manifested in Jesus's words and deeds. Jesus desires mercy and forgiveness (e.g., 5:23–24, 43–47; 9:13; 12:7, 20; 18:27, 33; 20:34; 23:23; 26:28). He sums up the entire law and the prophets through the hermeneutics of love (22:37–40). The will of the Father, then, is clearly manifest in the practice of mercy and forgiveness. Thus, we as disciples of Jesus embody God's will by the way we forgive.

76. In context, the idea of taking the cup indicates accepting God's judgment as Jesus asks the Father to take away the cup that makes him grieve (26:38). Cf. Isa 51:17; Jer 25:15–16; Ezek 23:33. For discussions on the nature of drinking the cup, see Raymond E. Brown, *The Death of the Messiah: From Gethsemane to the Grave: A Commentary on the Passion Narrative in the Four Gospels*, 2 vols., ABRL (New York: Doubleday, 1994), 1:168–70; Green, *Death of Jesus*, 260–62, 319.

77. In context, the purpose of Jesus's injunction to keep on watching and praying is to prepare for "temptation" or "trial" (πειρασμός): "so that you may not fall into temptation" (26:41; cf. 6:13). But the disciples fall asleep, and it makes them unprepared for the coming trial as they desert Jesus and flee (26:56). For a discussion on the implication of "sleep," see Brown, *Death of the Messiah*, 1:195–200.

78. Senior, *Passion of Jesus*, 78.

79. Discipleship in Matthew is particularly related to Jesus's teaching. The disciples in Matthew are characterized as hearers and doers of God's will revealed in Jesus's teaching (e.g., 7:21; 12:50). See Ulrich Luz, "The Disciples in the Gospel according to Matthew," in *The Interpretation of Matthew*, ed. Graham N. Stanton (Edinburgh: T&T Clark, 1995), 122–23.

80. The nature of bearing one's cross in Matthew is to lay down one's life for the sake of Jesus (10:39). Just as Jesus lays down his life for his people's sake, so his followers are called to embody it.

81. As Donald Senior puts it, "Sufferings that will be experienced in the course of the community's mission provide a tie into the passion of Jesus" ("The Death of Jesus and the Meaning of Discipleship," in *The Death of Jesus in Early Christianity* [Peabody, MA: Hendrickson, 1995], 237). In a similar vein, Carroll and Green observe, "[W]hen Jesus authorizes his disciples to undertake their mission of healing and preaching" (e.g., 10:1), the underlying assumption is that "the disciples will experience opposition and persecution, even to the point of death, precisely because of their connection to him (10:16–25)" ("His Blood on Us," 41).

82. Cornelis Bennema, *Mimesis in the Johannine Literature: A Study in Johannine Ethics*, LNTS 498 (London: Bloomsbury T&T Clark, 2017), 175; Heil, *Death and Resurrection*, 110; Matera, *Passion Narratives*, 142–48.

83. On the nature of Jesus's sacrificial death, Senior observes that the use of περί denotes Matthew's conception of Jesus's death "as sacrificial because περί is more closely associated with the vocabulary of sacrifice in Isaiah 53" (e.g., Isa 53:4, 10). Although Matthew does not develop a theology of atonement, the addition of εἰς ἄφεσιν ἁμαρτιῶν indicates "an emphasis on the sacrificial as well as sacramental nature of Jesus' death" (cf. Exod 24:8; Jer 31:38). See Senior, *Passion Narrative*, 81–82. See also Senior (*Why the Cross?*, 45): "the word *peri* is used in the Septuagint (Greek) version of Isaiah 53:4 (AT) where the Servant is described as carrying sickness 'for us' (*peri*) and bearing suffering 'for us' (*peri*)." Jesus's atoning death is also observed by W. D. Davies and Dale C. Allison Jr. (*Matthew 1–7: A Critical and Exegetical Commentary on the Gospel according to Saint Matthew*, ICC [London: T&T Clark, 2004], 210). Also, that Jesus sheds his blood points to a violent death, which Matthew presents as sacrificial.

84. For instance, Exod 25:8 reads: "have them make a sanctuary, so that I may dwell among them" (NRSV).

85. Leviticus 16:2: "tell your brother Aaron not to come just at any time into the sanctuary inside the curtain before the mercy seat that is upon the ark, or he will die; for *I appear* in the cloud upon the mercy seat" (NRSV; emphasis mine).

86. Whether the torn veil is the outer veil or the inner veil has been debated. On this issue and the significance of the veil in scholarship, see Frank J. Matera, *The Kingship of Jesus: Composition and Theology in Mark 15*, SBLDS 66 (Chico, CA: Scholars Press, 1982), 137–38, 197 n. 63; Brown, *Death of the Messiah*, 2:1109–13; Gurtner, *Torn Veil*, 47–71.

87. Stephen Motyer observes that scholars "feel compelled to choose between rival explanations of the rending—*either* signifying the destruction of the Temple, *or* pointing to new access to God" ("The Rending of the Veil: A Markan Pentecost?," *NTS* 33, no. 1 [1987]: 157 n. 3; emphasis original). See, e.g., Davies and Allison, *Matthew 19–28*, 631. Davies and Allison contend that the rending of the veil points to the destruction of the temple in 70 CE because it vindicates Jesus's prophecy about the temple (24:2; 27:40; cf. 1 En. 90:28–29; Jub. 1:27). Charles L. Quarles also insists that "a gracious removal of the barrier that separated sinners from God" is "least likely." Instead, the rending of the temple veil signifies that the temple is "now open and vulnerable to desecration" ("Matthew 27:51–53: Meaning, Genre, Intertextuality, Theology, and Reception History," *JETS* 59, no. 2 [2016]: 272). However, both

views—the destruction of the temple and new access to God—are complementary in Matthew. Matera observes the vocabulary changes from ἱερόν (24:1) to ναός (26:61; 27:40, 51): "It would appear that by the tearing of the curtain of the *naos* [Matthew] had more in mind than the destruction of the *hieron*" (*Kingship of Jesus*, 138). Matera goes on to say that "on the basis of the temple theme it is manifest that in some sense the temple and its cult have come to a conclusion with the death of Jesus. But at the same time the destruction of the temple, symbolized in the tearing of the curtain, means that God has revealed his hidden glory to all" (139).

88. The difference between the Holy Place and the Holy of Holies connotes a sense of separation (בדל, e.g., Exod 26:33). See Lev 10:10; 11:47; Ezek 22:26; 42:20, where the priests separate (בדל) the clean from the unclean. The distinction between the Holy Place and the Holy of Holies points to two different spaces of sanctity in a cultic sense (cf. 1 Macc 9:54). Gurtner suggests the priestly, cultic function at work in the inner veil: "the veil *executed its cultic-separation role by prohibiting physical and visual accessibility to the holy of holies* (and thus to God's presence within)" (*Torn Veil*, 64–65; emphasis original). In this light, one of the functions of the inner veil is to limit access to God's very presence. Cf. Gen 1:6; 3:24; Rev 2:7.

89. Gurtner, *Torn Veil*, 52–53. He argues that in the LXX, "καταπέτασμα is the 'default' term for the inner veil (פרכת)," and when the LXX translator does not use καταπέτασμα to refer to the inner veil, the translator uses "a locative genitive clarifying to which part of the tabernacle the curtain belonged, as a means of distinguishing it from the primary καταπέτασμα" (46). For a detailed syntactical analysis of the use of καταπέτασμα in the OT, see Gurtner, *Torn Veil*, 49–71.

90. The cross-reference in the margin of Matt 27:51 in NA[28] points to Heb 6:19. In Heb 6:19–20, Jesus is depicted as the chief priest.

91. As noted above, Matt 26:28 alludes to Exod 24:8, where Moses sprinkles the blood of a sacrifice for the forgiveness of sins (cf. Exod 34:9–10; Lev 1–7).

92. Scholars who argue for the outer veil suggest that the centurion and those with him could see the tearing of the veil only if it was the outer veil since the inner veil was not visible from view (27:54). See, e.g., Howard M. Jackson, "The Death of Jesus in Mark and the Miracle from the Cross," *NTS* 33, no. 1 (1987): 23–24; David Ulansey, "The Heavenly Veil Torn: Mark's Cosmic *Inclusio*," *JBL* 110, no. 1 (1991): 124. However, there is no way the centurion and those with him could see the outer veil either, given the layout of Jerusalem and the temple. In any case, the text does not say that they see the temple veil torn. Instead, the centurion and the soldiers with him could possibly know the rending of the veil from distance by the report of the priests working at the temple at the time. Regarding the role of the priests in the Holy Place, see Lev 16:1–5; Num 4:20; 18:1–7.

93. Paul Lamarche, "La mort du Christ et le voile de temple selon Marc," *NRTh* 106 (1974): 596; my translation: "Through the death of Christ, the veil is torn apart, the Holy of Holies is revealed to us, and by the faith of Christ, it is given to us to enter freely into the habitation and intimacy of the true God."

94. In Second Temple and Rabbinic Judaism, the symbolic referent for the veil is the heavenly firmament in Gen 1:6. On the connection between the veil and the

heavenly firmament, see Lamarche, "La mort du Christ," 588; Gurtner, *Torn Veil*, 89–93. Cf. Josephus, *J.W.* 5.212–14.

95. Even to the chief priests who are permitted to access the Holy of Holies, the mercy seat is hidden from sight by the cloud because of God's glory (Lev 16:12–13; cf. 1 Kgs 8:11). Aaron's sons, Nadab and Abihu, die because of God's glory and presence (Lev 10:1–2). This suggests that God's lethal glory limits our access to God's very presence. But this is not to say that we are entirely prohibited from participating in God's glory. Matthew implies that we can participate in God's glory through sharing in Jesus's suffering and death (e.g., 20:21–23). Cf. On believers' participation in God's glory in Paul's letters (Rom 8 and 2 Cor 3–5), see Ben C. Blackwell, *Christosis: Engaging Paul's Soteriology with His Patristic Interpreters*, WUNT 2/314 (Tübingen: Mohr Siebeck, 2011; Grand Rapids: Eerdmans, 2016), 157–61, 183–97. Citations refer to the Eerdmans edition.

96. Jack Dean Kingsbury, *Matthew: Structure, Christology, Kingdom* (Minneapolis: Fortress, 1975), 76.

97. The rending of the veil at Jesus's death (27:51) and the rending of heaven at Jesus's baptism (3:16–17) form a narrative *inclusio*. For example, (1) in both scenes, a voice is heard (Jesus is Son of God)—at the baptism, it is the voice of God (3:17), and at Jesus's death, it is the voice of the centurion and those with him (27:54); (2) in both scenes, something descends—at the baptism, it is the Spirit (3:16), and at Jesus's death, it is the rending from top to bottom, from heaven to earth. For further discussion on the parallel connection between the rending of the veil at Jesus's death and the rending of heaven at Jesus's baptism, see, e.g., Matera, *Kingship of Jesus*, 139; Motyer, "Rending of the Veil," 156; Jackson, "Death of Jesus," 21–24, 27. Additionally, Ulrich Luz suggests that the opening of heaven in 3:16 may allude to Ezek 1:1–4 (*Matthew 1–7: A Commentary*, trans. James E. Crouch, Hermeneia [Minneapolis: Fortress, 2007], 143).

98. With the opening of heaven, the Spirit descends on Jesus and God's voice is revealed from heaven (3:16–17).

99. Leon Morris notes that what happened at Jesus's death is "earth-shaking" (27:51–52). Thus, what happened—"*torn in two from top to bottom*"—should be more than a minor tear: "[Matthew] is speaking of a bisected curtain, a curtain that no longer functioned to keep what lay on the other side of it a secret from all those outside" (*The Gospel according to Matthew*, The Pillar New Testament Commentary [Grand Rapids: Eerdmans, 1992], 724; emphasis original). Cf. Donald A. Hagner, *Matthew 14–28*, WBC 33B (Dallas: Word, 1995), 849.

100. The dead are described as "holy ones" (ἁγίων, 27:52), presumably, pious Jews. Cf. Isa 4:3; Dan 7:18, 22; Did. 16:7. On this issue, see Davies and Allison, *Matthew 19–28*, 633. Matthew tells us that the dead are not only raised by the power of God but also enter the "holy city," namely, Jerusalem (27:53; cf. 4:5; Luke 4:9). Jesus's death "for many" (περὶ πολλῶν, 26:28) thus effects the raising of the "many bodies" (πολλὰ σώματα) of the holy ones so that they bear witness of God's salvific action in Jesus's death "to many" (πολλοῖς) to whom they appear (27:52–53). This also confirms that Jesus's death enacts the salvific power of the Father in heaven on the earth. The location of Jerusalem in 27:53 has been a matter of scholarly debate.

For example, some scholars insist that in 27:53, the holy ones enter the city in heaven like Enoch and Elijah, since that the saints in ancient times resume their lives on earth is not likely. Nolland contends, "The neatest solution is to imagine them translated to heaven as were Enoch and Elijah" (e.g., Gen 5:24; 2 Kgs 2) (*Gospel of Matthew*, 1217). But in Matthew's conception, it is more likely that the holy ones enter the *earthly* Jerusalem because the "holy city" (ἅγιος πόλις) in Matthew always refers to the earthly Jerusalem as in 4:5. For Matthew, the heavenly Jerusalem is not in view elsewhere in the narrative. See Heil, *Death and Resurrection*, 89; Luz, *Matthew 21–28*, 568. Further, it would make more sense that the holy ones appeared to many who live on earth to bear witness of God's salvific action that just happened to them.

101. Regarding intertextuality at work in Matt 27:51–53, Senior points out that there is "striking concurrence" of Ezek 37 and Matt 27:52–53: (1) "the dead of the house of Israel" (Ezek 37:11); (2) "a reference to the *return* of revivified people to Israel" (Ezek 37:12, 14); and (3) "its purpose to manifest God's power and holiness" (Ezek 37:6, 13–14)—"the breath of life" (Ezek 37:5–6, 8–10, 14; cf. Matt 27:50) and "re-opening of graves" (Ezek 37:12). See Senior, *Passion Narrative*, 320. In a similar vein, France points out that "Matthew's wording here especially calls to mind Ezek 37:13, 'when I open your graves and bring you up out of your graves, my people,' though there resurrection is a metaphor for national restoration rather than a promise of personal life after death" (*Gospel of Matthew*, 1082). For further discussion on the connection between Ezek 37 and Matt 27, see Dale C. Allison Jr., "The Scriptural Background of a Matthean Legend: Ezekiel 37, Zechariah 14, and Matthew 27," in *Life beyond Death in Matthew's Gospel: Religious Metaphor or Bodily Reality?*, ed. Wim Weren, Huub van de Sandt, and Joseph Verheyden, BTS 13 (Leuven: Peeters, 2011), 153–55; Alberto Mello, *Évangile selon Saint Matthieu: Commentaire midrashique et narrative*, LD 179 (Paris: Cerf, 1999), 485. See Timothy Wardle ("Resurrection and the Holy City: Matthew's Use of Isaiah in 27:51–53," *CBQ* 78, no. 4 [2016]: 666–81, esp. 673–80), who argues for the influence of Isa 52:1–2 on Matt 27:52–53. Wardle observes, "Half of Matthew's formula citations are dependent on Isaiah (1:22–23; 2:23; 4:14–16; 8:17; 12:17–21; part of 21:5), and, when Matthew cites specific prophets, he names only Isaiah and Jeremiah" (671).

102. In the OT, the promise of resurrection is directly linked to a promise of restoration (e.g., Hos 6:1–3; Ezek 37:1–14). For further discussion, see Kevin L. Anderson, *"But God Raised Him from the Dead": The Theology of Jesus' Resurrection in Luke-Acts*, Paternoster Biblical Monographs (Carlisle: Paternoster, 2006), 48–91. In a similar vein, Hamilton writes that by alluding to Ezek 37, where "dry bones rise and walk into the holy city," Matthew envisions that Ezekiel's promise of return, "the ancient hope *of Israel* for restoration," is realized "in the death [and resurrection] of Jesus" (*Death of Jesus*, 225; emphasis original). Cf. Rev 22:14; Jub. 3:12–14; 1 En. 25:5; 4 Ezra 8:52.

103. Regarding the significance of the centurion's and the soldiers' confession of Jesus as Son of God, Ulrich Luz observes that "only God himself can reveal him as his Son, and it is to this revelation that the human confession responds" (*Matthew 21–28: A Commentary*, trans. James E. Crouch, Hermeneia [Minneapolis: Fortress, 2005], 570). Thus, the centurion and those with him (i.e., the gentile soldiers) could

confess Jesus as Son of God on the basis of what God has done. In context, Jesus is confronted by his mockers to demonstrate his power to save himself if he were the Son of God (27:40–43; cf. 4:3, 6). Matthew shows that God verifies who Jesus is ("Son of God"), particularly through his Son's obedient death. Jesus as Son of God, then, is aligned with his obedience. David D. Kupp observes, "It is the obedience of God's covenant people which evokes his presence" (*Matthew's Emmanuel: Divine Presence and God's People in the First Gospel*, SNTSMS 90 [Cambridge: Cambridge University Press, 1996], 131). Jesus's obedient death, then, is the means by which God's presence is extended to us.

104. On the inclusion of gentiles in the people of God, see Craig L. Blomberg (*Matthew: An Exegetical and Theological Exposition of Holy Scripture*, NAC 22 [Nashville: Broadman, 1992], 421), who opines that the rending of the veil signifies inclusion of gentiles in the people of God. Cf. 8:5–13; 28:19–20; Eph 2:11–19. Cf. David C. Sim argues that "the Romans at the cross symbolize the eschatological fate of imperial Rome. . . . it does not involve the dubious proposition that Matthew would have used such wicked characters [who humiliated and executed Jesus] in his narrative as models of Gentile faith. Moreover, this interpretation is in line with the evangelist's view that Rome, the ally of Satan in the cosmic conflict, will be condemned and judged by Jesus the Son of Man" ("Rome in Matthew's Eschatology," in *The Gospel of Matthew in Its Roman Imperial Context*, ed. John K. Riches and David C. Sim, JSNTSup 276 [New York: T&T Clark, 2005], 105). Matthew's portrayal of the Romans, however, is not uniformly negative in the narrative (e.g., 8:10–12; 9:13; 27:19).

105. We should remember that it is the same power Jesus himself exercises (e.g., 8:1–9:38), and it is also the same power (ἐξουσία) he shares with the disciples (10:1; cf. 10:25). See Luz, *Matthew 21–28*, 624.

106. Jonathan T. Pennington contends that Jesus's power in both realms—heaven and earth—has been "inaugurated" by his resurrection: through his death and resurrection, Jesus's "earthly authority has been expanded, hence the commissioning of the disciples" (*Heaven and Earth in the Gospel of Matthew* [Grand Rapids: Baker Academic, 2007], 205). What theosis allows us to see, however, is that Jesus's earthly authority and heavenly authority are not separable even during his earthly life. Throughout the narrative, Jesus unfolds God's heavenly forgiving power (9:1–8), commissioning and empowering the disciples with the authority he has received from the Father (10:1, 5; 18:18), power that is associated with his anointing with the Spirit in baptism for the forgiveness of sins (3:16). Thus, when he dies and is raised, Jesus does not become something that he was not before dying. Jesus's life-long heavenly authority is rather completed and vindicated precisely in the resurrection. Thus, heaven and earth come to be united by Jesus's exercising of God's forgiving power revealed in both his earthly and heavenly authority.

Conclusion

Through this study, I have demonstrated how a focus on theosis clarifies and advances Matthean teaching of forgiveness, with respect to the transformative dynamics between God and the human and thus between heaven and earth. This study is not focused on whether Matthew has a doctrine or idea of theosis in the first century CE, but on whether an aspect of Matthew's theology can be called theosis. Thus, although a patristic idea of theosis is brought to bear on Matthew's Gospel, the conceptualization is shaped by the particular Matthean usage evident in the text. Building on the patristic concept of theosis, I explored a theological vision set forth within Matthew's text through a hermeneutical lens provided by this understanding of theosis. To show this, I employed a narrative approach to examine Matthew's presentation of forgiveness in the progression of the narrative, his use of the OT, and his characterization of Jesus as God-with-us, healer, and forgiver.

What theosis allows us to see in the Lord's Prayer is that our relation to God as Father expresses our participation in God's life rather than only our imitation of the Father. We receive the Father's forgiving life in and through Jesus, such that we come to share in God's own forgiveness. I thus suggested that human forgiveness is not the condition of God's forgiveness but the mode of it, since human forgiveness embodies and extends God's own forgiveness (6:12, 14–15). In this way, embodying forgiveness is a way of theosis, which takes place with God's initiative and the work of God in our response, not as a consequence of conditions that we meet before God acts.

I also suggested that a theosis framework provides a more nuanced understanding of Jesus's forgiving and healing of the paralyzed person. That is to say, Jesus's action of forgiveness and healing is the very expression of God's forgiveness (9:2, 6). In this dynamic, it is not a matter of entirely sequential agencies, God and then Jesus or vice versa but one of theosis, the extension of God's own forgiving power working itself out in and through Jesus. Also, Jesus's healing entails not only the healing of the paralyzed person's body but also the transformation of the person's relationships and life conditions as he is able to join his community (9:7). Further, I suggested that when discipleship in Matthew is conceived with the framework of theosis, discipleship is not a matter of merely imitating Christ but one of theosis, the extension of God's own power working itself out through Jesus in our lives as we participate in God's powerful life (9:8; 10:1).

A theosis framework further clarifies the transformative dynamics of God and the human and thus heaven and earth in Jesus's discipline of his church. I challenged the excommunication reading (18:15–17) and suggested that the church's discipline involves restoration and reconciliation of our relationship with God and with others—that is, a way of theosis. I then challenged the view that heaven and earth are merely contrastive or conflicting realities (18:18–20). I also explored Jesus's relation to the Spirit and suggested that a theosis framework offers a more nuanced understanding of the relation between Jesus and the Spirit (18:20), with respect to the transfer and extension of power at work among the Spirit, Jesus, and his followers. Moreover, as in the Lord's Prayer, the parable of the unforgiving servant shows that human forgiveness is the very mode in which we reflect God's own forgiveness rather than a condition we meet in order to earn God's forgiveness (18:23–35).

Finally, I suggested that the death of Jesus can be usefully interpreted through the lens of theosis. What theosis allows us to see at the Last Supper is that the meal is a vivid expression of Jesus's forgiveness, a transformation of life that heals the conditions of life for sinners and welcomes them into the community of Jesus as God's family, sharers in the life of God (cf. 12:50). Also, when Jesus's blood of the covenant for the forgiveness of sins is conceived with the lens of theosis, the death of Jesus is an important means through which God and the human are united as God's covenant people and his family (26:28; cf. Exod 24:8; Jer 31:31–34). As the narrative unfolds, Matthew shows a further aspect of theosis, with respect to discipleship as participation in Jesus's cruciform life. That is to say, Jesus empowers us to reflect and enact his own cruciform life by embodying his forgiveness, even the loss of his life in the way we give of our own. Furthermore, the death of Jesus invites us to see the transformative, relational dynamics of heaven and earth, which can be seen more clearly through the lens of theosis (27:51–54; 28:18). God acts in and through Jesus's death, such that the veil is torn, the dead are raised, and the Romans come to know who Jesus is—Son of God. Thus, the culminating act of God in Jesus—the oneness of God and Jesus—takes place at the death of Jesus. Since Jesus embodies both divine and human life (cf. 1:23), his death for the forgiveness of sins is one of theosis as God decisively reveals himself in human flesh. In this way, a theosis framework clarifies and advances Matthean teaching of forgiveness.

THEOLOGICAL IMPLICATIONS FOR THE LIFE OF THE CHURCH

Embodying forgiveness as a way of life is significant for the life of the church. L. Gregory Jones observes that more than ever, we live in a world that "is in desperate need of a truthful embodiment of costly forgiveness."[1] Jones points out that "there have been comparatively few theological discussions of forgiveness in this century."[2] In this regard, part of this study's contribution is to shed light on a theology of forgiveness envisioned in Matthew's Gospel that may be useful for the life and practice of the church. I noted at the outset that this work is an exercise in theological interpretation of Scripture, with the result that this study has theological implications for the church. As Matthew invites us to embody God's forgiveness, we as the church communally need to be shaped by its transformative message. I suggest two implications for the life of the church.

First, the practice of forgiveness has transformative potential, with respect to our relationship with God. Matthew's Gospel envisions the formation of Jesus's community as participating in the Father-Son relationship—that is, divine family. This transformative, relational participation is done through embodying forgiveness in Matthew. To put it another way, through the practice of forgiveness, we become children and heirs of God's own life (5:44–45; 12:50). Forgiveness in Matthew is thus an important means for shaping God's household. We have seen in this study that family language is an important element of theosis. Matthew's presentation of Jesus as "the Son" is a key to understanding Jesus's unique relationship with the Father (e.g., 3:17; 7:21; 11:27; 12:50; 16:16; 26:39). Jesus says that we can come to know God in and through him (11:27). This suggests that the knowledge of God occurs in relationship with Jesus, the Son. Accordingly, our relationship with Jesus enables and empowers us to see and know God.[3] Having seen Jesus's life of love and forgiveness experienced in us, we are able to embody his merciful forgiveness. Our bond with Jesus, then, provides the means by which we participate in God's life. Thus, the intimate, privileged access to the Father Jesus has is shared with his followers, particularly through our embodying Jesus's merciful forgiveness (e.g., 5:44–45; 9:13; 12:7; 26:26–28). Through the embodied practice of forgiveness revealed in Jesus, then, we reflect and enact what it means to live as children of God. In this way, we are shaped and transformed in a way that reflects and enacts God's forgiving life, character, and power.

Second, the embodied practice of forgiveness effects healing in the life of the church. In particular, the Korean church has suffered much from schisms and conflicts throughout history. A Korean church historian, In Soo Kim, notes, "It is truly sad that the Presbyterian Church, in particular, [was] divided three times in the 1950's. In 1951, the Koryo faction (Koryo Presbyterian Church) separated itself, followed by the Ki-jang (Christ Presbyterian Church) in 1953, and finally in 1959, the Tonghap (Union) and Hapdong (Joint) separated into two."[4] Scholars have observed that divisions in the Korean church are due in part to different theological views and theological diversity.[5] While there may be various reasons for schisms in the history of the Korean church, one important factor is the lack of a theology of forgiveness and reconciliation.[6] The lack of a theology of forgiveness has kept the church from encouraging acts of tolerance and repentance, resulting in schisms and polarization in the church. In this context, the practice of forgiveness is vital for the life of the church, one that may open a way to heal and repair the ongoing, deep-seated divisions in the church, thereby transforming the condition of the life of the Korean church. As Jones aptly points out, through embodying forgiveness, we can hope to "unlearn habits and patterns of domination and diminution of others, of sin and evil, and learn to embody habits and practices of Christian *communion*."[7] Consequently, forgiveness as an embodied way of life enables us to be united and reconciled with others, by the way it unites us with God as envisioned in Matthew's Gospel (cf. 5:23–24).

LOOKING AHEAD: FUTURE RESEARCH ON THEOSIS IN MATTHEW'S GOSPEL

In addition to *forgiveness*, themes like the name of God and the name of the Lord can be other possibilities for reflection on theosis in Matthew's Gospel, since the name of God bears his identity, nature, and power (e.g., 1:23; 6:9; 7:21–22; 28:19). Matthew shows that in the name of God, we wield God's own authority and power—prophesy, cast out demons, heal and baptize people (e.g., 7:21–22; 28:19). Here, the name of God is depicted as the source, power, and impetus for our participation in what God does. Thus, for future research on theosis in Matthew's Gospel, the theme of the name of God or the Lord offers an inviting locus for considering Matthew's theological vision through the lens of theosis.

NOTES

1. L. Gregory Jones, *Embodying Forgiveness: A Theological Analysis* (Grand Rapids: Eerdmans, 1995), xvii.
2. Ibid., xiii.
3. To see God is to know God as seeing is not simply limited to "sensory perception" but is followed by "cognitive perception"—knowing, which further inspires us

to embody God's character. For further discussion, see Cornelis Bennema, *Mimesis in the Johannine Literature: A Study in Johannine Ethics*, LNTS 498 (London: Bloomsbury T&T Clark, 2017), 95. Similarly, W. D. Davies and Dale C. Allison Jr. point out, "To see God is to know him," involving an intimate relationship with God (*Matthew 1–7: A Critical and Exegetical Commentary on the Gospel according to Saint Matthew*, ICC [London: T&T Clark, 2004], 456).

4. In Soo Kim, *History of Christianity in Korea* (Seoul: Qumran Publishing House, 2011), 503. According to Kim, "The fact that the church that was unified as one for more than half a century divided three times within less than a ten year period, this can only be seen as the work of Satan" (503).

5. See, e.g., Sebastian C. H. Kim and Kirsteen Kim (*A History of Korean Christianity* [Cambridge: Cambridge University Press, 2015], 200): "The splits in the Protestant churches were not solely due to differences in theology, but a growth in theological diversity was an important factor and the new groups defined themselves in distinction from one another primarily by theological arguments." Kim and Kim note that "at the beginning of the twenty-first century, Korean Protestantism had a reputation for separatism and was split into more than seventy different groups" (279).

6. During the period of Japanese imperialism, for instance, Korean Christians were forced to participate in Japanese Shinto Shrine rituals. Yet, some courageous pastors refused to participate in these rituals, with the result that they were tortured and killed. Since Korea's independence in 1945, the Korean church has been divided due to the issue of participation in Shinto Shrine rituals, even to this day. Some Korean church leaders claim that pastors who participated in those rituals are betrayers and thus not eligible to serve as pastors. Those who wanted to separate themselves from those pastors involved in shrine worship in the past were largely former prisoners under Japanese ruling power. Thus, the anti-Japanese pastors could not accept the once pro-Japanese pastors. At the General Assembly held in April 1950, "There was a huge commotion regarding the moderator of the two divided presbyteries and the issue of Koryo Theological Seminary" (Kim, *History of Christianity*, 466). The two divided groups fought each other during the meeting, turning the meeting hall into a "battlefield." At the end, they had to "bring police in and point guns at people in order to stop the fight" (466). While it is right to acknowledge the martyrdom and resistance of courageous pastors against Japanese imperialism, it is also important to pursue a process of forgiveness of pastors who participated in Shinto Shrine rituals, a process that involves their repentance of their sins before the church.

7. Jones, *Embodying Forgiveness*, xv (emphasis mine).

Bibliography

Aasgaard, Reidar. “Brothers and Sisters in the Faith: Christian Siblingship as an Ecclesiological Mirror in the First Two Centuries.” In *The Formation of the Early Church*, edited by Jostein Ådna, 285–316. WUNT 183. Tübingen: Mohr Siebeck, 2005.

———. “Brotherhood in Plutarch and Paul: Its Role and Character.” In *Constructing Early Christian Families: Family as Social Reality and Metaphor*, edited by Halvor Moxnes, 166–82. London: Routledge, 1997.

Achtemeier, Paul J., Joel B. Green, and Marianne Meye Thompson. *Introducing the New Testament: Its Literature and Theology*. Grand Rapids: Eerdmans, 2001.

Allen, Leslie C. *Jeremiah: A Commentary*. OTL. Louisville: Westminster John Knox, 2008.

Allison Jr., Dale C. *Studies in Matthew: Interpretation Past and Present*. Grand Rapids: Baker Academic, 2005.

———. *The New Moses: A Matthean Typology*. Eugene: OR: Wipf & Stock, 1993.

———. “The Scriptural Background of a Matthean Legend: Ezekiel 37, Zechariah 14, and Matthew 27.” In *Life beyond Death in Matthew's Gospel: Religious Metaphor or Bodily Reality?* edited by Wim Weren, Huub van de Sandt, and Joseph Verheyden, 153–88. BTS 13. Leuven: Peeters, 2011.

———. *The Sermon on the Mount: Inspiring the Moral Imagination*. New York: Crossroad, 1999.

Anderson, Janice Capel. *Matthew's Narrative Web: Over, and Over, and Over Again*. JSNTSup 91. Sheffield: JSOT Press, 1994.

Anderson, Kevin L. *“But God Raised Him from the Dead”: The Theology of Jesus' Resurrection in Luke-Acts*. Paternoster Biblical Monographs. Carlisle: Paternoster, 2006.

Bakhtin, Mikhail M. “Response to a Question from the *Novy Mir* Editorial Staff.” In *Speech Genres and Other Late Essays*, edited by Caryl Emerson and Michael Holquist, 1–9. Translated by Vern M. McGee. 2nd ed. Austin: University of Texas Press, 1986.

Barclay, John M. G. *Paul and the Gift*. Grand Rapids: Eerdmans, 2015.

———. *Paul & the Power of Grace*. Grand Rapids: Eerdmans, 2020.

———. "The Gift Perspective on Paul." In *Perspectives on Paul: Five Views*, edited by Scot McKnight and B. J. Oropeza, 219–36. Grand Rapids: Baker Academic, 2020.

Bartchy, S. Scott. "Slaves and Slavery in the Roman World." In *The World of the New Testament: Cultural, Social, and Historical Contexts*, edited by Joel B. Green and Lee Martin McDonald, 169–78. Grand Rapids: Baker Academic, 2013.

Barth, Markus. *Das Mahl des Herrn: Gemeinschaft mit Israel, mit Christus und unter den Gästen*. Neukirchen-Vluyn: Neukirchener Verlag, 1987.

Beasley-Murray, G. R. *Jesus and the Kingdom of God*. Grand Rapids: Eerdmans, 1986.

Beaton, Richard. *Isaiah's Christ in Matthew's Gospel*. SNTSMS 123. Cambridge: Cambridge University Press, 2002.

Bennema, Cornelis. *Mimesis in the Johannine Literature: A Study in Johannine Ethics*. LNTS 498. London: Bloomsbury T&T Clark, 2017.

Betz, Otto. *Jesus der Messias Israels: Aufsätze zur biblischen Theologie*. WUNT 42. Tübingen: Mohr Siebeck, 1987.

Blackwell, Ben C. *Christosis: Engaging Paul's Soteriology with His Patristic Interpreters*. WUNT 2/314. Tübingen: Mohr Siebeck, 2011. Reprint, Grand Rapids: Eerdmans, 2016.

———. "Immortal Glory and the Problem of Death in Romans 3.23." *JSNT* 32, no. 3 (2010): 285–308.

Blomberg, Craig L. "Jesus, Sinners, and Table Fellowship." *BBR* 19, no. 1 (2009): 35–62.

———. *Matthew: An Exegetical and Theological Exposition of Holy Scripture*. NAC 22. Nashville: Broadman, 1992.

———. "Matthew." In *Commentary on the New Testament Use of the Old Testament*, edited by G. K. Beale and D. A. Carson, 1–109. Grand Rapids: Baker Academic, 2007.

Blount, Brian K. *Then the Whisper Put on Flesh: New Testament Ethics in an African–American Context*. Nashville: Abingdon, 2001.

Bock, D. L. "Son of Man." In *DJG*, edited by Joel B. Green, Jeannine K. Brown, and Nicholas Perrin, 894–900. 2nd ed. Downers Grove, IL: InterVarsity Press, 2013.

Boersma, Hans. *Heavenly Participation: The Weaving of a Sacramental Tapestry*. Grand Rapids: Eerdmans, 2011.

Bolyki, János. *Jesu Tischgemeinschaften*. WUNT 2/96. Tübingen: Mohr Siebeck, 1998.

Bonhoeffer, Dietrich. *Christ the Center*. Translated by Edwin H. Robertson. New York: Harper & Row, 1978.

Bornkamm, Günther. "The Authority to 'Bind' and 'Loose' in the Church in Matthew's Gospel." In *The Interpretation of Matthew*, edited by Graham N. Stanton, 101–14. Edinburgh: T&T Clark, 1995.

Brown, Jeannine K., and Kyle Roberts. *Matthew*. THNTC. Grand Rapids: Eerdmans, 2018.

Brown, Raymond E. *The Death of the Messiah: From Gethsemane to the Grave: A Commentary on the Passion Narrative in the Four Gospels*. 2 vols. ABRL. New York: Doubleday, 1994.

Bryan, Steven M. "Onomastics and Numerical Composition in the Genealogy of Matthew." *BBR* 30, no. 4 (2020): 515–39.

Byers, Andrew J. *Ecclesiology and Theosis in the Gospel of John*. SNTSMS 166. Cambridge: Cambridge University Press, 2017.

Carroll, John T., and Joel B. Green. "'His Blood on Us and on Our Children': The Death of Jesus in the Gospel according to Matthew." In *The Death of Jesus in Early Christianity*, 39–59. Peabody, MA: Hendrickson, 1995.

———. "Why Crucifixion? The Historical Meaning of the Cross." In *The Death of Jesus in Early Christianity*, 165–81. Peabody, MA: Hendrickson, 1995.

Carter, Warren. "Jesus's Healing Stories: Imperial Critique and Eschatological Anticipations in Matthew's Gospel." *CurTM* 37, no. 6 (2010): 488–96.

———. *Matthew and the Margins: A Socio-Political and Religious Reading*. The Bible & Liberation Series. Maryknoll, NY: Orbis Books, 2000.

Charette, Blain. *Restoring Presence: The Spirit in Matthew's Gospel*. Journal of Pentecostal Theology 18. Sheffield: Sheffield Academic, 2000.

Christensen, Michael J. "The Problem, Promise, and Process of *Theosis*." In *Partakers of the Divine Nature: The History and Development of Deification in the Christian Traditions*, edited by Michael J. Christensen and Jeffery A. Wittung, 23–31. Grand Rapids: Baker Academic, 2007.

Chung, Woojin. *Translation Theory and the Old Testament in Matthew: The Possibilities of Skopos Theory*. Linguistic Biblical Studies 15. Leiden: Brill, 2017.

Clarke, Andrew D. "Equality or Mutuality? Paul's Use of 'Brother' Language." In *The New Testament in Its First Century Setting: Essays on Context and Background in Honour of B. W. Winter on His 65th Birthday*, edited by P. J. Williams, Andrew D. Clarke, Peter M. Head, and David Instone-Brewer, 151–64. Grand Rapids: Eerdmans, 2004.

Cohen, Shaye J. D. "The Significance of Yavneh: Pharisees, Rabbis, and the End of Jewish Sectarianism." *HUCA* 55 (1984): 27–53.

Cohick, Lynn H. "Women, Children, and Families in the Greco-Roman World." In *The World of the New Testament: Cultural, Social, and Historical Contexts*, edited by Joel B. Green and Lee Martin McDonald, 179–87. Grand Rapids: Baker Academic, 2013.

Collins, Adela Yarbro. "Polemic against the Pharisees in Matthew 23." In *The Pharisees*, edited by Joseph Sievers and Amy-Jill Levine, 148–69. Grand Rapids: Eerdmans, 2021.

Collins, Paul M. *Partaking in Divine Nature: Deification and Communion*. London: T&T Clark, 2010.

Darr, John A. *On Character Building: The Reader and the Rhetoric of Characterization in Luke-Acts*. Literary Currents in Biblical Interpretation. Louisville: Westminster John Knox, 1992.

Davies, W. D. *The Setting of the Sermon on the Mount*. Cambridge: Cambridge University Press, 1964.

Davies, W. D., and Dale C. Allison Jr. *Matthew: A Critical and Exegetical Commentary on the Gospel according to Saint Matthew*. 3 vols. ICC. London: T&T Clark, 2004.

Dinkler, Michal Beth. *Literary Theory and the New Testament*. New Haven: Yale University Press, 2019.

Dodd, C. H. *The Parables of the Kingdom*. Rev. ed. London: Collins, 1961.

Dowd, Sharyn E. "Is Matthew 18:15–17 about 'Church Discipline'?" In *Scripture and Traditions: Essays on Early Judaism and Christianity in Honor of Carl R. Holladay*, edited by Patrick Gray and Gail R. O'Day, 137–50. Leiden: Brill, 2008.

Dupont, Jacques. "La paralytique pardonné (Matthieu 9:1–8)." *NRTh* 82 (1960): 940–58.

Edwards, J. Christopher. *The Ransom Logion in Mark and Matthew: Its Reception and Its Significance for the Study of the Gospels*. WUNT 327. Tübingen: Mohr Siebeck, 2012.

Finlan, Stephen. "Can We Speak of Theosis in Paul?" In *Theōsis: Deification in Christian Theology*, edited by Stephen Finlan and Vladimir Kharlamov, 68–80. Princeton Theological Monograph Series 52. Eugene, OR: Pickwick, 2006.

———. "Second Peter's Notion of Divine Participation." In *Theōsis: Deification in Christian Theology*, edited by Stephen Finlan and Vladimir Kharlamov, 32–50. Princeton Theological Monograph Series 52. Eugene, OR: Pickwick, 2006.

———. "Deification in Jesus' Teaching." In *Theōsis: Deification in Christian Theology*, edited by Vladimir Kharlamov, 21–41. Princeton Theological Monograph Series 156. Eugene, OR: Pickwick, 2011.

Finlan, Stephen, and Vladimir Kharlamov. "Introduction." In *Theōsis: Deification in Christian Theology*, edited by Stephen Finlan and Vladimir Kharlamov, 1–15. Princeton Theological Monograph Series 52. Eugene, OR: Pickwick, 2006.

Forkman, Göran. *The Limits of the Religious Community: Expulsion from the Religious Community within the Qumran sect, within Rabbinic Judaism, and within Primitive Christianity*. ConBNT 5. Lund: Gleerup, 1972.

France, R. T. The Gospel of *Matthew*. NICNT. Grand Rapids: Eerdmans, 2007.

Fretheim, Terence E. *Exodus*. IBC. Louisville: Westminster John Knox, 1991.

Furstenberg, Yair. "The Shared Image of Pharisaic Law in the Gospels and Rabbinic Tradition." In *The Pharisees*, edited by Joseph Sievers and Amy-Jill Levine, 199–219. Grand Rapids: Eerdmans, 2021.

Givens, Tommy. *Light in the Shadow of Death: A Reading of the Gospel of Matthew*. Grand Rapids: Eerdmans, forthcoming.

———. "The Election of Israel and the Politics of Jesus: Revisiting John Howard Yoder's *The Jewish Christian Schism Revisited*." *Journal of the Society of Christian Ethics* 31, no. 2 (2011): 75–92.

———. *We the People: Israel and the Catholicity of Jesus*. Minneapolis: Fortress, 2014.

Gorman, Michael J. *Abide and Go: Missional Theosis in the Gospel of John*. The Didsbury Lectures 2016. Eugene, OR: Cascade, 2018.

———. *Inhabiting the Cruciform God: Kenosis, Justification, and Theosis in Paul's Narrative Soteriology*. Grand Rapids: Eerdmans, 2009.

———. "Romans: The First Christian Treatise on Theosis." *JTI* 5, no. 1 (2011): 13–34.

Green, Joel B. *Body, Soul, and Human Life: The Nature of Humanity in the Bible*. STI. Grand Rapids: Baker Academic, 2008.

———. *Conversion in Luke-Acts: Divine Action, Human Cognition, and the People of God*. Grand Rapids: Baker Academic, 2015.

———. *Discovering Luke: Content, Interpretation, Reception*. Discovering Biblical Texts. Grand Rapids: Eerdmans, 2021.

———. "Healing and Healthcare." In *The World of the New Testament: Cultural, Social, and Historical Contexts*, edited by Joel B. Green and Lee Martin McDonald, 330–41. Grand Rapids: Baker Academic, 2013.

———. "Kingdom of God/Heaven." In *DJG*, edited by Joel B. Green, Jeannine K. Brown, and Nicholas Perrin, 468–81. 2nd ed. Downers Grove, IL: InterVarsity Press, 2013.

———. "Narrative Criticism." In *Methods for Luke*, edited by Joel B. Green, 74–112. Methods in Biblical Interpretation. Cambridge: Cambridge University Press, 2010.

———. "Practicing the Gospel in a Post-Critical World: The Promise of Theological Exegesis." *JETS* 47, no. 3 (2004): 387–97.

———. *Practicing Theological Interpretation: Engaging Biblical Texts for Faith and Formation*. Theological Explorations for the Church Catholic. Grand Rapids: Baker Academic, 2011.

———. "Rethinking 'History' for Theological Interpretation." *JTI* 5, no. 2 (2011): 159–74.

———. *The Death of Jesus: Tradition and Interpretation in the Passion Narrative*. WUNT 2/33. Tübingen: Mohr Siebeck, 1988. Reprint, Eugene, OR: Wipf & Stock, 2011.

———. *Why Salvation?* Reframing New Testament Theology. Nashville: Abingdon, 2013.

Gurtner, Daniel M. *The Torn Veil: Matthew's Exposition of the Death of Jesus*. SNTSMS 139. Cambridge: Cambridge University Press, 2007.

Habets, Myk. "Reforming Theōsis." In *Theōsis: Deification in Christian Theology*, edited by Stephen Finlan and Vladimir Kharlamov, 146–67. Princeton Theological Monograph Series 52. Eugene, OR: Pickwick, 2006.

Hagner, Donald A. *Matthew*. 2 vols. WBC 33A & B. Dallas: Word, 1995.

Hahn, Robert A. *Sickness and Healing: An Anthropological Perspective*. New Haven: Yale University Press, 1995.

Hallonsten, Gösta. "Theosis in Recent Research: A Renewal of Interest and a Need for Clarity." In *Partakers of the Divine Nature: The History and Development of Deification in the Christian Traditions*, edited by Michael J. Christensen and Jeffery A. Wittung, 281–93. Grand Rapids: Baker Academic, 2007.

Hamilton, Catherine Sider. *The Death of Jesus in Matthew: Innocent Blood and the End of Exile*. SNTSMS 167. New York: Cambridge University Press, 2017.

Hannan, Margaret. *The Nature and Demands of God's Sovereign Rule in the Gospel of Matthew*. LNTS 308. London: T&T Clark, 2006.

Hays, Richard B. *Echoes of Scripture in the Gospels*. Waco, TX: Baylor University Press, 2016.

———. *The Faith of Jesus Christ: The Narrative Substructure of Galatians 3:1–4:11*. 2nd ed. Grand Rapids: Eerdmans, 2002.

———. "The Gospel of Matthew: Reconfigured Torah." *HTS* 61 (2005): 165–90.

———. *The Moral Vision of the New Testament: Community, Cross, New Creation: A Contemporary Introduction to New Testament Ethics*. San Francisco: HarperSanFrancisco, 1996.

Heil, John Paul. "The Blood of Jesus in Matthew: A Narrative-Critical Perspective." *PRSt* 18, no. 2 (1991): 117–24.

———. *The Death and Resurrection of Jesus: A Narrative-Critical Reading of Matthew 26–28*. Minneapolis: Fortress, 1991.

Hogan, Larry O. *Healing in the Second Tempel* [*sic*] *Period*. NTOA 21. Göttingen: Vandenhoeck & Ruprecht, 1992.

Horrell, David G. "From ἀδελφοί to οἰκος θεοῦ: Social Transformation in Pauline Christianity." *JBL* 120, no. 2 (2001): 293–311.

Horsley, Richard A. "Building an Alternative Society: Introduction." In *Paul and Empire: Religion and Power in Roman Imperial Society*, edited by Richard A. Horsley, 206–14. Harrisburg, PA: Trinity Press International, 1997.

Hoskins, Paul M. "A Neglected Allusion to Leviticus 4–5 in Jesus's Words Concerning His Blood in Matthew 26:28." *BBR* 30, no. 2 (2020): 231–42.

Huizenga, Leroy A. *The New Isaac Tradition and Intertextuality in the Gospel of Matthew*. NovTSup 131. Leiden: Brill, 2009.

Jackson, Howard M. "The Death of Jesus in Mark and the Miracle from the Cross." *NTS* 33, no. 1 (1987): 16–37.

Jenson, Robert W. "Theosis." *Di* 32, no. 2 (1993): 108–12.

Jeremias, Joachim. *New Testament Theology: The Proclamation of Jesus*. London: SCM, 1971.

———. *The Eucharistic Words of Jesus*. Translated by Norman Perrin. The New Testament Library. London: SCM, 1966.

Johnson, Sherman E. "The Biblical Quotations in Matthew." *HTR* 36, no. 2 (1943): 135–53.

Jones, L. Gregory. *Embodying Forgiveness: A Theological Analysis*. Grand Rapids: Eerdmans, 1995.

Keating, Daniel A. *Divinization in Cyril: The Appropriation of Divine Life*. Oxford: Oxford University Press, 2005.

———. "Typologies of Deification." *International Journal of Systematic Theology* 17, no. 3 (2015): 267–83.

Kharlamov, Vladimir. "Clement of Alexandria on Trinitarian and Metaphysical Relationality in the Context of Deification." In *Theōsis: Deification in Christian Theology*, edited by Vladimir Kharlamov, 83–99. Princeton Theological Monograph Series 156. Eugene, OR: Pickwick, 2011.

———. "Introduction." In *Theōsis: Deification in Christian Theology*, edited by Vladimir Kharlamov, 1–20. Princeton Theological Monograph Series 156. Eugene, OR: Pickwick, 2011.

———. "Rhetorical Application of Theosis in Greek Patristic Theology." In *Partakers of the Divine Nature: The History and Development of Deification in the Christian Traditions*, edited by Michael J. Christensen and Jeffery A. Wittung, 115–31. Grand Rapids: Baker Academic, 2007.

Kim, C. H., and Kirsteen Kim. *A History of Korean Christianity*. Cambridge: Cambridge University Press, 2015.

Kim, In Soo. *History of Christianity in Korea*. Seoul: Qumran Publishing House, 2011.

Kim, Kangil. "A Theology of Forgiveness: Theosis in Matthew 18:15–35." *JTI* 16, no. 1 (2022): 40–56. doi:10.5325/jtheointe.16.1.0040.

Kingsbury, Jack Dean. *Matthew: Structure, Christology, Kingdom*. Minneapolis: Fortress, 1975.

———. "The Developing Conflict between Jesus and the Jewish Leaders in Matthew's Gospel: A Literary-Critical Study." *CBQ* 49, no. 1 (1987): 57–73.

Kunjanayil, Paul. "The Interconnection between the Emmanuel Theme and the Forgiveness of Sins Theme in the Gospel of Matthew." *Studia Biblica Slovaca* 13, no. 1 (2021): 20–48.

Kupp, David D. *Matthew's Emmanuel: Divine Presence and God's People in the First Gospel*. SNTSMS 90. Cambridge: Cambridge University Press, 1996.

Ladd, G. E. *The Presence of the Future: The Eschatology of Biblical Realism*. Grand Rapids: Eerdmans, 1974.

Lamarche, Paul. "La mort du Christ et le voile de temple selon Marc." *NRTh* 106 (1974): 583–99.

Lenski, Gerhard. *Power and Privilege: A Theory of Social Stratification*. 2nd ed. Chapel Hill: University of North Carolina Press, 1984.

Litwa, M. David. "2 Corinthians 3:18 and its Implications for Theosis." *JTI* 2, no. 1 (2008): 117–33.

Longenecker, Bruce W. *Remember the Poor: Paul, Poverty, and the Greco-Roman Word*. Grand Rapids: Eerdmans, 2010.

Luz, Ulrich. *Matthew: A Commentary*. 3 vols. Translated by James E. Crouch. Hermeneia. Minneapolis: Fortress, 2001, 2005, 2007.

———. "The Disciples in the Gospel according to Matthew." In *The Interpretation of Matthew*, edited by Graham N. Stanton, 115–48. Edinburgh: T&T Clark, 1995.

———. *The Theology of the Gospel of Matthew*. Translated by J. Bradford Robinson. New Testament Theology. Cambridge: Cambridge University Press, 1995.

Lyonnet, Stanislas, and Leopold Sabourin. *Sin, Redemption, and Sacrifice: A Biblical and Patristic Study*. AnBib 48. Rome: Pontifical Biblical Institute, 1970.

Macaskill, Grant. *Union with Christ in the New Testament*. Oxford: Oxford University Press, 2013.

Marcus, Joel. "Authority to Forgive Sins upon the Earth: The Shema in the Gospel of Mark." In *The Gospels and the Scriptures of Israel*, edited by W. Richard Stegner and Craig A. Evans, 196–211. JSNTSup 104. Sheffield: Sheffield Academic, 1994.

Marshall, I. Howard. *Last Supper and Lord's Supper*. Exeter: Paternoster, 1980.

Mason, Steve. "Josephus's Pharisees." In *The Pharisees*, edited by Joseph Sievers and Amy-Jill Levine, 80–111. Grand Rapids: Eerdmans, 2021.

Matera, Frank J. *Passion Narratives and Gospel Theologies: Interpreting the Synoptics through their Passion Stories*. Theological Inquiries: Studies in Contemporary Biblical and Theological Problems. New York: Paulist, 1986.

———. *The Kingship of Jesus: Composition and Theology in Mark 15*. SBLDS 66. Chico, CA: Scholars Press, 1982.

Mbabazi, Isaac K. *The Significance of the Interpersonal Forgiveness in the Gospel of Matthew*. Eugene, OR: Pickwick, 2013.

McGuckin, J. A. "The Strategic Adaptation of Deification in the Cappadocians." In *Partakers of the Divine Nature: The History and Development of Deification in the Christian Traditions*, edited by Michael J. Christensen and Jeffery A. Wittung, 95–114. Grand Rapids: Baker Academic, 2007.

McKnight, Scot. "Covenant." In *Dictionary for Theological Interpretation of the Bible*, edited by Kevin J. Vanhoozer, 141–43. Grand Rapids: Baker Academic, 2005.

Mello, Alberto. *Évangile selon Saint Matthieu: Commentaire midrashique et narrative*. LD 179. Paris: Cerf, 1999.

Mendez-Moratalla, F. "Repentance." In *DJG*, edited by Joel B. Green, Jeannine K. Brown, and Nicholas Perrin, 771–74. 2nd ed. The IVP Bible Dictionary Series. Downers Grove, IL: InterVarsity Press, 2013.

Moberly, R. W. L. "What Is Theological Interpretation of Scripture?" *JTI* 3, no. 2 (2009): 161–78.

Mohrlang, Roger. *Matthew and Paul: A Comparison of Ethical Perspectives*. SNTSMS 48. Cambridge: Cambridge University Press, 1984.

Montanari, Franco. *The Brill Dictionary of Ancient Greek*. Edited by Madeleine Goh and Chad Schroeder. Leiden: Brill, 2015.

Morgan, Teresa. *Literate Education in the Hellenistic and Roman Worlds*. Cambridge: Cambridge University Press, 1998.

———. *Roman Faith and Christian Faith: Pistis and Fides in the Early Roman Empire and Early Churches*. Oxford: Oxford University Press, 2015.

Morris, Leon. *The Gospel according to Matthew*. The Pillar New Testament Commentary. Grand Rapids: Eerdmans, 1992.

Motyer, Stephen. "The Rending of the Veil: A Markan Pentecost?" *NTS* 33, no. 1 (1987): 155–57.

Moyise, Steve. "Intertextuality and the Study of the Old Testament in the New Testament." In *The Old Testament in the New Testament: Essays in Honour of J. L. North*, edited by Steve Moyise, 14–41. Sheffield: Sheffield Academic, 2000.

Nellas, Panayiotis. *Deification in Christ: Orthodox Perspectives on the Nature of the Human Person*. Translated by Norman Russell. Crestwood, NY: St Vladimir's Seminary Press, 1987.

Neyrey, Jerome H. "God, Benefactor and Patron: The Major Cultural Model for Interpreting the Deity in Greco-Roman Antiquity." *JSNT* 27, no. 4 (2005): 465–92.

Nolland, John. *The Gospel of Matthew: A Commentary on the Greek Text*. NIGTC. Grand Rapids: Eerdmans, 2005.

O'Neill, J. C. "The Lord's Prayer." *JSNT* 51 (1993): 3–25.

Park, Eugene Eung-Chun. "Rachel's Cry for Her Children: Matthew's Treatment of the Infanticide by Herod." *CBQ* 75, no. 3 (2013): 473–85.

Pennington, Jonathan T. *Heaven and Earth in the Gospel of Matthew*. Grand Rapids: Baker Academic, 2007.

———. "The Kingdom of Heaven in the Gospel of Matthew." *Southern Baptist Journal of Theology* 12, no. 1 (2008): 44–51.

———. *The Sermon on the Mount and Human Flourishing.* Grand Rapids: Baker Academic, 2017.

Pokrifka-Joe, Todd. "Probing the Relationship between Divine and Human Forgiveness in Matthew." In *Forgiveness and Truth: Explorations in Contemporary Theology*, edited by Alistair I. McFadyen, Marcel Sarot, and Anthony Thiselton, 165–72. Edinburgh: T&T Clark, 2001.

Porter, Stanley E. "Further Comments on the Use of the Old Testament in the New Testament." In *The Intertextuality of the Epistles: Explorations of Theory and Practice*, edited by Thomas L. Brodie, Dennis R. MacDonald, and Stanley E. Porter, 98–110. Sheffield: Sheffield Phoenix, 2007.

Powell, Mark Allan. "Binding and Loosing: A Paradigm for Ethical Discernment from the Gospel of Matthew." *CurTM* 30, no. 6 (2003): 438–45.

———. "Table Fellowship." In *DJG*, edited by Joel B. Green, Jeannine K. Brown, and Nicholas Perrin, 925–31. 2nd ed. Downers Grove, IL: InterVarsity Press, 2013.

———. "The Religious Leaders in Luke: A Literary-Critical Study." *JBL* 109 (1990): 93–110.

Quarles, Charles L. "Matthew 27:51–53: Meaning, Genre, Intertextuality, Theology, and Reception History." *JETS* 59, no. 2 (2016): 271–86.

Rawson, Beryl. *Children and Childhood in Roman Italy*. Oxford: Oxford University Press, 2003.

———. "Children in the Roman *Familia*." In *The Family in Ancient Rome: New Perspectives*, edited by Beryl Rawson, 170–200. Ithaca, NY: Cornell University Press, 1986.

Rendtorff, Rolf. *The Covenant Formula: An Exegetical and Theological Investigation*. Translated by Margaret Kohl. OTS. Edinburgh: T&T Clark, 1998.

Roberts, J. J. M. *First Isaiah: A Commentary*. Hermeneia. Minneapolis: Fortress, 2015.

Runesson, Anders. *Divine Wrath and Salvation in Matthew: The Narrative World of the First Gospel.* Minneapolis: Fortress, 2017.

Russell, Norman. *Fellow Workers with God: Orthodox Thinking on Theosis*. Foundations Series 5. Crestwood, NY: St. Vladimir's Seminary Press, 2009.

———. *The Doctrine of Deification in the Greek Patristic Tradition*. Oxford: Oxford University Press, 2004.

Saldarini, Anthony J. *Matthew's Christian Jewish Community*. Chicago: University of Chicago Press, 1994.

Sanders, E. P. *Jesus and Judaism*. Philadelphia: Fortress, 1985.

Schneider, Gerhard. "'Im Himmel—auf Erden': Eine Perspektive matthäischer Theologie." In *Studien zum Matthäusevangelium: Festschrift für Wilhelm Pesch*, edited by Ludger Schenke, 285–97. Stuttgart: Katholisches Bibelwerk, 1988.

Schweitzer, A. *The Quest of the Historical Jesus: A Critical Study of Its Progress from Reimarus to Wrede*. Translated by F. C. Burkitt. London: A & C Black, 1910.

Scott, Bernard Brandon. "The King's Accounting: Matthew 18:23–34." *JBL* 104, no. 3 (1985): 429–42.
Senior, Donald. "The Death of Jesus and the Meaning of Discipleship." In *The Death of Jesus in Early Christianity*, 234–55. Peabody, MA: Hendrickson, 1995.
———. *The Passion of Jesus in the Gospel of Matthew*. The Passion Series. Wilmington, DE: Glazier, 1985.
———. *The Passion Narrative according to Matthew: A Redactional Study*. BETL 39. Leuven: Leuven University Press, 1975.
———. *What Are They Saying about Matthew?* Rev. ed. New York: Paulist, 1996.
———. *Why the Cross?* Reframing New Testament Theology. Nashville: Abingdon, 2014.
Shin, Sookgoo. *Ethics in the Gospel of John: Discipleship as Moral Progress*. BibInt 168. Leiden: Brill, 2019.
Sim, David C. "Rome in Matthew's Eschatology." In *The Gospel of Matthew in Its Roman Imperial Context*, edited by John K. Riches and David C. Sim, 91–106. JSNTSup 276. New York: T&T Clark, 2005.
Siorvanes, Lucas. *Proclus: Neo-Platonic Philosophy and Science*. Edinburgh: Edinburgh University Press, 1996.
Smyth, Herbert Weir. *Greek Grammar*. Revised by Gordon M. Messing. Cambridge: Harvard University Press, 1984.
Spencer, F. S. "Forgiveness of Sins." In *DJG*, edited by Joel B. Green, Jeannine K. Brown, and Nicholas Perrin, 284–88. 2nd ed. Downers Grove, IL: InterVarsity Press, 2013.
Stack, Judith V. *Metaphor and the Portrayal of the Cause(s) of Sin and Evil in the Gospel of Matthew*. BibInt 182. Leiden: Brill, 2020.
Stanton, Graham N. "The Communities of Matthew." *Int* 46, no. 4 (1992): 379–91.
Starr, James. "Does 2 Peter 1:4 Speak of Deification?" In *Partakers of the Divine Nature: The History and Development of Deification in the Christian Traditions*, edited by Michael J. Christensen and Jeffery A. Wittung, 81–94. Grand Rapids: Baker Academic, 2007.
Stern, Frank. *A Rabbi Looks at Jesus' Parables*. Lanhan, MD: Rowman & Littlefield, 2006.
Strange, C. R. "Athanasius on Divinization." *StPatr* 16, no. 6 (1985): 342–46.
Sung, Chong-Hyon. *Vergebung der Sünden: Jesu Praxis der Sündenvergebung nach den Synoptikern und ihre Voraussetzungen im Alten Testament und frühen Judentum*. WUNT 2/57. Tübingen: Mohr Siebeck, 1993.
Syreeni, Kari. "Between Heaven and Earth: On the Structure of Matthew's Symbolic Universe." *JSNT* 40 (1990): 3–13.
Tannehill, Robert C. "Beginning to Study 'How Gospels Begin.'" *Semeia* 52 (1990): 185–92.
Thompson, Marianne Meye. "On Writing a Commentary." *JTI* 15, no. 2 (2021): 333–45.
———. *The Promise of the Father: Jesus and God in the New Testament*. Louisville: Westminster John Knox, 2000.

Ulansey, David. "The Heavenly Veil Torn: Mark's Cosmic *Inclusio*." *JBL* 110, no. 1 (1991): 123–25.

van der Watt, J. G., and D. S. du Toit. "Salvation." In *DJG*, edited by Joel B. Green, Jeannine K. Brown, and Nicholas Perrin, 826–32. 2nd ed. Downers Grove, IL: InterVarsity Press, 2013.

Vanhoozer, Kevin J. "What Is Theological Interpretation of the Bible?" In *Dictionary for Theological Interpretation of the Bible*, edited by Kevin J. Vanhoozer, 19–25. Grand Rapids: Baker Academic, 2005.

Verhey, Allen. *Remembering Jesus: Christian Community, Scripture, and the Moral Life*. Grand Rapids: Eerdmans, 2002.

———. *The Great Reversal: Ethics and the New Testament*. Grand Rapids: Eerdmans, 1984.

Volf, Miroslav. *Free of Charge: Giving and Forgiving in a Culture Stripped of Grace*. Grand Rapids: Zondervan, 2005.

Wallace-Hadrill, Andrew. "Patronage in Roman Society: From Republic to Empire." In *Patronage in Ancient Society*, edited by Andrew Wallace-Hadrill, 63–87. Leicester-Nottingham Studies in Ancient Society 1. London; New York: Routledge, 1989.

Wardle, Timothy. "Resurrection and the Holy City: Matthew's Use of Isaiah in 27:51–53." *CBQ* 78, no. 4 (2016): 666–81.

Weiss, J. *Jesus' Proclamation of the Kingdom of God*. Edited by R. H. Hiers and D. L. Holland. Philadelphia: Fortress, 1971.

Whittaker, C. R. *Land, City and Trade in the Roman Empire*. Aldershot: Variorum Ashgate, 1993.

Williams, Rowan. *Christ on Trial: How the Gospel Unsettles Our Judgment*. Grand Rapids: Eerdmans, 2000.

Wilson, John A. "The God and His Unknown Name of Power." In *Ancient Near Eastern Texts Relating to the Old Testament*, edited by James B. Pritchard, 12–14. Princeton: Princeton University Press, 1969.

Zerwick, M., and M. Grosvenor. *A Grammatical Analysis of the Greek New Testament*. SubBi 39. 5th ed. Rome: Gregorian & Biblical Press, 2013.

Ancient Sources Index

About the Author

Kangil Kim received a PhD from Fuller Theological Seminary, a ThM from Emory University, and an MDiv from Presbyterian University and Theological Seminary in Seoul, South Korea. His publications have appeared in several academic journals, including the *Journal of Theological Interpretation* and *Religions*.

Milton Keynes UK
Ingram Content Group UK Ltd.
UKHW011425231123
433133UK00004B/40